Letters to a Young Psych

Written in the form of letters from an experienced analyst to a young colleague, *Letters to a Young Psychoanalyst* expands the psychoanalytic frame to include South American, French and British theory, and examine a wide variety of theoretical and clinical topics.

Letters to a Young Psychoanalyst is ground-breaking in more than one respect. It re-examines major psychoanalytic theories in the light of rich clinical practice, and in the light of the practice of friendship, while portraying the practice of analysis as the choice of a personal code of ethics. Covering such core issues as transference, trauma, hysteria, the influence of the mother, and love and hate, and drawing on the work of notable analysts such as Winnicott, McDougall, Pankow and Ferenczi, the book explores the many facets of the healing function of psychoanalysis in practice and discloses the workings of the psyche in human existence.

This book considers psychoanalysis a humanist endeavour, focusing on its healing function and using captivating examples to illustrate different modes of commitment on the part of the analyst. Rejecting a view of psychoanalysis as a painful and laborious process, the book insists instead on the joyous and passionate nature of the work of psychic elaboration. Uniquely, the transmission of knowledge and skill which it provides, constituting a veritable training, is not at all didactic in tone. It places the two interlocutors, as well as the reader, on the same level: people who share the desire to remain attentive to themselves and to others, and who believe that empathy heals, within the setting of therapy and in human relations in general.

Written in a remarkably engaging and accessible style, *Letters to a Young Psychoanalyst* will appeal to psychoanalysts and psychoanalytic psychotherapists, students of all levels studying in these fields, as well as lay readers wishing to understand fundamental psychoanalytic concepts.

Heitor O'Dwyer de Macedo is a French psychoanalyst and former theatre director of Brazilian origin, based in Paris.

Letters to a Young Psychoanalyst

Lessons on psyche, human existence, and psychoanalysis

Heitor O'Dwyer de Macedo

Routledge
Taylor & Francis Group

LONDON AND NEW YORK

First published 2017
by Routledge
2 Park Square, Milton Park, Abingdon, Oxon OX14 4RN

and by Routledge
711 Third Avenue, New York, NY 10017

Routledge is an imprint of the Taylor & Francis Group, an informa business

© 2017 Heitor O'Dwyer de Macedo

The right of Heitor O'Dwyer de Macedo to be identified as author of this work has been asserted by him in accordance with sections 77 and 78 of the Copyright, Designs and Patents Act 1988.

This book is a translation of a work previously published in French as *Lettres à une jeune psychanalyste* by Editions Stock (2008).

Translation into English by Agnès Jacob.

British Library Cataloguing in Publication Data
A catalogue record for this book is available from the British Library

Library of Congress Cataloging in Publication Data
Names: Macedo, Heitor O'Dwyer de, author.
Title: Letters to a young psychoanalyst : lessons on psyche, human existence, and psychoanalysis / Heitor O'Dwyer de Macedo.
Other titles: Lettres âa une jeune psychanalyste. English
Description: Milton Park, Abingdon, Oxon ; New York, NY : Routledge, 2017. |
Includes bibliographical references and index.
Identifiers: LCCN 2016010636| ISBN 9781138671188 (hbk : alk. paper) | ISBN 9781138671195 (pbk. : alk. paper) | ISBN 9781315617183 (ebk)
Subjects: LCSH: Psychoanalysis.
Classification: LCC RC506 .M25313 2017 | DDC 616.89/17–dc23
LC record available at https://lccn.loc.gov/2016010636

ISBN: 978-1-138-67118-8 (hbk)
ISBN: 978-1-138-67119-5 (pbk)
ISBN: 978-1-315-61718-3 (ebk)

Typeset in Times New Roman
by HWA Text and Data Management, London

To Leslie,
who helped me become all that a man can be.

Contents

Introduction

Taking Rainer Maria Rilke's publication *Letters to a Young Poet* as a model, I conceived the idea that this non-academic style might be perfectly suited for presenting my view of psychoanalysis. Initially, my hope was to spark an interest in Sigmund Freud's work and transmit to a novice a specific concept of the theory and practice of psychoanalysis.

Although I still hold to my original intention – to describe in the simplest and most subjective terms my relation to psychoanalysis – I am no longer certain that a reader who first encounters the notion of the unconscious in these pages will have a clear idea of concepts I consider obvious.

My doubts arose due to reactions to some of these letters, expressed by friends whose various fields of interest are far removed from my own. Although, in most cases, they were interested and pleasantly surprised, at times they pointed out the opacity of passages which I took to be banal descriptions of my practice. I reviewed the text keeping these observations in mind and had to admit that it is not always possible to talk (or write) about psychoanalysis without using the terms (concepts) on which a psychoanalyst builds his reflections. Therefore, a degree of opacity remains, despite my efforts to illustrate each concept presented by describing the use I make of it and the sense I attribute to it. Here, Freud's terminology is not intended to serve as a metalanguage, but rather as a springboard for rekindling the discussion. In other words, if what I perceive as banal and simple appears difficult to understand, it is because we enter a sphere where the obvious is not easy to accept: infantile sexuality; the wish to kill; hate; the intimate link between madness and love as well as between madness and creativity; and where we must accept these conditions as constitutive of human sensibility and of the human psyche.

Since we cannot do away with these difficulties, I ask the reader to rely on the same method he uses to read a novel in a foreign language – that is, instead of letting each unknown word become an obstacle, the reader continues on, trusting that the meaning will become apparent as the text unfolds.

Two lines of thought converge in these letters: the interconnection between theory and practice in the work of a psychoanalyst, and my conception of the meaning and the responsibility inherent to this occupation – its ethics; the letters are my way of paying tribute to those who trained me, and to the inheritance with which I was entrusted and which it now falls to me to transmit.

This book attempts to convey the passion and joy at the heart of the psychoanalyst's work, without which, in my opinion, it would not be possible to engage in this practice. Strictly speaking, the book does not offer an introduction to psychoanalysis – Freud left us his remarkable *Introduction* – but it does invite the reader to enter the workshop of a psychoanalyst, with its clutter and occasional achievements. My intention was to show that psychoanalytic theory and practice are in no way esoteric. They constitute a form of human reflection and endeavour like many others, handcrafted and founded on a certain know-how and, in this case, on the doctrine of Freud (giving rise to the difficulties mentioned earlier), involving both risk-taking and rigour, as well as a passionate interest in all the exquisite fragilities that compose a human existence.

This being so, the present work opens a perspective far removed from the wild idea of trusting science to discover a universal drug that will eliminate human suffering. This book is addressed to all those who continue to believe that the end of the most singular of subjectivities would in no way solve the challenges encountered by the living, but would, in fact, constitute its "final solution". I am also addressing young analysts who choose to devote themselves to this endangered discipline at a time when this activity has been discredited by irresponsible policies and by the perverted and cynical exercise of psychoanalysis in certain circles.

Certain patients who chose me as a witness and guide on the voyage leading to their encounter with the unconscious, and colleagues who shared their experiences as analysts with me, might recognise themselves in these pages. I hope they will view the clinical illustrations in which they appear as the acknowledgement of my indebtedness to them.

The letters are of two types: those that are based on a clinical situation; and those that develop a point of theory. The references, as well as the development or discussion of an issue roughly outlined in the body of a letter, are presented in the Notes section at the end of each letter.

After reading the manuscript, my daughter thought it best that the Introduction should include elements of the biographical information scattered throughout the book. She pointed out, rightly, that these facts have shaped my "manner" of practicing psychoanalysis. I agree and comply.

I was born in Brazil and arrived in France in September 1968, from a country under military dictatorship. In Brazil, I was a stage director. I believe I was good at directing theatre productions, but I was, above all, good at directing actors. In France, I studied psychology in order to work in hospitals, but I am convinced that it is my theatre background that made me the psychoanalyst I am. Some people take this statement for an affectation, but it is the plain truth. Although the analysts I met taught me to care for myself and to reflect on my clinical practice, it was my work with actors that provided my initial frame of reference in my encounter with patients.

The interlocutor

Dear friend,

I agree to try being, in your own words, "the privileged interlocutor accompanying a young psychoanalyst on her journey".

The notion of becoming travelling companions suits me. It is a good illustration of what takes place, or can take place, when a psychoanalyst speaks of his work with another psychoanalyst.

I like your way of describing your work with your patients, and am therefore willing to embark on this adventure on two conditions. First, that you agree for us to interrupt the journey if our theoretical interests become too divergent, or utterly contradictory. Second, that you agree for us to meet at least once every two months. Psychoanalysis is a practice of the spoken word, and I would find it insufficient for us to have nothing but written exchanges.

Now let me speak of the clinical material you sent me. The presentation is clear and vivid. You succeed in conveying quite well the atmosphere of the sessions, their affective tone and the importance of what is at stake.

About the adolescent girl you mention, I don't understand your reason for suggesting to her that she should contact you after the school holidays, instead of making an appointment right away. Why do this, after the enormous progress you helped her accomplish – that you accomplished together – by making it possible for her to reveal, in the analytic space, the complications of her history and the shame of her symptoms? Your proposal, coming as it does after the disclosures made in the sessions, is in contradiction with what I imagine to be the quality of the relation established between you in the course of these intense encounters.

This is clearly a symptomatic act. By forcing her to postpone her request until the holidays are over, you place yourself among those who have let her down, who have abandoned her in the course of her life.

I suppose that you are troubled to read this. So I will elaborate on these symptomatic acts committed by the psychoanalyst in the process of analysis. Most often, these acts are induced by the material presented by the patient. This means that unconsciously the patient "wishes" to repeat the trauma and that the archaic nature of the material – which generally brings to the forefront the suffering of the child, or even the infant he once was – activates in the psychoanalyst a certain repressed content associated with his most primitive conflicts.

Naturally, the question that arises is: shouldn't the analyst, thanks to his own analysis, be protected from this return of the repressed? I raise the question because it is a common concern in all psychoanalytic communities, related – of course – to their most mediocre members, those for whom time spent on the couch was not very productive.

It is easy to see that this perspective combines the most unbridled superego with an idealised conception of the technique. Most surprisingly, knowing that we are not committing a stupid act does not prevent us from feeling guilty, or even incompetent, each time our narcissism is undermined during the analytic process.

The fact is that although errors can sometimes be avoided in working with certain patients, some errors are necessary, inescapable. How could we treat the very real devastating effects of early traumas if these effects do not readily spring forth in the relation between the analyst and the patient, in this sphere that in our jargon we call the transference situation?

It is for this reason that patients "wish" to see their trauma reappear during the analytic process: so that it be contained; so that the extent of the disaster be measured; so that the right words be spoken and heard. In this respect, it can be said that, unconsciously, the patient actively and insistently provokes this resurgence, attempting to involve the therapist in his psychic world.

I believe it is crucial for the therapist to let himself be pulled into this significant enactment. As I said earlier, this involvement is part of the work, no matter how trying it may be for our narcissism. From the patient's perspective, this repeated insistence represents the hope that this time the outcome will be different and that the other – in this instance the analyst – will admit being responsible for the trauma. What is at work here is the life force aspect of the compulsion to repeat, the aspect regulated by Eros.

But, of course, the anti-life force is not absent from this enactment. Thanatos wants things to be repeated in exactly the same fashion, and wants the analyst to be the pathetic representative of the initial destruction – which would justify the disavowal of any attempt to take charge of one's life, and would open the way to inhibition, fear, apathy and suicide.[1]

But all these considerations regarding the patient do not dispense the psychoanalyst from understanding his own unconscious mechanisms as they are reflected in his actions. The distinguishing characteristic of psychoanalysis consists of the importance granted by the analyst to the psychic work making it possible to identify the unique fashion in which a particular psychoanalyst becomes drawn into the infantile history of a particular patient. Contrary to any other form of therapy, in psychoanalysis understanding the patient requires psychic elaboration of what is at stake on the part of the analyst as well, in advance or in parallel with elaboration on the part of the analysand.

Since in most cases the unconscious roots of the analyst's actions are to be found in the material produced by the analysand, I can provide two hypotheses where you are concerned. First hypothesis: you were also abandoned in your childhood, and you are doing to this young girl what was done to you. Probably because you are envious of what she received from you, the very thing that you were never given in your early years (like parents who cannot bear to give their children better parents than the parents they themselves had). Second hypothesis: your masochism prevented you from agreeing to represent an ego ideal for the patient, or from enjoying the fruits of all the creativity you deployed – and undermining the relation was your way of destroying what you had so painstakingly built.

As for the prognosis, the best thing that could happen would be that you don't hear from her at the start of the school term. This would allow you to take the initiative in arranging a meeting with her – which would facilitate the working through of the parapraxis. Unfortunately, it is more likely that she will contact you. In that case, you will have to work through together the sadomasochistic relation enacted in the transference.

To be continued passionately…

Your friend,

Note

1   These concepts are discussed in Letter 5, *Couch or chair*, and are developed in greater detail in Letter 10, *Winnicott's concept of* continuity of being: *transference and the treatment of trauma.*

Letter 2

The young psychoanalyst

Dear friend,

You are right to point out that more and more often we are asked to act as psychoanalysts in a context that makes the psychoanalytic process impossible. In these situations, as Winnicott said, we are psychoanalysts doing something other than psychoanalysis. But it is precisely because it is a psychoanalyst who responds to this type of impossible request that it may be possible to establish a truly psychoanalytic process.

Why impossible? Based on the doctrine as such, the only requests suitable for psychoanalysis are those that can be treated using the reference points provided by the theory of repression: erotic experience or fantasy; repression; return of the repressed; anxiety; inadequate defence against anxiety; and a symptomatic compromise between anxiety and ego defences. But today it is often the case that defences do not fit this paradigm; moreover, we have the mistaken impression that nothing matters to these individuals. This being so, what type of clinical work could be suitable for these zombies?[1]

Are young analysts any less dismayed than their elders when other therapists send them very difficult cases, particularly those they no longer want, or do not want to accept?

It is clear that money is not the reason they accept these cases. In general, when he first starts to practise as an analyst, the novice psychoanalyst has other sources of revenue. Very often, it is a more experienced colleague, someone who is older, who sends the patient. "It's a very interesting case, I am certain you will learn a great deal from it. But it's not an easy case, and the patient can't pay very much."

No, the reason for accepting all sorts of patients is not money, but the need for the second protagonist participating in this exceptional dialogue. In a remarkable conference at Maison des Centraux in Paris, François Perrier identified this obvious fact as nearly the baseline of psychoanalytic training. Not the absolute baseline because, he reminded us, before meeting patients the psychoanalyst has to buy, or rent, a couch.

Once the couch is in place and the patient keeps his appointments, another analyst must be found to discuss what transpires in the sessions. And so, Perrier concluded with the simplicity that comes from lengthy experience, if you have a couch, a patient and a psychoanalyst friend with whom to discuss the content of the sessions, you are a practising psychoanalyst.

Let us note that here François Perrier encapsulates, in a simple and straightforward fashion, the essence of a practice that Freud considered impossible when he formulated the theory of repression. Suggesting that the other analyst be a friend suddenly reveals the complexities and requirements of our work. This observation could also spark fruitful reflection on the qualities of the relation between the supervising analyst, the interlocutor, and the novice psychoanalyst.

But what I want to stress here is this availability of the young analyst, which allows him to welcome everyone. It reflects a position of absolute creativity that, hopefully, will not diminish with time. It is an uncomfortable, even trying, position but preferable to that deadening respect of protocol that some of us have known, and which practically forces the analyst to thank his patients for having sacrificed, as he did, precious time to the institutional rules governing the proper conduct of analysis.

The experience of young analysts has much to teach us about requests for analysis made in a context not lending itself to a psychoanalytic approach. Their experience sheds valuable light on the factor guaranteeing that the framework established at the start of the process will not compromise the subsequent psychoanalytic process. What is clearly revealed here, above all, is the lack of distinction between clinical practice and theoretical practice, and the fact that this occupation requires constant invention. Of course, young analysts can console themselves – a small comfort – with the thought that they lack the technical skill that can only be acquired with time. But while waiting for this endowment, never acquired once and for all, how does it come to be that awkward, sometimes disastrous handling of the clinical situation does not prevent psychic elaboration on the part of the patient?

The clinical situation can easily accommodate a multitude of tentative approaches thanks to the setting in which the work takes place. I am referring to the setting passed on to us by Freud – sessions at regular intervals, of a comfortable duration that remains constant – that we take for granted. But I am also thinking of the use we make of this frame of reference, depending on our particular desire to be an analyst, on our personal passion for the unconscious.

In truth, this occupation, which is never practised in a conventional fashion, shapes our daily lives and intimate existence, forges our convictions and lays the foundations of our personal ethics. So that the young analyst, with his first patients, remembers what he has read, remembers his own analysis, situations recounted by colleagues, refers to his own experiences – and tries to piece all this together, around the patient. This type of makeshift procedure, yours, in no way differs from that which experienced analysts have to invent when they see new patients. "Young" or "old", if we are to succeed, we must let the patient in, allow him to enter our internal world. In short, the framework is inscribed in the psychic reality of the analyst. It is this inscription that safeguards the setting in which we practise.

A question of space, then. And therefore of bridges, passageways that connect different places and spaces. When a patient lacks passageways between his various internal spaces, the psychoanalyst can make his own available as a sphere of communication and contact between psychic regions previously isolated from one another.   .

Lending one's own psychic space as a zone of contact and communication between the internal regions of the subject, and between the latter and the external world, implies trusting that this "space graft" will incite the subject to internalise this architecture of passageways and transit zones that he has come to know through, and in, the other. Awakening this interest will depend on the quality of the psychic experience associated with this "graft", this very particular loan.

When the analyst proceeds in this manner, he rejects all doctrines based on an asepticised, rigid use of the analytic framework. Instead, he follows the logic of what Jacques Lacan called the analytic act – a term that describes the actual experience of any analyst who accepts the discomfort, responsibility and extravagance of his function.

Every analytic society always grants young colleagues the right to absolute symbolic solicitation from their elders, placing them in the role of hysterics. In fact, Freud's capacity for surprise was what allowed a hysteric to invent psychoanalysis. And we know that hysterical symptoms take on the characteristics of a particular era. Therefore, continuing to let hysteria steer our course is the best way to keep an open perspective.

This, then, my young friend, is one of the reasons we profit from working with novice analysts like you. Granting you the role of real interlocutors with whom we can share real experience, and who can make us question what we take for granted, is what prevents us from growing old.

And so I count on you.

Note

1   The question of zombies is discussed more fully in Letter 32, *Totalitarian regimes and psychosis.*

The setting

Dear friend,

To comply with your request, I will elaborate on the question of the analytic setting in borderline cases. The following is a clinical illustration.

One day, I received a call from a mother asking me to see her son urgently and reminding me that I had seen him when he was three. I did, in fact, seem to have a clear recollection of a very energetic little boy whose problems were straightened out in the space of four sessions. Since I don't have much time and since "I remember the little boy so well", I suggest to the mother that her son call me so that I can give him the name of a colleague. The mother answers that he will not call, that he asked her to call me and that he won't see anyone else. I still resist, saying that my time is limited, that sometimes it's best to make a change, and so on. At this point, the mother bursts into tears, tells me that her son engages in morbid self-mutilating behaviour, and that she and her husband are desperately worried. Of course, I set a date for an appointment. I feel very guilty and ask myself what I missed when the boy was three, for things to have progressed to this level of pain.

A few days later I meet an adolescent typical of his contemporaries: very wide pants that drag on the ground; a matching jacket and a skateboard under his arm. He is not, in fact, a boy I saw when he was three, as his mother had said, but rather a child I saw three years ago, brought to me by his parents who were worried about their son's withdrawal at home and his increasing disinterest in schoolwork. I saw him regularly for several months, during which time I learned a great deal about video games; this was followed by sessions which he never missed and during which he kept silent. After a while, I learned that on the day of the sessions, always a Saturday, his father drove him to his appointments – from their home located quite far in the suburbs – and that they spent the afternoon together. We discussed this and agreed that there was no need for us to continue the sessions just so that he could spend time with his father; they could have this precious time together even if the sessions stopped. His father agreed completely. The boy took an interest in his schoolwork again and became communicative at home, but we both knew that nothing had been said about the reasons for his withdrawal or his possible depression. He was leaving, but he knew that he could come back – if ever he wanted to discuss the things he had not been ready to discuss this time (and which I had not been able to discern).

And so he came back. Right from the start, it was clear that he wanted to waste no time. During our first session, I hesitated between using the formal form of address ("*vous*") or the familiar "*tu*". During the second session, I still hesitated; I explained to him that this must be due to the fact that I had last seen him three years ago, when he was still a child. I added that now he is a young man, I prefer addressing him as an adult, and that I would now consider it natural for him to contribute to paying for the sessions. Therefore, I would agree to work with him provided he paid for one out of every two sessions. He said he could not afford to pay the amount his parents had been paying me. I assured him that this was not what I had in mind, but that I was referring to an amount he could pay himself using his allowance or earnings from doing odd jobs. We agreed to meet once a week, and that he would pay me five euros once every two sessions. Before leaving, he asked me, "What if I can pay for all the sessions?" I told him that would be excellent.

The youth who arrived for the next scheduled session was alert and brimming with energy. He told me right away that he had stopped his self-mutilating rituals. From that point on, we engaged in difficult, even painful, but exciting work.

Establishing this setting was the result of an interpretation on the part of the patient. The same is true for me; since then, I only work with adolescents if they agree to contribute to paying for their analysis, with the intention of paying for all the sessions to the extent their resources allow, in the medium term. But given that I have to earn a living, I cannot accept many clients who pay five euros. However, in the case of the youths with whom I conducted analytic work, these conditions created a quality of commitment unusual at their age.

I do not yet fully understand the importance of these conditions for adolescents, and I would appreciate your thoughts on this. But I am certain of two things.

The first is a founding concept: the object of psychoanalytic work is the unconscious. Freud invented the unconscious and the tools to reach it, others refined the concept and introduced new elements, but the most exciting aspect of the work of psychoanalysts consists in their personal manner of using these tools – their knack, so to speak – for helping patients deal with anxiety, and for creating the distance necessary to hear them. In other words, the most exciting thing is always the way in which a psychoanalyst reinvents psychoanalysis for the particular person he has before him.

The second point is that I don't think that analysis consists solely of transference and interpretations of the transference. There is transference and there is the analytic setting. The rules are part of the setting, but the setting is more than the rules. The analyst's theory is part of the setting and, as Michel Neyraut so pertinently remarked, the theory is also part of the analyst's countertransference.[1]

In addition, the analyst's biography is another part of the setting, as are all the factors that determine his way of thinking and his sensitivity. The setting is composed of all this, and of something more, something that makes it possible to manoeuvre within the space of the transference, the rules, the theory and the analyst's biography in a manner that does not compromise the essence of the process. Some analysts call this a therapeutic alliance. Freud referred to friendship on one occasion; I use this term very often. Winnicott spoke of transitional space. I believe that asking an adolescent to pay for his analysis is such a sign of respect that the psychic work is inscribed in the setting from the start. From that point on, both protagonists participate in its elaboration. Initiated by the agreement that founded the analytic pact, such an elaboration goes beyond this process, becoming part of the human condition: two people somewhere in the world are doing something that is important to them because they decided to do it together. This thing has no greater or lesser importance than any other things that others are doing at the same time, things that are all part of life.

I would have liked to be able to invent, for each one of my patients, an analytic pact capable of creating at once a relation endowed with this fundamental quality. Too great an expectation or naïvety? I don't know. But I believe that the psychoanalyst's desire for the best outcome should not come in conflict with a passion for the precarious.

I described my work with this young man at a meeting among colleagues. During the discussion that followed, I was asked whether the fact that I did not meet with the parents again was due to the work I had done with them during the previous therapeutic period. This was, in fact, the case. François Dolto and Gisela Pankow have taught me that working with children and psychotic patients (including adults) requires including the parents in the therapeutic process whenever possible. By doing so, the analyst reinforces their self-esteem, helps them to withstand the competition with the therapist – it is always hurtful to bring one's child to therapy – and addresses the unconscious envy linked with the child's diminished suffering. From the patient's standpoint, involving the parents in the therapy allows him to share with the therapist the concrete difficulties he encounters in dealing with the symptoms, and in some cases even the parental violence (what is known as real and actual superego).

One of the therapists present at the meeting was sceptical about asking the young man to pay for his sessions, saying that the youth might feel authorised to obtain the money by any means, including selling drugs or prostitution. I have trouble imagining that sharing the cost of the therapy, or even paying for all the sessions at a rate based on pocket money, can be an invitation to delinquency. I believe, in essence, that this objection is related to different conceptions of transference. In my view, in this situation the analytic pact redefined the sphere of the transference by creating a new manner of being-in-the-world for this young man. I am not excluding the possibility of perverse behaviour on the part of adolescents, but I don't think it should be considered to be outside the sphere of influence of the transference, and consequently impossible to work through. In all clinical borderline situations, the work is set forth by the analyst – he is the one who sustains the transference – and therefore depends on both his commitment and his creativity.

Your friend,

Note

1 Neyraut, M. (1974), *Le Transfert*. Paris: PUF, coll. "Le Fil rouge", 1974.

Letter 4

Françoise Dolto and psychoanalytic amorality

Dear friend,

Not surprisingly, my first meeting with Françoise Dolto left me speechless.

It was the start of the 1970s. I was working at the Marcel-Rivière Institute as a full-time intern. One of the psychiatrists I enjoyed working with offered to take me to the seminar Dolto was giving to members of the École Freudienne.

It took me several months to realise what a great gift I had been given. I had recently arrived from Brazil, where Melanie Klein was considered the reigning authority on child psychoanalysis, and where no one had heard of Françoise Dolto.

The seminars were held at 21 rue Cujas, where her husband, Boris Dolto, had his physiotherapy school. Françoise presented to the group, in detail, the content of sessions she conducted with a young patient – what would later become her book *Dominique: Analysis of an Adolescent*.[1]

During the discussion period, with the assurance and heedless attitude of youth – I was then 26 – I expressed, in halting French, my strong disagreement with what she had just told us. I said I was surprised that, faced with a case of psychosis, she had not used Margarite Sechehaye's symbolic realisation technique – which I had just studied at length.

Here is the fiery exchange that ensued: "Mrs Sechehaye is perverse. Are you in analysis?" – "Yes." – "Does your analyst know that you attend these seminars?" – "No." – "Do you conduct analysis with children?" – "No." – "In that case, when you will work with children, call me and I will give you individual supervision." – "Why do you say that Mrs Sechehaye is perverse?" – "We will discuss that at another time. Thank you for coming. Goodbye."

And that was that. I was left sitting there until the end of the seminar, stunned. Admonished and accepted, an infinity of possibilities before me. Françoise Dolto can be summed up in this exchange: abrupt and respectful, uncompromising and full of generosity – brilliant.

When I started to work with children, I contacted her, of course. And she, of course, kept her promise. It was the beginning of an intense working relationship and a sincere friendship. She made me experience a kind of freedom I had never known before. This had to do, no doubt, with her way of being present to others. She was with you at once, with all her confidence and all her remarkable attention.

Her attentiveness involved the intense concentration typical of well-loved children – although this had not been true in her case – who do not fear being constantly surprised by the endless discovery of the world.

This kind of openness to the unexpected is a great strength. It is a clear, unquestionable, directly perceptible strength. It did not intimidate me, but expanded my world, made me stronger, more serene and more demanding.

Her chair was behind the couch; in front of the couch there was a small table covered with sheets of paper, pencils and modelling clay – the materials she used with children. (There were no toys in sight.) She listened, seated comfortably at one end of the little table, considering you with a serious expression, with the serious demeanour of a child, her hands in her lap or stretched out on the table, her fingers moving or busy with something – discreetly betraying boundless contained energy. She would interrupt unexpectedly, to ask a question, to relate a pertinent clinical situation or to suggest an elaboration on the problem. She could speak at length, sometimes emphatically. But dialogue was always possible, always animated and enthusiastic. Never an all-knowing attitude; never. Rather, and very often, she would encourage further elaboration, or confirm a very personal clinical approach.

During these supervisory encounters, Dolto assumed she was speaking to a psychoanalyst, since the person before her was there to talk about his analytic practice. This ethical stance had profound and immediate consequences. Being granted this kind of confidence from the outset, with nothing demanded in return, filled us with the joy of speaking freely, made us feel more alive, rendered our experience more vivid and our work more real. It also made us acutely aware of our debt and our boundless responsibility. And it underscored our unavoidable solitude.

I held her in great esteem.

(Regarding Margarite Sechechaye, she recounted a disturbing event: lunch at her home, on rue Saint-Jacques, where "Renée", her famous patient, took a dose of drugs with the approval of her "analyst". For me, that was the end of Sechechaye.)

A few months later, I started attending the psychotherapy consultations she conducted at the Trousseau Hospital. Several generations of analysts were trained in this unit where I saw extraordinary things happen, including Sabine's therapy.

Sabine was a little girl who had stopped speaking at the age of four, after witnessing a sexual encounter between her mother (who at the time was prostituting herself to make a living) and a client. Sabine had been in therapy with Françoise Dolto for several years; in fact, she was known to more than one "generation" of trainee analysts who attended the sessions at Trousseau. Those of us who served as interlocutors during the consultations, at Dolto's request, were not always able to attend every Tuesday session. But we almost always managed to be there for the sessions with Sabine (as I choose to call her).

We were touched by this little girl, who was now nine, and by her mother. We did not understand what transpired during the sessions. Neither did Françoise Dolto. She always took some time to reread the notes from the previous session, to discuss them with the analysts present, to go over the entire case file. For years, at *each session* with Sabine, there was the sense of urgency we often feel with children – urgency but not haste: the wholehearted commitment of the analyst to the work of analysis, his desire to find the right track, the one that would allow him to glimpse, through transference, the fragment of reality holding the subject captive.

Those who attended the Tuesday sessions at Trousseau will never forget the tension and anguish to which Dolto was subject to before each session, and which was another expression of her complete availability. With Sabine, these states reached their greatest intensity.

The session I am about to describe took place after several years of analytic work. Three? Four? I don't remember exactly. Sabine had brought her teddy bear that day. Françoise understood that the child wanted to play at having a tea party and, with her usual skill, started to sculpt plates, forks, knives, spoons, bowls. This took time. Françoise Dolto enjoyed working with modelling clay. It gave her a chance to rest and relax, all the while continuing to talk to the child, explaining what she was doing or what she intended to do. Sabine's eyes, big and beautiful like those of her mother, followed the movements of her analyst's skilful fingers. Dolto asked her what was the name of the teddy bear. Sabine, of course, made no reply. Dolto then asked Madame Arlette, a nurse whose assistance at the Trousseau consultations was invaluable, to go and see the mother to find out the name of the bear. We saw Madame Arlette returning, with or without the name. Now, the table is set. Sabine starts to feed the little stuffed animal. Françoise Dolto voices the silent conversation between Sabine and her "baby". The child is very concentrated on the game, which consists of feeding her teddy bear. At one point, Sabine lifts the spoon to her mouth. What could be more natural, after all? A little girl is playing at feeding her toy bear, and does what mothers often do with their babies, tasting or pretending to taste their food.

But Françoise Dolto sees things differently. Before the spoon reaches the child's lips, Dolto's hand gives Sabine's little hand a *real* slap. Madame Dolto is angry, very angry. She is almost shouting. What she says is this: that the food for the teddy bear is food for pretending, while what Sabine eats is food for people. So where had she gotten the preposterous idea of eating pretend food that can't help her grow and become a woman?

Dolto stops talking. She continues to be there as usual, present and available. But also angry, very angry. Some of us wonder what could be the matter with her that day, to make her scold this little girl we all like so much. As for Sabine, she is considering Françoise Dolto without showing any surprise, in total silence, as usual. She seems to be reflecting profoundly on this lady who is still so angry. And suddenly she says, "You are right, Madame", before the assembled adults who shed tears of joy while Dolto, without pausing and as if nothing unusual had happened, pursues this dialogue that we had spent years waiting for, and that our emotion now prevented us from hearing.

In this instance, a real intervention dissociated the imaginary space from the symbolic space, and prevented the child from identifying with the infantile. Of course, this type of intervention relies on rigorous technique, on the necessity of separating aspects that must remain distinct throughout the therapeutic process. We know that what we call the psychoanalyst's desire is indissociable from his ethical position. Working with children is one of the most extreme forms of psychoanalytic practice because it requires a clear conception of the theoretical genesis of a subject. In other words, the psychoanalyst must have a precise theory on psychic health, meaning a theory on how maturational stages, ego development and thought processes are integrated. This integration extends from the time of the mother's perfect adaptation to the needs of the baby, to the child's autonomy. It must be remembered that, at the very beginning, the psychic space of the mother constitutes the environment.

To answer your question on Freudian amorality, I will relate another exceptional clinical situation that took place at Trousseau. This story illustrates what can be shocking about psychoanalysis to people with conventional ideas or to those who use ideas and theories to avoid thinking. It also illustrates Dolto's complete confidence in the Freudian method, her remarkable creativity and her great openness to everything that contributes to constituting a human subject. Above all, it is a concrete example of what acknowledgement of all aspects of the unconscious entails: major restructuring of the premises of thought.

But before recounting the story, I have to remind you of the context of the sessions held at Trousseau: there were between eight or ten of us, psychoanalysts, present in the room. In other words, although we were working with the intimate, even atrocious aspects of the intimate, the analytic scene took place in public, before witnesses. Therefore, there could be secrets, but no confidentiality.

The story concerns the tragic life of a twelve-year-old schizophrenic girl Dolto had been treating for several years. When I saw her for the first time in consultation, she was animated, amusing and participating actively in her analysis.

Her mother was a pretty, petite woman, pleasant and silly; thanks to the progress accomplished, she consented to some distance between herself and her daughter, a degree of separation. This allowed her to meet a man who became her companion.

The presence of a man in the household, a man who took care of the mother and on whom she focused her attention, had remarkable effects. The young girl flourished, became very spirited and made great strides in her studies.

The mother was very proud and brought her companion to the therapy sessions. He was a pleasant man, timid and unpretentious. He had an occupation, and seemed happy and fond of his wife.

Things continued to go well for a time. And suddenly, to everyone's stupefaction, everything stopped. The young girl became apathetic, withdrawn, distant.

Françoise Dolto searched for answers. She met with the educators from the day hospital, who were just as puzzled by this turn of events. The couple acting as a foster family, where the girl stayed for two weeks during the last school holidays, had no answers either. They were vivacious people, very pleased to be at the consultation, before an audience, and very distressed when they saw the child, who arrived late.

The mother and her companion were devastated, crushed by shame. Françoise Dolto listened to them, comforted them, went over the events of the past two months once again. But she found nothing that could explain such a major setback.

And one day, inexplicably, Dolto guessed the truth:

– Sir, how long have you been acting like a lover with your wife's daughter?

This terrible sentence, which the precision of its carefully chosen words makes unforgettable, was spoken in a manner that precluded any objection and, at the same time, invited discussion. The tone of voice carried no blame, no judgment. But no compassion or complicity either. The sentence was spoken because it was true, and because with a psychoanalyst one looks for the truth – no matter how horrifying.

From that point on, Françoise Dolto embarked on clinical work that was impressively rigorous, clear-sighted and compassionate. We were confronted with the horror of raw human misery. There was the child, in whom something seemed irrevocably broken. There was the mother/spouse, in total shock, suffering a triple blow: wounded by what had happened to her daughter, and by the double failure of her companion – as a man and as a parent.

Dolto's genius transformed this man's actions into a means of access to the place inside him where he was insane. This transformation was also at work within us, the analysts witnessing the sessions.

I would not go so far as to say that I still found the man likeable. In fact, I hated him. But for the duration of each session I was deeply interested in him, in his psychic functioning on which Dolto, patiently and relentlessly, was trying to make him reflect, so that he could identify it and describe it. At the end of the sessions, he was exhausted. So were the rest of us. (Françoise Dolto seemed fine.) The man was exhausted, yes, but more consolidated; his eyes were no longer empty. Sometimes, at the end of a session, he even moved with the physical ease of a child who had been safely carried by someone.

This man was not a pervert. He was governed by another sort of idiocy, combined with a symbolic misery that could not respect any value, or be affected by any feeling. The reign of pleasure and the senses: a spineless ogre.

The sessions involved all three of them: the man; the woman; and the child. The girl was gradually coming out of her lethargy, returning to her relation with the analyst. The woman, clearly encouraged by the work accomplished with her companion, commented more often, and spoke more freely than she had ever done. Dolto let each of them speak in turn. She often addressed the young girl directly, made interpretations, tried to separate the child's existence from that of the two adults, to separate her living being from the object of the massacre.

On one occasion, to our horror, Dolto understood that the man had repeated his previous actions. It was horrible, but after this session, after what the analyst told him – "Your father's madness overpowered you once again" – the man was able to take control of the search that Dolto had initiated and conducted in his place. In his own way, with his limitations, his fears and his shame, he began to speak truthfully.

For those of us who were present, these sessions were unbearable, hellish episodes. We were shaken, but we had faith. In what? That was the question.

There was only one person who had no faith at all. One man who found all this more unbearable than we did. He did not believe in it, insisted that it was impossible to be cured, that an analyst should not waste time with such a thing. What he expressed was so pathetic, so absurd, so final that no one contradicted him. In this situation, it would have been indecent to invoke the question of a cure.

Dolto's genius allowed her to accept that disaster and scum are part of life, and that the inhuman is part of the human. This way of seeing things did not produce a fatalistic attitude. The calamity that befell these three people was a tragedy. And there is no cure for a tragedy. But because the calamity was created by its protagonists, it was possible to reflect on it, try to find its roots, try to avoid its recurrence.

But can we consider the child one of the agents of the tragedy? Of course not. Françoise Dolto was very clear on this point: the parents must never be set aside; like it or not, the child will have to deal with them in order to grow up, separate from them or reject them – so that it is best that the analyst help the child set in motion or accomplish this work.

Tragedy is incurable. But an analyst like Françoise Dolto has the certainty that one can live with it. Given that, for her, this was a real, embodied truth – and not simply a wish – the analytic exchange could transform it into a possibility.

Although there is no explanation for genius, I always believed that Dolto's genius had its roots in her familiarity with the Bible. She must have learned from the Bible, as Gisela Pankow had done, to transform the most ordinary details of daily life into a founding myth of the subject. It was the well from which she drew the ever-renewed vitality of a code of ethics that included amorality.

Your friend,

Note

1   Dolto, F. (1973), *Dominique: Analysis of an Adolescent* (trans. I. Kats). New York: Outerbridge & Lazard.

Couch or chair

Dear friend,

Your question as to whether to place the patient on the couch or on the chair is part of the many things a novice analyst usually wants to explore. If we think about the history behind these two options, we can easily see that this question is secondary. The important question is why we use the couch, since this position, where a person lying on the couch is speaking to someone who sits behind him, seems absurd and surrealistic to most people.

I will tell you about my own experience. When I started to work as a psychoanalyst, at the end of the 1960s, a period when we were very interested in possible modalities for working with psychotic patients, the usual advice was that they should never be asked to lie on the couch.

Later, I met Gisela Pankow, who understood the nature of psychoanalysis as very few people did; she asked her psychotic patients to lie on the couch. What she considered essential were the evaluation sessions. It was important to take all the time necessary to clearly identify the major defensive organization of the patient – what she called making a diagnosis. I will give you an amusing, but instructive, illustration.

My office was full of psychotic and perverse patients sent by Pankow. One day, she sent an attractive young woman, a physician working both in a hospital and in private practice. Given this woman's social status, I thought that this time Pankow had consented to refer a true neurotic for analysis with me. Therefore, at the end of the first session, I suggested that we start therapy the following week, and that we see each other three times a week. She agreed and I was very pleased. At the first session, she lay down backwards – that is, she placed her head where the feet should be, and her feet on the cushion, where people usually put their head – and announced: "I have a psychotic sister and a brother who attempted suicide."

My first thought was to ask her to sit in the chair. But since she was a doctor, I told myself that I couldn't do that because she would realise that I consider her psychotic. So I told myself that I should think of her as a baby who has trouble finding a comfortable position to fall asleep, and I helped her to lie comfortably on the couch.

What is amusing here is my belief that she would consider herself psychotic if I asked her to sit in the chair. Such is the power of theories in vogue at a certain time! What is instructive is that I cannot say what I would do today – that is, I don't know if I would ask her to sit in the chair or not. The difference is that now I have much more experience, and therefore more freedom in handling difficult clinical situations. But I still can't be certain of what I would do in a similar situation; the nature of each particular situation depends on a multitude of factors.

Victor Smirnoff,[1] whom I met a few years later, believed that what was important was to make sure the patient would not regress massively as soon as he lay on the couch. This observation, coming from such an eminent clinician, reminds us that asking someone to recline has effects, that it is not a neutral request. The fact that he wanted to prevent sudden regression, before transferential landmarks are in place to allow working it through, shows his concern not just for the patient, but primarily for his own psychic well-being.

In fact, it was to protect his psychic well-being that Freud asked his patients to lie down, so that he would not have to maintain eye contact with them for an entire day of analytic work. But Piera Aulagnier used to say that she asked patients who tended to bore her to sit facing her – so that she would not fall asleep, and be able to concentrate better.

As for me, well-being is my first consideration as well. In general, in the case of patients who recognise the existence of an internal world (made of dreams, and memories) in constant conflict with reality (the desire of the other, and the limits of a particular culture) – in other words, those for whom anxiety is a fact of life – I place them on the couch from the start, or as soon as I can.

With all the others, for whom the major difficulty springs from the effects of a trauma, the first priority is to assess the type of presence necessary. Our presence to them, of course, but also the degree of their presence to us, so that we can work in the best conditions possible.

Presence is made up of perceptions of body language and of eye contact; it has to do with our way of greeting the person, of opening the door, with our tone of voice, with the appropriate use of silence and, if need be, our ability to envelop the person in a flow of words that warms him and puts him at ease.

In the case of these patients marked by the effects of trauma, ritualisation of the analytic scene renders the analysis and the relation to the analyst unreal, because it resonates with the defences these patients invented as a protection against the agent of violence. For these subjects, in whom the effects of traumatic violence have destroyed all spontaneous expression, our actual existence is the fundamental condition allowing them to risk admitting that the analyst recognises their existence as a reality. The risk they take is the risk of hope, and therefore of loss of this hope, which would be a repetition of the traumatic collapse.

It is the unprecedented nature of the analytic relation that will allow the patient to recognise the projective character of certain convictions. He will seize, *as an actual experience*, the distinction between fantasy and perception, or between the symbolic reality of a relation – that which he builds with the analyst – and the infinite imagined possibilities of an encounter.

All these observations confirm that our comfort is related to the transferential dynamic. This is why the same factors could motivate me to conduct the sessions face-to-face or with the patient on the couch. I can ask a woman patient to lie on the couch because she is so beautiful and seductive that I can hardly focus on what she says. I ask an equally beautiful patient to be seated because she uses her seductiveness to hold her melancholic depression at bay. I want to hear her melancholia without forgetting that she is an attractive woman, so that she can connect these two disconnected dimensions: her depression and her sensuality.

What are the other things I can tell you? Usually, people who have been in analysis previously prefer to stay seated. I am willing to comply, if I think that their decision is not unalterable. When patients are tedious, I ask them to lie on the couch: they were children whose parents could not imagine a future for them – I want them out of sight to be better able to dream a life for them. Although I am rather inflexible concerning the initial position of a patient, I can modify my decision later: once my suggestion has been accepted, as the work progresses we may both prefer to discuss certain things with the patient either seated or lying on the couch – although few patients have experienced such flexibility in the analytic setting.

In short, it can be said that the couch can only be used when the analyst feels that the patient has granted him the position of interpreter; when this is the case, the decision about chair or couch becomes secondary, in my view. But asking someone to lie on the couch without being confirmed in the role of interpreter leads nowhere – in other words, it is a sure way to head for disaster.

Sometimes, patients perceive an analyst in the role of interpreter from the outset. (This can facilitate initiating the process – provided the patient also grants this position to the particular analyst he is seeing.) But, more and more often, this is far from being the case.

Not long ago, just before the holidays, I saw a new patient who decided to start analysis following an event that had troubled her deeply. Wanting to surprise her mother on her birthday, she went to the country her mother was visiting at the time. She arrived in the midst of festivities and found her mother, who did not recognise her, and exclaimed: "Who is this?"

As Françoise Dolto used to say, in some situations you have to be touched by grace. The last day before your vacation, one hour left before you leave, and all this suffering left unattended! I was lucky to think of telling her: "Your mother must be someone who has a lot of trouble dealing with her emotions. Your arrival was a pleasant surprise, but the emotion was so intense and unexpected that she preferred not to believe it was real, to treat your presence as if it was a dream." I had guessed right. With such a mother, it was obvious that the analysis would quickly reveal traumas and childhood privations, but I knew that now we had overcome this predicament together, I could, if I wished, ask her to lie on the couch as soon as we resumed the sessions. And this is, in fact, what I did.

Enjoy your vacation.

Note

1   French psychoanalyst of Russian origin. See Letter 22, *Victor Smirnoff: an example to follow.*

Letter 6

Transference

Dear friend,

The issue of the analyst's transference seems to constitute the focal point of the numerous questions you raise in your reply to my previous letter. You are saying that, in your understanding, once I have been granted the role of interpreter, my decision to choose the couch or the chair is determined by my transference towards the patient. You explain that as far as you are concerned, you need to treat psychotic patients face-to-face, given the multitude of signs one can read on their faces, signs with which you need to maintain contact or which allow you to foresee an anxiety attack that would prevent the patient working through. Finally, you ask if analytic work with children and psychotics has changed the original conception of transference.

I once wrote an article about a patient who asked me to read a book she liked, and about the fact that doing this allowed us to get through a difficult period in the analysis.[1] Commenting on this manner of dealing with a situation, contrary to orthodox practice – which requires that the relation to the patient be limited to what is said during the sessions – I pointed out that it was the direct result of my practice with children – who often bring to the sessions not only their drawings and clay sculptures, but also personal possessions that are important to them. When I thought about this again after reading your letter, I realised that I wouldn't know how to treat the situation differently. Reflecting on the meaning of this inability to imagine another form of clinical treatment could begin to answer your questions.

At first, I told myself that I couldn't imagine another form because there simply wasn't one. Of course, this is not true, but it shows that my work with psychotic patients and children has shaped my conception of transference. In fact, I have noticed that I always speak about analysis from this clinical perspective. And I must add that in my opinion optimal psychoanalytic training includes the following stages: being in analysis; a long period of practice with psychotic patients; work with "normally afflicted" patients; and only after all this, work with children.

Later, I told myself that another option is to refuse the situation altogether. I was thinking of psychoanalysts who make it a rule never to answer questions, receive gifts, etc. In these conditions, for the sake of what you call a "fictional" typical analysis, the formal analytic setting becomes a procrustean bed that excludes chance and the unexpected from the process.

But in fact, openness to chance and to the unhoped-for is a fundamental requirement for working with children and psychotic patients. Practicing this type of work long enough becomes a form of training that leads to the construction of a setting suitable to all patients.

For analysts trained, like you, by working with psychotic patients, the work with neurotics, the listening for products of the imagination – what we call fantasies – constitutes one particular aspect of analytic work, among others. What we learn from psychotic patients and children allows us to modify our transference, giving us more freedom to adapt the setting so as to work more comfortably. This is why, as you so rightly point out, in most cases we prefer to work with schizophrenics face-to-face in order to discern from their facial expressions the possible onset of an anxiety attack. But we might sometimes ask a particular schizophrenic patient with whom we have already established a strong bond to lie on the couch for a more or less lengthy period, in order to better explore a fantasy identified through analytic interpretation.

Speaking of this freedom we have acquired, I see an illustration of it in your work with your "dangerous" patient, the one whose delusion involves an actress he sees everywhere. You could have decided to ask him to lie on the couch after he said that your legs made him want to touch your body, given that your fitting interpretation – "but I do have to put my legs somewhere" – prompted him to speak about his mother. But you chose to keep him seated, no doubt in order to continue exploring the difference between the delusional and real aspects of his relation to you, or in order not to disturb the setting which allowed the fantasy to surface.

Let us return to the central question you raise in your letter. No, I do not think that analytic work with psychotic patients and children has changed the original perception of transference. But this work did allow the development of an aspect of the process on which Freud insisted and of which his friend Ferenczi[2] would have approved. In *The Dynamics of Transference*,[3] he states that the analyst, like any new person in the patient's life, represents a new libidinal hope (the text was written in 1912!). In short, we can say that pathology is characterised not so much by repetition as by the immense energy employed by the patient in refusing to recognise that which is unexpected and different. True analytic work implies the presence, on the part of both analyst and analysand, of the desire to think, to analyse. (Of course, my interpretation of Freud's text is influenced by everything we have learned since.) But it remains comforting to know that Freud was aware of this aspect of the transferential relation.

My understanding of transference included, from the start, a distinction between *psychotherapeutic process* and *analysis*.[4] I inherited this perspective from Gisela Pankow. I encountered it initially when I read her first book, and later during the immensely instructive "supervision" period I spent with her. Gisela Pankow, who was attempting to work psychoanalytically with severely psychotic patients, was always concerned with the conditions that make the work possible. She would ask these patients to sculpt using modelling clay; she had learned the technique and part of the theory from Françoise Dolto. Using this technique allowed her to create a *space* between her and her patients, a space in which she could work with less risk of a fatal physical confrontation with the patient.[5]

Having adopted this theory, I think of the therapeutic and analytic space as being "external" to both protagonists and serving as a common ground where the patient and the analyst can reflect together on the patient's infantile experiences.

The distinction I make between the therapeutic space and the space of analysis is simple. I call *therapeutic space* the time we spend being primarily therapists. And I call *analytic space* the time we dedicate primarily to helping the patient find meaning in his life thanks to his discovery of the unconscious.

Sometimes – and not only when working with psychotic patients – it takes a long while before the therapeutic space can serve as an intermediary zone between the analyst and the patient. This was the case with a young girl who, for months on end, recounted in detail the tortures inflicted on her by her mother, her brother and her stepfather. I had the feeling that she was physically inside me. She borrowed my space, explored all the corners of its landscape, deposited something in one place and something else in another, she came back to put these bits together and left again. She made herself comfortable, settled in by the fireside, to let herself remember, to tell herself all these horrors which acquired reality, became part of her life, were located in a precise time and space, and could now constitute her past. During this entire time, I was unable to speak. It was my turn to bear what was being done to me. Sometimes, after a session, I had to vomit. Finally, one day, disgusted and angry, I told her: "I hate your mother, I hate your brother, I hate your stepfather." From that moment on, her life changed completely. Of course, anger and disgust were the emotions she felt as a child, before she could name them. But her suffering had to spend all this time inside me before she could hear these words as words she had been waiting for, and before these words could create a barrier, a closure – detaching her, separating her permanently from the reality of the nightmare.

When the therapeutic space is not an intermediary zone between us and the patient, we are doing the work of two people. We support, protect and carry the patient. We become a container, a house where he comes to stay. We lend him our way of thinking and feeling. We grant him necessary, never-before-possible respite, time in which to learn a new way of relating to himself and to others, without unfathomable anxiety and a relentless sense of persecution. He receives a space, transplanted from a donor, until his own existence becomes real. We provide an envelope, a shelter, like a mother does for the baby she is carrying. We lend him our world. A psychic world for two.

This view of the analytic process is inconceivable for those who consider psychoanalysis solely a process of disassembling, that is, the work of deconstructing the defences set in place by the subject in order to live. But if the therapeutic aspect holds such a dominant place – the scandal of Eros – in the case of these therapists we can no longer speak of psychoanalysis. When Freud encountered this type of objection, he would say: "Theory is all well and good, but this [clinical reality] exists as well."

Warm regards,

Notes

1 "Un nouveau découpage des scènes", *Topiques*, No. 53, 1994.
2 Sándor Ferenczi (1873–1933), Hungarian psychoanalyst, a disciple and later a friend of Freud, his only real interlocutor, with whom he continued to invent psychoanalysis. Ferenczi was the inventor of trauma theory and treatment. See Letter 7, *The Ferenczi predicament*.
3 Freud, S. (1912), *The Dynamics of Transference*, S.E., 12: 99–108. London: Hogarth.
4 This distinction was originally made in my first book *Ana K, histoire d'une analyse*, Paris: Gauthier-Villars, 1977.
5 Gisela Pankow's first book was entitled *L'Homme et sa psychose*, Paris: Aubier, 1969.

The Ferenczi predicament

Dear friend,

I will begin with some simple advice which concerns the best way of becoming acquainted with Ferenczi: my advice is to start by reading the entire *Correspondence* with Freud. This will allow you to judge for yourself the immense importance of the role played by Ferenczi in the invention of psychoanalysis. Then, before coming back to this correspondence by reading Freud's essays as well as those of Ferenczi – since the correspondence was written in parallel with these texts – and in order to provide a context for this ambitious study, you can refer to three essential texts. The first, "Ferenczi: False Problem or Real Misunderstanding", by Wladimir Granoff, was published in French in 1961 in the journal *La Psychanalyse* (issue 6). At the time, the *Correspondence* had not yet been published in its entirety and it was this text that revealed to the analytic community the place held by Ferenczi in Freud's life: from 1908 on, the co-inventor of psychoanalysis and tireless explorer of the possibilities of analytic practice, and of its applicability to borderline cases, to psychosis, and to psychosomatic responses.

This article played a crucial historical role in France as well. Through Ferenczi's notions about the child in the adult – meaning that the analytic process must find the child the patient carries inside him – Granoff brought into question the clinical possibilities of theories on the signifier. He did so in his elegant, elliptical manner, but it was a hard blow and Lacan recognised what was at stake. All the more so since, at Granoff's prompting, the same issue of the Journal included a translation (by Granoff's wife) of "The Confusion of Tongues between Adults and Children", an essay in which Ferenczi reiterates the importance of trauma as a factor in the genesis of psychic pathologies – a view Freud found intolerable. This initial divergence between Granoff and Lacan heralded the break that would take place a few years later, when the International Psychoanalytical Association refused to renew Lacan's psychoanalytic training position – a decision in which Granoff played a crucial role.

The second text I advise you to read in order to ground your practice is *"Les enjeux et les conséquences"*, another article by Granoff, published in Études Freudiennes, issue 34, in September 1993. This issue published the presentations and discussions at a symposium on the publication of the Freud/Ferenczi

Correspondence[1] in France. Granoff's reinterpretation of his 1961 article, and his ensuing conclusions, are very interesting.

The third text I recommend is Judith Dupont's preface to Ferenczi's *Clinical Diary*[2] written in 1932, one year before his death. Judith Dupont outlines in very precise terms the effects on the analytic community of Ernest Jones's biased presentation of the relationship between Freud and Ferenczi. While you read the *Correspondence*, or afterwards, you can study Monique Schneider's *Le Trauma et la filiation paradoxale*,[3] a fascinating account of what was and continues to be at stake given the theoretical differences, and even disputes, between Freud and Ferenczi.

Let me try to give you an introduction to this entire matter.

Someone trying to describe, today, Ferenczi's place in the history of psychoanalysis encounters the same difficulty as the person who attempts to see the fingers of a hand held up against his nose. Since Ferenczi's ideas are now part of the theoretical corpus, for an analyst, assessing its value amounts to assessing the value of psychoanalysis. To illustrate, this is what Freud said at the end of his life: "[Many subjects discussed for a number of years] have become part of the literature under his name or mine."[4] I hope that this gives you an idea of the extent of the problem: recognising the essential nature of an inexhaustible question whose defining characteristic is a lack of definition.

Yet the Ferenczi predicament is quite real. First, because it designates the clinical practices Ferenczi initiated, whose interest lies not only in the answers they provide, but also in the permanent questions they raise. In addition, there is the question of Ferenczi's relationship with Freud.

When Wladimir Granoff wrote his article in 1961, the clinical area identified and explored by Ferenczi was not yet defined. In fact, Granoff's work was decisive, as had been that of Michel Balint, Ferenczi's analysand, in attributing to the latter the formulation of the most difficult and most forward-looking questions studied by researchers in the psychoanalytic field at the time. Granoff chose (or circumstances forced him to choose) as a starting point Freud's relationship with Ferenczi. There was no mention of the latter's major contributions: introjection; negative transference; countertransference; etc. Instead, Granoff focused on the question on everyone's mind at the time: Freud's opinion of Ferenczi. This question had been given an answer by Ernest Jones – Freud's biographer, Ferenczi's analysand, jealous of the latter's relationship with Freud, and long-time President of the International Psychoanalytic Association. But Jones's answer was built on fragmented quotes from the *Correspondence*, to which he had access, and was clearly given in bad faith. Granoff did not even bother to quote him, preferring to use Freud's own texts to show the difference between the two men in Freud's view. He then concluded: "To say that [Ferenczi] was the favourite disciple is an incorrect interpretation. He was Freud's interlocutor, the only one." Even if one was in Paris, and not in London, where Jones's reign was still felt in 1961, it took great courage to say: "Freud invented psychoanalysis, but Ferenczi practised psychoanalysis." Why courage?[5]

First, because this way of presenting things differentiates between Ferenczi the man and the question he raises – although only the man he was could have raised the question: that is, that the practice of psychoanalysis requires constant confrontation between established theory and what happens in the transference/countertransference domain. In addition, this way of presenting things places the Freud–Ferenczi relationship on a different foundation. The presumed confidence and loyalty existing between the two men allow each of them to raise clinical questions contributing to their theoretical reflections. This assumption is fully confirmed by the *Correspondence*, which shows that Sándor's therapeutic concerns meet with Sigmund's interest, support and encouragement. Moreover, the fact that Granoff associates the two men in his research could be taken as a warning against any attempt to return to Freud without taking into account the clinical work developed by Ferenczi. A foreshadowing of things to come.

The main objective of Granoff's 1961 commando offensive was to free Ferenczi from the role Jones' official account had assigned to him: that of Freud's eternal analysand. Granoff accomplished his mission with the speed and efficiency expected of a commando operation: two quotes where Freud acknowledges the crucial role Ferenczi would play in the creation of psychoanalysis, one sentence portraying Jones in no more than a stewardship role, and finally Freud's judgement of *Thalassa*: "His most brilliant work, his richest reflection [...] could be the most daring, the most courageous explanation of analysis ever attempted."[6]

With this mission complete, Ferenczi regained his rightful status as a giant, and the second part of the commando operation could be set in motion.

This mission was more complex. The goal was to place a time bomb at the heart of a theoretico-clinical system whose dangers had become clear to Granoff. The operation required great skill, subtlety, adroitness and self-control, because once the countdown started, the agent had no place to go and could do nothing but wait for the explosion. Granoff lived up to his objectives in admirable fashion. There was something of a sleight of hand in his masterful manner of turning a phrase so that his intention did not become immediately obvious. He came back to Freud, but the context and the flow of his writing intentionally misled the listener, who supposed that he was talking about the Freud/Ferenczi relationship again, but this was no longer the case. Now, he was talking about the published work: Freud's texts and Ferenczi's texts. Granoff barely compared them; he had a different objective: to present, almost casually, the inventory of the clinical themes explored by Sándor Ferenczi: trauma; the splitting of the ego and even its fragmentation; the importance of the environment; the desire to heal; the child in danger; the child in distress; and, finally, the child in the adult. Who could be upset by this? Freud? The text does not say – and, as I will demonstrate, Freud was not always opposed to this. And what became of these clinical themes? In 1961, were they merely ghostly presences in the history of analytic theory? Not at all. In fact, quite the opposite. All these questions were being developed in London by the famous "Middle Group" whose most illustrious members included Michael Balint, Donald Winnicott and Wilfred Bion. Granoff, who spoke English perfectly, was well aware of the Group and its work. In fact, he would be the one to introduce Winnicott in France a few years later. But in 1961 he said nothing of his intentions; he did not reveal them until 1993. Why?

Granoff shared this long silence – should we say secret? – with Lacan, who was also aware of the work conducted in London as a direct outgrowth of Ferenczi's clinical work – which Jones prevented from being recognised as such. Ferenczi disturbed Lacan. The child in the adult was a problem for him, not for Freud. Granoff's discussion of this matter was aimed at Lacan. Granoff's article juxtaposed quotes from Freud and Ferenczi in such a way as to point out the impasses from which it was Lacan who could not escape (not Freud). Granoff notes, for history, Lacan's dodging and hasty avoidance of such dilemmas, and refers implicitly to the disastrous consequences this silence could have in the clinical practice of those who trained with Lacan. Granoff's warning produced the unfortunate effect we all know.

Today, more than forty years later, when the entire *Correspondence* is available to us, on re-examining the Freud/Ferenczi relationship we can clearly see that the latter was Freud's disciple (not his student), co-creator of psychoanalysis and its institutions, loyal friend and... eternal analysand. This last factor was the mainspring of both his inventiveness and the dilemmas he could not avoid – Judith Dupont goes so far as to say that they killed him. And now I will tell you what I believe was problematic for Freud in his relationship with Ferenczi. (I will not discuss Ferenczi's perspective, which is presented in great detail in the *Correspondence*, as well as in the *Clinical Diary* and in his letters to Groddeck.)

First, what is evident is that the sincerity, even shamelessness, with which Sándor writes to Freud is motivated by two factors: the desire to continue his own analysis and consequently live better, but also the desire to understand his patients better and consequently develop more polished theories based on his practice. The *Correspondence* testifies to the fact that the two men saw no separation between psychoanalysis and a personal code of ethics based on a love of truth that required examination of all their passions.

I find these letters completely convincing. They convince me that there is no other way to work, to write, when we want to grab hold of the unconscious and to understand its hold on us. I was equally convinced when I read Freud's letters to Fliess, his friend and substitute analyst. Freud assigned the place of the father to Fliess. But given that Fliess was incapable of taking on this role, Freud theorised that this place is important in the life of a subject. In time, dear friend, you will come to see that we often develop theories based on failures in our analytic work. Another consequence of the failures that occurred in Freud's relationship with Fliess was Freud's ability to bear the homosexual love of his friends and disciples, and to encourage their innovative work; Ferenczi benefitted greatly from this capacity.

Ferenczi was asking Freud to be the mother he had not had. For Freud, this was doubly difficult: first, because the fact that he himself had had a good mother made it hard for him to imagine that a mother could be destructive; and second, because his own experience tended to designate the father as the one who engenders the subject. Thanks to this inadequacy in his relationship with Freud, Ferenczi would become the first to develop a theory regarding the importance of the mother as an environment, in constituting the child and the subject, and the first to accept this role in transference. Therefore, when Freud suggested that Ferenczi do the same thing as he himself had done when he broke off his relationship with Fliess – that is, choose the "good" internal father over the "bad" transferential father – he was making an absurd, impossible request. Ferenczi's concern was with the mother, good and bad, a role he assigned to Freud in transference, and which the latter, given his history and the expectation he had had in relation to Fliess, was unable to identify or to take on, so as to make it possible for Ferenczi to go beyond this unconscious request.

But the fact that Freud was unable to deal with the archaic manifestations of the relationship to the mother in transference did not prevent him from supporting his Hungarian friend in his clinical research in this field, or from sharing his interest in telepathy – which is present in both maternal empathy and in transferential identification. As you can imagine, this did not facilitate things for the analysand Ferenczi.

We can see this in the *Correspondence*: Freud never discouraged Ferenczi's technical attempts to treat trauma, nor his desire to be cured. It would have been absurd for him to do so, for at least two reasons. First, from the scientific point of view, presenting psychoanalysis as a therapy that can treat and cure psychic illnesses was necessarily of interest to the researcher in Freud, even if he himself had decided to bypass this question – which had nevertheless been a central theme in *Studies on Hysteria*,[7] his first book. Second, there was the fact that the cases Ferenczi treated were outside the parameters of neurosis. Ferenczi's grievances in regards to Freud were never related to a lack of support for his research, but only to a didactic attitude disguising the lack of clinical inventiveness needed to free him from the constraints imposed by the deficiencies of his relationship with his mother.

Freud was also able to show concern for the real child in the therapeutic process, as evidenced by his work with the patient known as the Wolf Man, during which Freud confirmed the reality of the reconstructed memory of a scene that had occurred in the first year of the subject's life. He also agreed that in the traumatised child the analyst must look for a living child on whom the subject can learn to reconstruct his internal world – a concept which constitutes the nucleus of Freudian theory. In addition, Freud did not object to the notion of repression of affect, since he found the idea of *need for punishment* as an explanation for *unconscious sense of guilt* unsatisfactory. In that case, where was the problem?

Ferenczi became a problem when he asserted that Freud was unable to recognise his negative transference, masked by idealisation – a statement that forced Freud to confront his own idealisation of Ferenczi, in whom he saw not only a potential son-in-law, but also a man with remarkable intellectual qualities and a talented clinician. Ferenczi became a problem when he made a public presentation in which he once again asserted the importance of trauma as opposed to fantasy – even if the clinical context to which he alluded was not neurosis, because what Freud wanted, understandably, was to keep away from the centre stage of theory a concept he had rejected in favour of the idea of fantasy generated trauma. Ferenczi is a problem if he proclaims publicly that analytic healing consists of curing a child of the psychic consequences of his relationship with a demented mother – because this requires reconsidering the entire theoretical edifice founded on the father, and Freud no longer had the time to do this work.[8] In addition, Freud would have to take responsibility, as Ferenczi's analyst, for the misfortunes his friend encountered in life. But to do so meant recognising the difficulty of the psychoanalytic method. This was too much to ask for.

Let us try to imagine what Freud could have felt. As Judith Dupont points out, the quality of their relationship did not allow for lasting hostility. But this would not have prevented Freud from thinking: "What a troublemaker, this Ferenczi." Or, as Granoff said in 1961: "With Ferenczi it seems that [things] had to be played out to the death. It's something that could be expressed like this: 'My relationship with Ferenczi was out of the ordinary; one of us had to die and, in the end, I can't say that I am sorry that it was him.'"[9]

There is, then, a tragic ending to this story. A faint-hearted man could feel there is mortal danger in risking innovation, in a departure from what is established in order to create something new. But we can also tell ourselves that tragedy was inherent to this period of the psychoanalytic movement – the historical moment of the encounter of two great thinkers, when it proved to be impossible to find enough room to contain the main ideas of their complementary research. It was a paradoxical historical moment when despite the immense richness and scope of each man's ideas, the possibility of building on each other's reflections remained limited and dependent upon the dual transferential relation that held them captive in a sterile existential situation without promise. Today, we can imagine other transferential contexts in which the disciple's discoveries do not inflict a mortal narcissistic injury on the one who acts as a teacher.

And so we come to the end of our topic. I hope that I have inspired you to discover the giant of Budapest who loved life and who, apparently, used to laugh like a child.

All my best,

Notes

1 *The Correspondence of Sigmund Freud and Sándor Ferenczi*. Cambridge, MA: Belknap Press, 1996.
2 *The Clinical Diary of Sándor Ferenczi,* (trans. M. Balint and N. Z. Jackson). Cambridge, MA: Harvard University Press, 1995.
3 Schneider, M., (1988), *Le Trauma et la filiation paradoxale,* Paris: Ramsay.
4 Quoted by Granoff in his 1961 article "*Ferenczi : faux problème ou vrai malentendu*" in *La Psychanalyse* magazine (no. 6).
5 Granoff, W., article *Ferenczi : faux problème ou vrai malentendu* in 1961 issue of *La Psychanalyse* magazine (No 6).
6 Freud, S. (1933), Obituary: Sándor Ferenczi, in *International Journal of Psychoanalysis*, 14: 297–299.
7 Breuer, J. and Freud, S. (2000), *Studies on Hysteria (1893–1895)*, (trans. J. Strachey). New York: Basic Books.
8 I think that Freud's theory of a protective superego rooted in paternal and maternal affection was his way of acknowledging his debt to the concepts introduced by his Hungarian friend. See Letter 35, *The Celestina superego and the Dulcinea superego*.
9 Granoff, W., article "*Ferenczi : faux problème ou vrai malentendu*" in 1961 issue of *La Psychanalyse* magazine (No 6).

Psychosis

The encounter with Gisela Pankow

Dear friend,

I understand your impression that nosography is perplexing. For a long time, I had two very different experiences in this regard. When I read psychiatric terms in Freud's texts, I found them useful. But when I heard the same terms used by some psychiatrists, I no longer understood what they meant.

So I consulted the authorities on the subject: first Emil Kraepelin; then Eugen Bleuler, for whom Freud had great respect; Ernst Kretschmer; and Henri Ey. What I learned left me both pleased and perplexed. I was pleased to discover the existence of a highly sophisticated clinical practice, and I was surprised at the simplistic, brutal and unimaginative nature of mainstream psychiatric practices.

It was not until I encountered Gisela Pankow that I was able to sort all this out. Fortunately, I was familiar with the work of psychotherapists conducting psychoanalytic therapy in hospitals, who belonged to the *institutional psychotherapy* movement started by François Tosquelles, a brilliant exile from Catalonia who had come to France to flee the Spanish Civil War. Almost all of these psychiatrists were also trained psychoanalysts, or in training with Lacan – who was more skilled than anyone at building bridges between psychiatric and analytic practice.

But let me come back to Pankow. I first encountered her through her book *L'Homme et sa psychose* (Man and His Psychosis).[1] I bought the book during the Easter holidays in 1972, when it first came out. The title had caught my attention and in the months that followed, the book never left me.

Everything in it seemed right to me. The style was simple, direct, instructive. You could feel Pankow's desire to convey an experience, to share it.

Psychiatric terminology is discussed early in the book. To resume, Pankow defines four types of psychosis: schizophrenia; paranoia; marginal psychosis; and hysterical psychosis. She describes how the last of these is often confused with schizophrenia, and identifies the factors that make it possible to distinguish them.

This book is a veritable training manual because the reader never feels excluded from the process of developing the content discussed. The book is written in the present tense, so that the reader can consider in parallel the clinical material, its possible origins, and the new theoretical formulations Pankow proposes. It is a book full of ideas, but free of ideology; it offers a wealth of knowledge without being dogmatic.

As far as the nosography is concerned, Pankow goes over the major pathologies from her perspective on psychosis. Her interpretation transforms semiology into a vivid description of a way of being in the world. For her, the diagnosis is not a category used to classify people based on their symptoms, so as to allow distancing; it is, rather, a tool making it possible to reach them where they are. Thus, Gisela Pankow confirms and renews the fundamental practices of imminent psychiatrists for whom these concepts are essential clinical tools. But she does so as a psychoanalyst, intending to go beyond a phenomenological description – the manner in which the psychotic is "present" in the world – and to undertake an investigation aimed at situating this way of being within a family history, where it constitutes an adaptative response whose significance is inscribed in what was regarded as the law through the generations.

To summarise Pankow's conception of psychosis, I would say that for her the psychotic is someone who causes our usual definition of space to be abolished. This destruction mirrors the destruction of his mental representation of the body. The schizophrenic is unable to recognise his body as a whole object. In other psychoses, recognition of this wholeness is possible; what is missing is recognition of the connection between parts of the body. There are also patients who recognise the wholeness of the body and the connection between its parts – that is to say, they recognise the body as unified form, but do not perceive the meaning of this connection because sensory experiences remain unconnected.

The dissociation of the body image is governed by very strict unspoken laws, often transmitted from one generation to the next: "It is forbidden to have ears – you must not hear – eyes – you must not see – a mouth – you must not speak – etc." The corollary to this is that each part of the body recognised as such is linked to fragments of history that have escaped destruction, periods when some connection to another human being was possible. Pankow understood that for psychotic patients time resides in a space.

The analytic treatment of psychosis requires a method that can connect these different spaces of the body, these segments of history. The dynamics involved in this act of connecting constructs a relation between areas of the body and parts of history. And because these *dynamics concern spaces*, it is essential to establish the place occupied by the analyst in the therapeutic process. Pankow considered it crucial that this place be outside the delusion – if only to prevent the analyst from being taken for a portion of the patient's body.

Pankow's brilliant idea was to ask patients to bring drawings and clay sculptures – a technique she borrowed from Françoise Dolto's work with children. Pankow considered clay models, which have a spatial dimension and can be placed in relation to one another as a means of access to the way in which the patient inhabits his body, experiences it and locates it in relation to the therapist's body.

A therapist who works with the patient on this prototypical representation of the latter's relation to space gives himself the distance that makes it possible to measure how far the patient has come, and identify the threshold beyond which the intolerable becomes frightening, disorganising and destructive. For instance, schizophrenics are afraid of all forms. Any determinate form fills them with an unfathomable, unnameable fear of losing their body image. Because they cannot recognise the body as a whole, any form is dangerous because it can "imprison" them.

The therapist must always keep in mind that he is dealing with the dialectics of segments of the body, the dialectics between the space of the analyst and the spaces of the patient, the dialectics between fragments of the body and fragments of history. He must attempt, tactfully, to build bridges between isolated segments of the body in order to gain access to a space of time in a story.

Thanks to these notions and to the vast experience on which they are built, in my work with a young woman diagnosed as schizophrenic – but who, in fact, suffered from hysterical psychosis, I was able to free her from her psychotic defences in a short time. I had taken extensive notes after each session, and I sent them to Gisela Pankow as a tribute.[2]

She "summoned" me, took me "in supervision" and included me in the group of analysts with whom she worked once a month. It was on these occasions that I understood what teaching is.

To be continued…

Your friend,

Note

1 Pankaw, G. (1969), *L'Homme et sa psychose*. Paris: Flammarion, 2011.
2 These notes became my book *Ana K, histoire d'une analyse*, op. cit.

Letter 9

Gisela Pankow and her teaching

My dear friend,

What is teaching?

To teach is to transmit to another, through a certain practice, a feeling about the world.

The desire to transmit involves respect, confidence and the ability to identify with the interlocutor. Generosity is no doubt needed as well. And because psychoanalysis involves the intimate realm, a refusal of all compromise must accompany the search for the truth.

In fact, the most important thing a psychoanalyst transmits through his passion for his work is his intransigence. In psychoanalytic practice, where extreme states are so often interwoven with the most exquisite subtleties, the analyst's intransigence determines the range within which he can navigate.

The same intransigence governs the nurturing qualities associated with our ability to wait and advance tentatively, with our persistence, tolerance and patience.

When intransigence is not rooted in dogmatism or in a rigid superego that masks great fragility and fear, and when, on the contrary, it is the foundation of our way of being in the world, its transmission involves our innermost being, depends on our limitations and reflects our humility in the face of the infinite forms of the real. Therefore, letting our intransigence speak is an act of courage. A very particular kind of courage.

I am reminded of Alécio de Andrade, a Brazilian photographer and friend, who was visiting Carlos Drummond, one of the greatest poets of the twentieth century, to discuss the text for his exhibition of photographs of children.[1]

It was seven in the morning – the poet rose early to do his writing. Drummond offered to serve breakfast: orange juice, coffee, toast, fried eggs. Alécio, impressed with the dexterity of the poet, who quickly produced four perfect fried eggs, exclaimed: "Unbelievable! How do you do it? I always break them before they go in the pan or afterwards." The poet thought for a moment and said: "It takes courage to break them."

Gisela Pankow decided to "give me supervision" before she met me. Reading my manuscript had filled her with joy; she had read it as I hoped she would when I sent it: as proof that her book served to convey her ideas to others.[2]

After expressing surprise at my young age – I was only twenty-eight and seemed much younger – she immediately added: "People who look very young for a long time were traumatised in their childhood. Now I see why you understood my work so well."

Now that we were acquainted she started to talk about my manuscript. It was my turn to be surprised: I had been told that she was impressive (and she was), but also surly, brutal, guarded – and I was seeing a woman brimming with enthusiasm, generosity, joy and energy. A joyful giant.

Everything about this German woman that could cause inhibition in some of my colleagues was exciting for the Brazilian I was, placed us on the same footing and gave me great satisfaction. She had no bourgeois mannerisms, nothing polished, roundabout, measured, calculated or small-minded. She was a peasant who spoke of psychoanalysis in the same precise, frank, serious and passionate way in which she might have discussed potato farming. She carried the traces of a life where Man depended on nature and where death could strike at any moment.

We soon agreed that something extraordinary had taken place when I read her book. She kept exclaiming: "Incredible!", "Unbelievable!" to express her joy and wonder at having been understood so well for once. She spoke of my talent, I spoke of her genius, very simply, without false modesty, like farmers or poets who admire the harvest of one another's garden.

After this initial rejoicing – with which she took her time – plans had to be made for my future. She asked me what I had done before coming to France, who my parents were, what my work had been, what I had studied, who my analysts were. She strongly advised me to leave the analyst I was seeing at the time – "He has become an analyst! When I knew him he was a psychologist without much talent. What you're saying is very interesting." (And I did, in fact, leave this analyst a few months later.) She also asked what I was doing now, where, how many hours I worked each day, each week, how many patients I had, how often I saw each one, and the length of the sessions.

And then she informed me of her plan. I was to come to see her every Sunday at five in the afternoon, I would be part of the group that met with her once a month, and I would also attend the seminars she held every Thursday evening at the Faculty of Medicine. And that was that.

I did not have to ask for anything. She made all the decisions and organised everything. Since I understood her work so well, she was going to look after me and guide me. Although she was moved by my appreciation of her writing, it was her sense of responsibility that motivated her to provide me with this training. All this was unspoken, but very clear to us both. This tacit understanding, like the rest, suited me perfectly.

Gisela Pankow was a strong, intelligent, possessive woman who demanded total reciprocity. My mother was the same type of woman; as a result, I like strong, intelligent women and am not intimidated by them. I know how to deal with their excessive jealousy. In addition, I had heard Pankow described in such glowing terms that I could not fail to appreciate the gift she was bestowing on me. I knew that this experience would cause a life-changing upheaval.

When I left her, three hours later, I felt proud, carefree, joyful and very grateful.

The following Thursday I went to the Faculty of Medicine. The room was full. A young intern was presenting his work with a schizophrenic patient. Pankow was attentive, well-disposed. When he finished, she asked some questions concerning aspects of the patient's personal history not discussed in his presentation. He was unable to answer. She asked about the patient's present circumstances. He could provide no information. Pankow was genuinely interested, she wanted to understand. Why couldn't he tell her anything? Because the patient had not said. Why hadn't he asked her? He doesn't ask questions. And why not? Because he waits for patients to tell him. Pankow loses her patience: "Really, you wait for them to tell you. What an idea! If you're not interested in people, why have you chosen this profession? You could work somewhere else, in a government agency or at the post office."

The audience was shocked by what she was doing. The analysts in the room identified with the students and were traumatised. But I found what she did healthy and liberating. I had had a similar experience with Françoise Dolto, and her honesty had helped me save time.[3] Faced with criticism, Pankow would retort: "I am not their analyst. If they have a problem with this, they can talk about it in analysis. Here, it's a training session. And that's that!"

Training based on practice, practical training. Gisela Pankow's anger was justified. How was it possible that in the early 1970s psychiatric students did not know, or had forgotten, that psychosis is different from neurosis, and that the neutrality and rule of abstinence proposed by Freud to treat neurotics – and blindly applied ever since – is useless with psychotics, or serves only to worsen the massacre caused by everyone's indifference to their suffering? Her anger and intolerance in the face of such ignorance was healthy. What was unhealthy was the silence and reserve shown by others, who seemed not to understand what was at stake: that this young student spouting foolishness already had considerable responsibilities in the clinical care of patients, and that soon he could become the head of his department and establish policies governing mental health.

Gisela Pankow was familiar with the relationship between psychiatry and psychoanalysis. For twelve years, she had been the assistant of Ernst Kretschmer – an important figure in psychiatry in Freud's lifetime. She had worked with him twelve hours a day, every day. She had constructed the mathematical model for his classification of psychopathy. Kretschmer liked her and allowed her to see patients, after work, to practise this thing called psychoanalysis. A crazy idea, trying to do psychoanalysis with psychotics! This is where she had acquired her experience; this is how she had become uncompromising. But unlike those she shocked and traumatised, Pankow had no ill will. Her anger, her violence, her brutality were born of the respect she had for her work and her patients. Purity. Ignorance of basic principles and lack of rigour outraged her, but after an outburst she held no grudge, she could discuss the matter and show indulgence, but she never lowered her standards. However, hollow pretence and imposture were sure to trigger her fury.

Pankow was a brilliant teacher, but she was not an academic. Her teaching reflected her love of life and her passion for her work. Like all genuine psychoanalysts, she didn't see herself as an analyst. When she spoke of her work she described her way of inventing it, how she had come to make an interpretation, how she had handled an extreme situation. What she taught to others, above all, was her uncompromising involvement in the transference/countertransference interplay. This would be followed by a description of its manifestation in the clinical situation, and by the theoretical conclusions she had drawn. Gisela Pankow is one of the few analysts whose writing and teaching testify to the fact that the theoretical framework in which the analysis is conducted is part of the countertransference – a concept Michel Neyraut would develop a few years later.[4]

One Sunday, when I arrived at her office, she was very pale. She said something terrible had just happened. The brother of a patient she had treated some time ago had telephoned and asked to see her. She said: "Today was the day of the appointment. He arrived, he rang downstairs. I pressed the button to open the street door. He rang again, saying that the door didn't open. I found that strange, because someone had come earlier and there had been no problem. [She comments: I immediately felt that there was something aggressive about him.] So I went downstairs, I opened the door, I tried the code and found that it worked, and we took the elevator. [She comments: Of course, I did not look at him, we were not in the session yet.] I had him come straight into the office. [She comments: When a person comes for the first time, I don't make them wait in the waiting room. You should not make a patient wait the first time because you don't know the person yet.] He came in, he sat down, I closed the door, I sat down, I took a sheet of paper, I looked at him. And when I looked at him I was certain that he was there to kill me. I asked myself who was going to find my body tomorrow. I said: 'And what will you do with my dead body?' [She comments: Because with a psychotic, you always have to place the focus beyond his desire.] He then took out a gun and said: 'I don't know why, but I have to kill you.' [She comments: Now that he had spoken, I knew the danger was past.] I said: 'Listen, you did not come from Germany to kill me; that was not part of our contract. Your name?' He answered. 'Your age?' He answered. I stopped, and noticed that he was still very excited. I said: 'After all, it's not my fault that your brother was the one who slept in your mother's bed and not you.'"

An amazing story, like many others told by analysts working with psychotic patients. The story is so fascinating, it is easy to find it magical. And yet, it is constructed on rigorous reasoning, like a theorem. Of course, there is Pankow's clinical genius, and all her experience. But what impresses me most is the persistence of her search, the way she takes her cues from her hypotheses regarding the patient's unconscious, her refusal to compromise, and her unshakable ethics.

As for what had taken place earlier, before any words were spoken, she possessed intimate knowledge of the family (she had been the brother's analyst), a theory of the analytic process (the need to place the focus beyond the patient's desire) and a sense of respect for the concrete reality of the meeting with the other.

Finally, *her interpretation created the setting*, which defined and circumscribed the situation from the outset. The meaning she provided was clear – you don't know why you want to kill me, so I will tell you: because you are jealous that it was your brother and not you who was the incestuous lover of your mother. After this, he spoke and she was sure that the danger of being killed had been eliminated (as I said, she remained steadfastly focused on her idea), and for an hour and a half the gun lay between them on the table.

This incident illustrates her character perfectly. The intense fear she had just experienced was already overshadowed by the pleasure she took in seeing thinking triumph over impulse, and by the opportunity to relate to the young analyst this clinical example of the handling of a situation illustrating certain crucial theoretical and technical points to implement with this type of patient. This was Pankow's teaching.

She knew that in order to practise this profession, it was essential to take care of oneself. She tried to teach this along with the rest. One day, seeing that I was very tired, she said: "You work too much. To do the work that we do, we can't allow ourselves to be tired; our patients need us. When I feel tired, I stop. I say something like: 'The cow is tired, she needs to rest to regain her strength and be able to give milk.' Psychotic patients understand this very well. Don't come next Sunday (the day of supervision). Go home, cancel your patients and go somewhere to rest for a week. That's that." I agreed, of course, but told myself that she was crazy to think that I could cancel my patients just like that, with a day's notice. The next day, Monday, she called me, saw that I was in my office with a patient, and said that I would have to pay for Sunday's supervision session, since I had not left town. She added that she would call later to see if I was still there. And what did I do? By the end of the afternoon I was on my way out of town. And I learned a lesson: that I am the most important tool in my work.

What Pankow wanted most of all to teach, to make clear, was that an optimal distance is needed if there is to be a psychoanalytic encounter between a very disturbed patient and another subject who plays the role of analyst. I was describing a session I had conducted the previous day with a paranoid patient; when I came to the part where I asked the patient where she had placed me in her sculpting with modelling clay, Pankow looked very concerned and asked me to call the patient and offer to see her right away – it was a Sunday: "If she is still alive. When you asked her where you are in her sculpting, you placed yourself inside her delusion. She must feel abandoned, desperate." To please her, I made the call right away – although I felt she was exaggerating. And the patient's mother found her daughter about to jump from her balcony. These are things one never forgets.

The events of the Second World War had taught Pankow that in situations of extreme pain people can "become" crazy to survive the horror. In the first chapter of her book *L'Homme et sa psychose*, she quotes Jean Cayrol's explanation of how he was able to withstand torture: "I was thinking about the apple tree in my garden."[5] And she adds: he was the apple tree in his garden, his body had become the apple tree in his garden. I had the opportunity to see this for myself in my work with patients from Latin America who had been tortured: to endure the pain, to survive, they had had to find a way to escape from their body physically. Claude Lanzmann, in his 1985 film *Shoah*, gives a number of examples of creative recourse to psychosis that allowed some prisoners in death camps to survive.[6]

The following story shows the power of a devastating reality to drive someone crazy. It concerns a patient Pankow had been seeing for two years. She often talked about him in the study group because she did not understand why, from time to time, he would become suicidal and would have to be hospitalised. Otherwise, he was a very intelligent man, full of life and good humour, very fond of his wife and children.

On one occasion, while this man was hospitalised, his wife called Gisela Pankow. She said she was desperate about these repeated crises and asked Pankow to write a certificate declaring that her husband was unable to manage his affairs. Given what Pankow knew about the man, she found the request to be strange. In order to give herself time to think, she asked the woman to come and see her. When? Right away – it was a Saturday.

The woman arrived and started talking. She appeared distraught, she cried, but Pankow felt that something was not right. When she described this meeting in the study group, she said she listened to the woman for hours, and that she would have listened twice as long if necessary. And finally the woman broke down. She became abusive. "It's all your fault. You've ruined my life." And she revealed that for years she had been the mistress of her husband's best friend. The two of them had decided to cause the husband to commit suicide, to gain access to his considerable fortune. But how? Leave it to her, she knew what to do. Little things: "But of course I told you, dear. It's strange that you don't remember." Or causing an important object to disappear and insisting that of course she had just seen it, what was he saying again, he seemed to become more absent-minded every day. And so on. Pure evil. (Do you know the character Celestina, the monstrous madam of a brothel, in the Spanish play of the same name written in 1499?[7])

Of course, the patient talked about his "forgetting", his "memory lapses". When his concern with them became overwhelming, when his "symptoms" became more frequent, Pankow recognised the warning signs of depression and suicidal desires. But she was unable to identify the cause – for good reason.

What did Pankow do? She called a taxi and left with the woman for Provence. At the clinic, in her patient's room, she told his wife: "Alright, you can tell him now." And after the wife's confession, she must have added her famous "that's that". How many analysts would have done what she did in a similar situation?

Enjoy your holiday,

Notes

1   The book describing the exhibition was published in France, by Seuil. At my request, in order to present Alécio's work to the European public, Françoise Dolto contributed a text entitled *Enfances* (The Faces of Childhood). (De Andrade, AS., *Enfances*, Seuil, 1986).

2 This was the manuscript of *Ana K, histoire d'une analyse*, op. cit.
3 See Letter 4, *Françoise Dolto and psychoanalytic amorality*.
4 Neyraut, M. *Le Transfert*, op. cit.
5 Pankow, G. *L'Homme et sa psychose*, op. cit., p. 61.
6 See Letter 31, *Hallucination as a defence and Claude Lanzmann's triple knowledge*.
7 See Letter 35, *The Celestina superego and the Dulcinea superego*.

Winnicott's concept of *continuity of being*

Transference and treatment of trauma

Dear friend,

You are asking for a "thread" to follow in reading D. W. Winnicott. I think that the notion of *continuity of being* summarises the foundation of his work. For example, this concept can be used to understand all aspects of the humanising function of the mother in her relationship to the infant, and later to the toddler. Her holding and handling, her capacity to identify perfectly with her infant, as well as her ability to recognise the importance of the experience of solitude, and afterwards anxiety – all these "techniques" or qualities of the mother serve to prevent impingements distorting the construction of the child's psychic space. In other words, the structuring and humanising function of the mother is an ego-support function, a protective barrier against traumatic invasion, and a barrier that ensures the continuity of being. A good-enough or adequate mother, or a mother who is not too persecutory, who allows her infant, and later her toddler, to experience the world at each encounter as a source that reinforces his feeling of being alive and his desire to live. In other words, the maternal function – *a function that can be exercised by the father* – consists of making sure that the world is presented to the infant, and later the toddler, in a way that makes the encounter creative and harmonious. Filtering the intensity of stimuli is part of the ego-support function of the mother; ensuring that the complexity of the world is presented gradually constitutes a filtering mechanism, a protective shield.

Another approach would be to say that the concept of *continuity of being* and its implications constitute the context in which misunderstanding, criticism and rejection of Winnicott's theory are rooted. The concept of a transition from complete adaptation of the mother to her infant's needs, to gradual disidentification from the mother culminating in independence, is seen by Winnicott's critics as an idealisation, even a Rousseauistic, angelic, sentimental conception of the mother.

Before continuing, let me say that from here on I will speak of Winnicott's ideas as they are reflected in the use I make of them in my analytic practice, and therefore in the way I interpret my experiences, both personal and social.

Of course, the best way to pay tribute to a way of thinking is to keep it alive in all our exchanges with the incredible diversity of the world. My reason for differentiating what I say from Winnicott's actual *oeuvre* is my desire to take responsibility for what I set forth – which will facilitate subsequent discussion.

Let us resume. This trajectory going from complete dependence to autonomy of the child is, in fact, a logical sequence of psychic processes culminating in the creation of a psychic space coinciding with the emergence of a subject. In Winnicott's view, the maternal function illustrates the importance of the encounter between the infant and the "other" (in France, this includes the "other" with a small "o" and with a capital "O"). It is another way of saying that the human is created by the human – a simple but often forgotten truth. Winnicott's formulation also reminds us that for an extended period of time this holding environment is constituted by the person who is the baby's primary caretaker – usually the mother.

The logical sequence of the psychic processes allowing the emergence of a subject as a differentiated psychic space is founded on the *ego-support function of the mother*. As he often does, Winnicott uses a paradoxical model to describe this function: on the one hand, it is an unavoidable illness befalling the mother, an illness allowing her to adapt perfectly to her baby's psychic needs – for instance, the mother awakens during the night just when her baby needs changing, or when he starts to develop a fever, etc., on the other hand, this function is inscribed in a constellation of desires that include other maternal investments: her relation to the world, to others, and her desiring of the child's father. When she gradually moves away from the psychic needs of her child, the mother does not do so to enable the child to adapt to her reality; on the contrary, what she desires is for the child to be different and separate from her. The various maternal techniques Winnicott identifies serve to protect the space in which the mother imagines and invents her child as radically distinct: able to be alone; able to bear a certain degree of anxiety; able to change through his encounter with the reality of life; and to transform this reality by humanising it. Thus, we can say that the notion of *continuity of being* includes a theory of primary identification. I formulate this theory as follows: *the first identification is identification to a place*. This place is located in the psychic space of the mother, a space reserved for the emergence of this particular subject and no other. Protecting the continuity of being means protecting the continuity of the self, and the self is the subject, the actual person.

In short, the existence of an ego-support maternal function protecting the infant, and later the toddler, from impingements and intrusions from the outside world is inseparable from the conditions needed for the emergence of the subject. Therefore, to say that this idea is angelic, comforting or naïve is more than a misunderstanding: it is a falsehood.

It is likely that in France the descriptive aspect of Winnicott's texts contributed to this confusion. Instead of reading these descriptions as clinical illustrations of the underlying theory, they were apparently taken for dogmatic injunctions as to the "correct behaviour" of a mother in relation to her baby. In addition, the normative intent mistakenly attributed to Nicolas Abraham's stages of development, and Jacques Lacan's demolition of *ego psychology* no doubt contributed to this misreading bordering on inanity, which transformed the most broad-minded theorisation of the work of psychoanalysis into ordinary psychopathology to be used by dim-witted psychologists. It did not matter that Winnicott wrote: "good-enough mother" or "not too persecutory mother", the widely-accepted reading continued to be "normative" or "idealised" mother. The same blindness would lead to absurd assertions such as: "There is no place for the father in his conceptualisation", or "The transitional object is the same thing as the fetish." Laziness, or ignorance, or bad faith – or a combination of all three – proclaimed that his conception of the Self was related to the most stupid of all criteria of emotional health: an adaptation of the psyche to the definition of reality given by an ideology.

Let me go over the main points constituting Winnicott's conception of the self. First, he considers the emergence of the self to be anterior to the scopic stage – that is, to the mirror stage described by Lacan (following in Henri Wallon's footsteps). Like Freud, Winnicott considers the Ego to exist before the Id – which explains the importance of the maternal ego-support function. Initially, the self and the subject are one. (Lacan has provided a remarkable description of the self/ subject relation, without discussing the paradox of their common genesis – which he recognises.[1])

I believe that Winnicott's notion of *continuity of being* refers to the theoretical genesis of a subject. By emphasising the importance for emotional health of a certain quality of presence, he provided conceptual tools allowing us to *understand* and to *treat* the more or less painful effects of discontinuity with the mother, of lacunae, of distortions and ruptures in her integrative presence.

I have already discussed in detail how the mother's ego-support function introduces a principle of spaces, and I have noted above that the first identification is identification to a place existing in the psychic space of the mother.[2] It must be added that Winnicott's discussion of genesis refers to an embodied subject. In fact, after Freud, with the exception of Georg Grodeck and before Piera Aulagnier, Winnicott was the only psychoanalyst to grant a central place in his theory to a psychic transposition of sensory experiences and physiological maturation processes – an interest that was no doubt due to his extensive experience as a pediatrician. (Melanie Klein also focused on the body, but an imaginary body.)

We often forget that Winnicott was the first to assert that the baby's relation with his primary caretaker is decisive for the emotional health of the subject. (Even Anna Freud thought that the role of the person who took care of the baby was unimportant. This non-recognition of the significant relation between the baby and the mother can be seen as an outgrowth of the theory of the psychic monad proposed by her father.)

Winnicott's theory of the emergence of the subject, which emphasises the importance of the initial human environment and of the psychic translation of bodily sensations – a translation facilitated or impeded by the initial environment – provides an answer to certain questions shared by a number of psychoanalysts: how do you think about trauma, how do you understand its causes and its effects? What place should you give it in transference? How is it possible to work through it, in order to free a subject trapped in seemingly unfounded deathly repetition?

Winnicott's primary concern was to reflect on the possibility of treating trauma by psychoanalytic means. The theory he developed regarding the problem of *continuity of being* focuses on a positive conception that can counteract the destruction caused by the traumatic disaster.

In other words, in the debate between Freud and Ferenczi concerning trauma, Winnicott sides with Ferenczi. For him, there is the reality of fantasy and the Real of trauma. (Talented clinician and shrewd diplomat, Winnicott never claimed any Ferenczian affiliation – I believe there is only one mention of Ferenczi in his work, because he knew that Ernest Jones, who had been Ferenczi's analysand, was envious and resentful of the latter's relationship with Freud. This resentment caused Jones, who was also the "initiator" of British psychoanalysis, to present Ferenczi as paranoid in his official biography of Freud. Winnicott's debt to Ferenczi is a subject that remains to be researched by a young psychoanalyst.[3])

To continue discussing the history of psychoanalytic theory, Lacan's notion of the subject is a transposition of Winnicott's concept of *self*; Lacan even acknowledges *continuity of being*, which he calls "unary trait". Piera Aulagnier's theory of the "I"[4] is her way of escaping the Lacanian episteme; her theorisation is a metapsychology of the subject, a subject within the filiation of the Winnicottian *self*, which retains its sensory and somatic roots, in short, a subject in a body, an *embodied subject*.

Winnicott's writing illustrates the treatment of trauma based on the theoretical possibility of integrating somatic and psychic processes. He describes how this is achieved when everything goes well, although experience has shown him that in most cases things do not go well: the body is not a reality for the subject, drives and sexuality frighten him and, as a rule, he is busy creating a false self, a counterfeit personality, a masquerade to protect a fragment of real existence, a hint of true intimacy.

Winnicott elaborates a theory of transitional space and transitional objects in order to underline the devastating consequences of the absence of a subjective object. A person who did not have the opportunity to create such an object belonging to both the internal world and to external reality will remain unable to define the boundaries between his internal world and the external world, and will be unable to feel his skin as both containing him and separating his body and the infinity of his sensations from the multitude of external worlds around him.

Presenting the mother as an ego-support function which protects the space into which the subject will emerge from encroachments is a way of drawing attention to the ever-present danger of trauma in infancy and early childhood, and to the fact that all experiencing of the world during this period could be potentially traumatic.

What Winnicott describes as the mother's "techniques" for adapting to her baby's psychic needs constitutes a theory of psychoanalytic practice, and more specifically, a theory of transference.

Like Freud, Winnicott believed that transference (with its interpretation) is the tool that makes it possible to conceptualise the manner in which the subject, through his fantasy activity, creates the other and creates himself in his relation to the other. In short, this is the analytic work which takes place in the sphere of neurotic repetition, where imaginary changes unfold in a stable framework. This framework is the result of accomplishments, of satisfactions experienced by the subject in his encounters with the other in the world, encounters which have become reference points that are proof of the continuity and permanence of these experiences in his internal reality. At this level of functioning of the psychic apparatus, the failures encountered by the subject in his relation to the other can usually be considered effects of his projection: he is the primary cause of the difficulties he encounters in his relation to the world – in short, the Freudian monad operates optimally.

Winnicott's contribution to the theory of transference – following in Ferenczi's footsteps – was to point out its ability to reveal trauma, and to serve as a tool in repairing the effects of the trauma suffered by the subject, or inflicted on him, in his early environment. An analyst adopting this perspective must be aware that in the analytic setting he occupies the position of the agent who created the trauma.

It is the patient who incites the analyst to take this place – I will come back to this incitation. Placing the therapist in this position is the only way for the patient to deal *in the present with certain aspects of the relation to the initial other*, aspects outside the scope of omnipotent fantasies. In this context, transference is a tool serving to seize non-symbolised and unhumanised fragments of experience contained in the Real. When transference plays this role, the analytic process is no longer a setting in which repetition unfolds, but rather the place of unprecedented speech and of the emergence of previously unintegrated experiences excluded from the psychic world of the subject. Integrating this experience into the psychic world makes it possible to experience *continuity of being*, affirming the feeling of being alive. (It is true that the lifting of repression produces the same effect.)

To illustrate this use of transference, I will give you two examples from memory. Winnicott told a patient surprised at the flood of tears that followed the recounting of a seemingly minor childhood incident: "You are shedding now all the tears you could not shed at the time." The second example is from *Therapeutic Consultations in Child Psychiatry*.[5] At the end of a session with a child, Winnicott realised that he had let the patient leave in a depressed state. He went out on the landing, but the child was not there – he had already taken the elevator. Winnicott ran down the stairs all the way to the basement to catch up with him, convinced that the child had mistakenly pressed the basement button, which turned out to be the case.

This example calls for two observations. The first is addressed to young psychoanalysts like you. This is a wonderful clinical story, but you should know that this type of transference often give rise such occurrences. They are the result of the fact that in such situations the transference concerns unaccustomed areas of the psyche, giving rise to events of a highly unusual nature.

The second remark concerns the content and the meaning of the clinical situation. Winnicott felt that urgent action was needed because he recognised that he had been assigned the place of the one who initially abandoned the child at a crucial time – that is, just when the child most needed someone's support. When a traumatic situation is replayed in the analytic setting, when the analyst holds the place of the person responsible for the trauma, he must leave this place so that the scenario taking place in his actual encounter with the child in the patient can diverge, come to an end or be overturned. The analyst's talent consists first of knowing that he holds this place, and then of finding a way to leave it.

The re-enactment of the traumatic situation is the patient's creation – a creation, not the result of any strange manipulation skills. Recreating the traumatic situation in analysis presupposes that the patient has great faith in the psychoanalyst, and that he is willing to take the greatest risk. In fact, if the analyst is unable to recognise the scenario which is being replayed, the patient is in danger of suffering the tragic consequences of renewed abandonment. We must remember that here we are not dealing with the arrangement and displacement of representations associated with repression. What is displaced here, what intersects, are fragments of the actual painful moments of a relation with the other which, while never forgotten, remain inconceivable because they engulf the subject. This explains the great damage that can be done by dashing the hope placed in the analyst for ending the vicious cycle of traumatic repetition.

The analyst's latitude for foreseeing the re-emergence of a traumatic situation in the analytic setting depends on the degree of disintegration of the patient's internal world. As you will see, at times this latitude is completely absent.

A very long time ago, I worked for years with a patient who had a melancholic psychic structure. I liked her very much and devised a therapeutic setting that accommodated her schedule, which was as complex as her imaginings. All my interest, all my devotion were not enough to convince her that I did not hate her, did not wish to get rid of her... and so on. I was often exhausted by these accusations. Her third session of the week was at seven-thirty on Friday mornings, an unusual time for me, but the only option if we were to meet three times a week. One Friday, I woke up at fifteen minutes past eight, exactly when the session would have ended. That afternoon she called me, concerned, to see if I was all right. The following Monday, without asking any questions, she lay down and, after a short silence, started to talk about the things we had been discussing in her sessions. I interrupted her to ask how she felt about my absence on Friday. She replied that I must have been unable to be there. I said that I had the impression that she really did not want us to discuss the matter. In an aggressive tone, and to put an end to the discussion, she said that even an analyst can be detained and unable to keep an appointment, and that she is not so daft as to think that I do not have a private life. I thanked her for showing concern for my problems, just as she had always shown concern for her mother's problems, but I insisted on the fact that we were there to talk about her feelings. She replied curtly that it was too soon to talk about it; I answered that I imagined that she had felt horribly alone, abandoned, rejected. She wept silently, said that it was awful, that she had thought of killing herself. So I told her what had actually happened, which resulted in putting an end to her distress and filling her with savage rage instead: she said she had always known that I did not care about her and that I was only interested in her money, that I wanted her to die just as her mother did, and so on. I agreed with her that the incident could be interpreted as proof that the accusations she has been making against me for years were justified.

I added that if we both felt that this was the only way of seeing things, we would have to put an end to the analysis – since I would be holding the place of someone who had truly wanted to destroy her, which would make psychoanalytic work impossible. But I said that there was another way of interpreting this event. We could consider that what happened was induced by her, that it was something she created to confirm her allegations and disqualify me as a person who could help her. In that case, the event ought to be considered part of the analytic treatment, and she should pay me for the session she caused me to miss. She said, and with good reason, that I was mad. I said I was willing to consider the possibility, but that for the moment we had no choice: she could either pay for the session and we would continue to work together, or she could refuse to pay and I would end her analysis. She paid for the session and the melancholic structure lost its hold.

I believe that this ability to induce events is linked with the "demonic character" always at work in humans, which Freud described in *Beyond the Pleasure Principle*.[6] A clinical observation reported by Bernard Penaud at a meeting of the Paris Psychoanalytic Society provides a most extraordinary illustration of this phenomenon. According to his design of psychodrama with children, the therapists acting as auxiliary egos were to have no contact with the parents of the children participating in the "plays". The parents only met in therapy with Bernard Penaud. But strangely, after a few sessions of psychodrama, the therapists took on intonations, gestures and postures identical to those of the parents they had never seen!

Before closing, I would like to share some thoughts about the current state of the world around us.

Being a psychoanalyst is a wonderful occupation. We trust in the principle that a proper understanding of the past can change the perception of the present and make it possible to invent a new future. But in our time there is no place for the past. Inspired by the Age of Enlightenment in the West, the nineteenth century created societies convinced that the barbaric could always be reduced and civilised, that progress was always possible. It was in this symbolic context that Freud invented psychoanalysis. Then came the First World War, which could have served as a disillusionment with preventive effects, but humanity disregarded the warning. The 1929 Crash followed, then Nazism and the Second World War with its unspeakable horrors. After the disaster, Western leaders implemented the lessons learned from the previous post-war period. Thanks to the United States, internal markets were rebuilt – based on the Marshall Plan – and social conditions were improved for all classes of the population; labour unions, with the experience they had acquired in labour struggles, were recognised as a counterpower and a partner in the reconstruction of economically exhausted nations.

Today, from an economic perspective, we are in a situation similar to that which existed prior to 1929, at least in one respect: political leaders are convinced, once again, that priority should be given to the market economy. But, in contrast to the 1950s, labour unions no longer organise events and they carry no political weight; communism, that represented a different model of society, offers no metaphor for an alternative future. In short, there is no counterpoise to the short memory, or lack of responsibility, of those in power. In addition, large corporations have lost their national identity and have become multinationals in the service of capital – the nation has lost its economic power. What Adam Smith called the invisible hand of capitalism no longer exists. As Eric Hobsbawm pointed out, this invisible hand was rooted in traditional societies and consisted of values such as trust, solidarity and honour.[7] These are not nostalgic observations, my young friend, but rather very vague foreshadowings of the new expectations to which our profession has begun to be confronted.

The late Helio Pellegrino, writing under the dictatorial regime in Brazil, asked himself what becomes of the Oedipal pact when the father is an assassin.[8] Of course, such extremes do not occur in our democratic nations of the First World. Here, what occurs is an increasingly more pronounced disintegration of the symbolic dimension; for a psychoanalytic reflection on this situation, I suggest that you read Michel Tort's remarkable book *Fin du dogme paternel* (The End of the Paternal Dogma), published by Aubier. (This disintegration brings about a profound change in the possibility of regarding Oedipus as a structuring agent of the psyche. Freudian theory equated the symbolic murder of the father with the moment when the Subject assumes his human destiny. But if the father is symbolically dead beforehand or, to say it differently, if the father no longer transmits solid reference points to the Subject, it is possible that the essential work of the psychoanalyst, in an effort to provide human origins, a *continuity of being*, will no longer concern murdering the father, but rather making it possible, above all, for a particular subject to be able to love *a* father. Of course, for this to happen, the father has to be likeable – which is not always the case.

But we shall forge ahead!

Notes

1 See Letter 28, *Loup Verlet: Psychoanalysis as a revolution of the conceptual framework.*
2 I am grateful to Laura Dethiville for her help in structuring the discussion presented in this letter.
3 See Letter 7, *The Ferenczi predicament.*
4 See my book *De L'Amour à la pensée – La psychanalyse, la création et D. W. Winnicott.* Paris: L'Harmattan, 1999.
5 Winnicott, D. W. (1971), *Therapeutic Consultations in Child Psychiatry.* London: Hogarth Press (reprinted London: Karnac Books, 1996).
6 Freud, S. (1920), *Beyond the Pleasure Principle.* London: The Hogarth Press.
7 See Eric J. Hobsbaum's superlative book *Age of Extremes: The Short Twentieth Century, 1914–1991.* London: Abacus, 1995. Many thanks to my friend Nicole-Edith Thévenin for our discussions concerning this book.
8 "*Pacte oedipien et pacte social*" (The Oedipal Pact and the Social Pact) in *Le Psychanalyste sous la terreur.* Paris: Matrice-Rocimante, 1988.

Reading *Beyond the Pleasure Principle*

The insistence of Eros

Dear friend,

You ask me if my theory of trauma, which I described as modelled on Winnicott in my previous letter, takes into account the theory developed by Sigmund Freud in *Beyond the Pleasure Principle*. I think the answer is yes, but you can be the judge.

Freud presents a theory that is simple and clear: the encounter between two people brings each of them an amount of new excitations which increases the level of tension present in each person. What becomes of this change in the vitality level of the two people? It can either reinforce life, or be reduced by life.

The origin of life

How does this reduction take place? Freud used the hydraulic model which allowed him to formulate the pleasure principle by demonstrating that the dominant tendency in psychic life is to reduce or eliminate unpleasant excitations. The process aims to re-establish a quantum of energy which must remain constant to ensure the functioning of the psychic apparatus. When the equation is weighted in this manner, it always favours pleasure. But Freud had to admit that this model was not helpful for theorising trauma. A binary system – increase and reduction – could explain the overall functioning of the apparatus. The pleasure principle sufficed to understand the dynamics leading to death – the end of all excitation – but after Freud introduced repetition compulsion and its insistence *beyond* the pleasure principle, life itself became enigmatic. Once the existence of mechanisms of repetition compulsion extending to life instincts and death instincts was recognised, Freud's theory of the libido had to be revised. The hydraulic metaphor was suitable for reflecting on experience, as long as the latter was confined to the limited duality basic needs/sexual drives, or to the sphere of transformations or combinatorial possibilities involving internal excitation (for instance, the resurfacing of a reminiscence) and external excitation (for instance, sexual arousal produced by another person).

The model of a psychic apparatus, which functions based on the pleasure principle to explain reduction of excitation due to actual experience, remained perfectly coherent with everything Freud had said about the death drive (since death can be seen as a way of ending all tensions, as the radical discharge in which the end of unpleasure coincides with the end of life). Every human being longs for the definitive absence of tension; Freud called this the *Nirvana principle*. But although the functioning of the apparatus according to the pleasure principle can explain the attractiveness of an end to life, it does not explain why death does not always triumph.

In other words, the idea of death instincts associated with repetition compulsion requires the *admission that life instincts are equally compulsive, insistent and repetitive*. The most compelling example of this is the tension accompanying the huge emotional investment required by romantic love or by the creation of an oeuvre. A similar tension is generated by loyalty to one's ethical choices, which are the building blocks of a life.[1]

Beyond the Pleasure Principle does more than introduce the idea of death instincts; associating the functioning of the apparatus with repetition compulsion changes the conception of the theory of the libido. I believe that this is an entirely new way of interpreting this text. And the conclusions we must draw are very important. You see, my young friend, if at a certain level sexual drives are repetitive and compulsive like the death instincts, it means that at this level they are opposed to the pleasure principle – whose aim is to eliminate unpleasure – and therefore, they too can be considered demonic.

I hope I can give you an accurate idea of the scope of the problem before us. The adjective *demonic* is often associated with death instincts. Seeing them as having this inexorable character redirects our conception towards a theory of resistance. Therefore, the analytic process is confronted from the start with sexual drives governed by the pleasure principle, on the one hand, and to this demonic repetition compulsion, deathly and indomitable, on the other. The clinical application of this point of view would consist of finding, through recourse to the libido, a way to limit this inexorable character and, if possible, to control it by integrating it into the dynamic structure that regulates psychic functioning based on the pleasure principle. From this perspective, whether a patient could be analysed would have to depend on the degree to which what is deadly in him is present. Of course, the dramatic way in which Freud phrased these concepts for didactic purposes might have led to such an interpretation.

We encounter the same problem when Freud describes the compulsive and repetitive nature of sexual drives. Why not return to the original theory of resistance asserting that, on the one hand, there are death instincts and on the other life instincts, or sexual drives, equally powerful and directed against death? In fact, this reading is phenomenologically grounded: either life triumphs over the tensions inherent to it, or destructive figures of drives, delusions and murder make their appearance. This metaphor of a battle may help to illustrate the dynamic nature of the new drive dualism, but it loses its effectiveness if we forget that, although there is combat and victory, the combat takes place in a sphere on which the principle of the elimination of unpleasure has no hold. When the aim is to change a psychic balance that includes the encounter with the Real, dealing solely with intrapsychic functioning is of no avail. Changing this balance requires encountering another balance, for example, in the person of a psychoanalyst, which gives you an idea of the degree of commitment the analyst must maintain throughout the analytic process.[2]

Let me say it again: in the economy of this new dualism, the functioning of sexual drives *escapes* regulation by the pleasure principle; this functioning, like that of the death instincts, exists *beyond* this principle and is governed by repetition compulsion. Although the death instincts/life instincts dualism includes the prior ego-instincts/sexual instincts dualism, this field is of a different nature than the earlier one, and is vastly wider. This does not prevent *a portion* of the sexual drives to be regulated by the pleasure principle and to function according to the laws of repression. In the same way, *a portion* of the ego instincts continues to be regulated by the pleasure principle. In other words, the theory on which the global functioning of the psychic apparatus had been founded now governs *only* one aspect of its functioning.

The limits of biology

In addition to the compulsive and repetitive nature of death instincts – a demonic nature from the viewpoint of the pleasure principle – Freud states that the only way of retaining the concept of death instincts – a concept made evident in clinical practice by the identification of the repetition compulsion mechanism – is to acknowledge the existence of life instincts in the newly constituted subject.

One must read and reread this passage of Freud's text to comprehend what an outrageous idea it was to admit the simultaneous existence of life instincts and death instincts.

The French philosopher Gaston Bachelard draws attention to the passages in a novel where the author describes a landscape. The comparative freedom he can exercise relative to the construction of the plot offers a glimpse of the writer's singularity.

This is exactly what happens when we read Section VI of this text.[3] We are always impressed by the simple, clear and rigorous manner in which Freud presents a complex problem, and we wonder how he arrives at a solution. For a psychoanalyst, this is a question of vital interest: what was Freud's method of interpretation? I believe that this segment of *Beyond the Pleasure Principle* provides some answers.

To this point, there had been, roughly speaking, two paths of investigation: first, the initial theory of drives developed by psychoanalysis and second, the identification of a clinical phenomenon, traumatic neurosis, which required the creation of the concepts of repetition compulsion and death instinct. The first path of reflection focused on connecting the new instinctual dualism – life instincts/death instincts – to the existing theoretical corpus. It was foreseeable that the idea of death instincts would meet with criticism that would attempt to reduce Freud's entire theoretical construction to hazy philosophical speculation. In order to prevent this, Freud drew on the most advanced principles of biological science of his era. He commented at length on the literature of the field, in the style of a laboratory researcher describing his slides. This is what gives the text its "scientific" tone.

This compulsory incursion into the world of biology provided Freud with two concepts: either death exists before life, or death is a conquest of life. Up to Paragraph 62, Freud chose the first option, and founded his theory of the existence of death instincts on it. Then, *contradicting* everything he had just elaborated based on biological science, he asserted that life instincts exist from the beginning of life. He came to this conclusion as a result of his clinical work in psychoanalysis, which also testified to the compulsive and repetitive nature of sexual drives. In short, to examine this question – which is, in fact, the question of the unconscious – biology can no longer serve as a point of reference. (And, once again, it is surprising to note that commentators did not remark on this reversal of opinion, which deserves closer attention.)

Recourse to myth

The biological paradigm is useful to Freud until he begins to speak of a human subject. The cellular biology of his era can provide him with a model presenting difference as the condition needed for reproduction, but this model cannot explain the repetitive and compulsive nature of sexual drives. Biology is powerless to explain why a human subject, to exist, live and die, desires and needs the existence of another. At this point in the text, Freud turns to Plato and presents the myth of the Androgyne:

> The original human nature was not like the present, but different. In the first place, the sexes were originally three in number, not two as they are now; there was man, woman, and the union of the two [...] [the androgyne]. Everything about these primaeval men was double: they had four hands and four feet, two faces, two privy parts, and so on. Eventually, Zeus decided to cut these men in two, "like a sorb-apple which is halved for pickling" [...] After the division had been made, the two parts of man, each desiring his other half, came together and threw their arms about one another eager to grow into one.[4]

Eros and the protective shield

This myth can serve to account for both the compulsive and repetitive nature of sexual drives, and the need to return to an earlier state. It was not unusual for Freud to turn to the poets in order to express his ideas. But the fact that he did this at the very moment when he rejected the biological paradigm is, it seems to me, a valuable indication of the path we analysts can follow when seeking a terminology to help us work through the transferential contexts that reveal the limits of our theoretical framework.[5]

Let me come back to my question: how is it that analysts who accept the theory of the functioning of the psychic apparatus based on a principle of insistence beyond the pleasure principle have never questioned what it is that insists and returns on the side of Eros?[6]

Indeed, either there is a mode of functioning of the apparatus *beyond* the pleasure principle, or there is not. If there is, it is simply inconceivable not to assert that *that which insists and returns coming from Eros is just as unbearable for the ego* as that which insists and returns coming from Thanatos. And what can come from Eros that insists and is so unbearable for the conscious system of the ego? The answer: the investment of unpleasure. What does this mean?

It means that the unpleasure which generally accompanies all tension has become a sign of a widening of the field of possibilities. Consequently, this tension is desired, it becomes the quintessential object, a vital object, and interest in unpleasure shifts to an interest in what unpleasure announces; anxiety which is always mixed with desire loses its heaviness and becomes a tool for preserving desire and its satisfaction. The certainty of death is divested of its shadow, and reinforces strength and vitality – a wild cat looking for its prey, which is life itself, with all its richness, its demands and its temporality.

In short, acceptance of this demanding insistence to represent and to link the representations together can be a source of joy, but requires enormous psychic work. A certain level of functioning of the thought process is rooted in this insistence where *the longing for thought is in fact a desire to experience joy.*[7] This involves a state of total availability to the other and to the real world, of course, but also to one's own sensations, emotions and feelings. Joy is the result of what has become an essential need: to receive fully the complexity of the encounter between the psyche and the unknown nature of the world. As I said earlier, joy can come into being when the unpleasure generally associated with any tension becomes a sign of the widening of the field of possibilities.

Our clinical work teaches us that to contain this level of tension and to feel its power intensely, without guilt, joyfully, requires the fulfilment of a number of psychic conditions. For instance, the constitution of the unconscious ego would have had to be associated with pleasure.

Winnicott explored the question of the place of pleasure in the constitution of the unconscious ego. For example, he pointed out that sexual instincts enrich the subject, provided that there is a place in him for their spontaneous reception, so that his experience of them is real and not frightening. In other words, Eros and pleasure are two different things. Eros unites, makes the link with Thanatos, and sets thought in motion. Pleasure brings release, abreaction, reduction of tension; it affects the balance between the amount of excitations present, without influencing their quality. It is thinking that concerns itself with the qualitative dimension.

But why is the insistence of Eros a problem in analysis? *Because investing in unpleasure as a sign of widening the range of possibilities requires the reorganisation of the negative energy characteristic of protective shields.*[8] In order for the subject to accept the immense threat to his life if he attempts to rearrange this basic energy, he must trust the other embodied by the analyst as another who, *for once*, will not let him down. In this context, the colossal work involved in changing a conceptual framework – work that can be easily seen to take place at the secondary process level of psychic functioning, can bring us closer to the vital question of a modification of this fundamental negativity. When a subject takes the psychic risk of crossing the boundaries set by a conceptual framework, in order to venture onto the territory of the unconceived, this implies, like any creative idea, that "there is some degree of suspension of the epistemological premises of this framework", and that "the subject has recourse to support that does not yet exist" (Loup Verlet). In other words, to cross the space above the abyss, the subject must accept the paradoxical position of being at once inside the conceptual framework whose limits he is crossing, and inside a new conceptual framework whose dimensions are still unknown to him.[9]

However, when I describe the insistence of Eros in this manner, am I not producing an aporia by invoking *life instincts and sexual instincts without representation*? But perhaps this objection points to a theory that can only conceive of the psychic apparatus in a context where its functioning is regulated by the pleasure principle, a context in which it is legitimate to associate sexual instincts with a certain type of representation.

But is my statement really an aporia? My hypothesis is based on Freudian theory, after all, and I believe it sheds light on certain passages of the essays written after *Beyond the Pleasure Principle*. For instance, this is what Freud wrote in *Remarks on the Theory and Practice of Dream Interpretation*, in 1923:

> In *Beyond the Pleasure Principle* I have dealt with this economic problem of how what are in every respect distressing experiences of the early infantile sexual period can succeed in forcing their way through to some kind of reproduction I was obliged to ascribe to them an extraordinarily strong upward drive in the shape of the "compulsion to repeat" a force able to overcome the repression which, in obedience to the pleasure principle, weighs down upon them – though not until "the work of treatment has gone half-way to meet it and has loosened the repression" (from *Beyond the Pleasure Principle*). Here we may add that it is the positive transference that gives this assistance to the compulsion to repeat.[10]

This quote is remarkable from the start. Instead of speaking of traumatic dreams, Freud illustrates repetition compulsion by referring to sexuality! He goes on to distinguish repression from repetition compulsion, and to underscore the contribution of positive transference. It is therefore clear that he is discussing the compulsive nature of Eros. He continues:

> Thus an alliance has been made between the treatment and the compulsion to repeat, an alliance *which is directed in the first instance against the pleasure principle*, but of which the ultimate purpose is the establishment of the dominion of the reality principle. [A psychic reality principle, to be clear.] (My emphasis.)[11]

In other words, psychic reality is constituted by these two modes of psychic functioning: functioning based on the pleasure principle, aiming at eliminating the tension produced by unpleasure; and functioning governed by the compulsion to repeat, where investing unpleasure generates, beyond pleasure, the joy of the desire to invest internal and external psychic reality. Freud concludes:

> As I have shown in the passage to which I am referring [in *Beyond the Pleasure Principle*], it happens only *too often* that the compulsion to repeat throws over its obligations under this alliance and is not content with the return of the repressed merely in the form of dream-pictures (my emphasis).[12]

Thus, if we are not dealing with the return of repressed material in dream images, we are speaking of a functioning where repetition compulsion in the service of Eros extends beyond the boundaries of representations.[13]

These concepts are essential in the treatment of borderline patients. If we agree with Freud that the ego is a *psychic action*, and that, as Winnicott states, certain conditions must be present in the environment for the unconscious ego to emerge, we can imagine a subject who, thanks to positive transference, is *forced to represent this necessary pleasure that the primal environment did not supply, and whose insistence is rooted in the pain of his psychic mutilations*. In short, if *basic psychic needs exist*, and are met with *pleasant techniques* of care and holding provided by the mother, we can suppose that this necessary pleasure, as yet unnamed and unrepresented, insists at the conscious ego level, which is alarmed by it. For such a subject, during the process of redistributing the energy of this negativity without which the psychic apparatus could not exist, and which must be reorganised to allow restructuring of the unconscious ego, *the analyst holds a place similar to that of the nurturing mother*. He is a container; as such, for the duration of this reorganisation, he becomes the unconscious ego of the patient: he protects him; contains his suffering and his desire to live; filters the intensity of pleasures so that they do not become alarming; he acts as a protective shield.[14]

Have a good trip and enjoy your holiday.

Your friend,

Notes

1 See Letter 33, *True love*.
2 A paradoxical example of the insistence of Eros is the clinical case concerning Georgette, described by Joyce McDougall. It took Georgette several years to remember that her father loved seafood. In the meantime, she exhibited very serious allergies to seafood; when she ate it, she was unconsciously swallowing the person of the father, sometimes the father's penis. (See Letter 17, *Perversion and somatisation: the work of Joyce McDougall*.) The clinical example concerning the melancholic patient I describe in Letter 10, *Winnicott's concept of* continuity of being: *transference and treatment of trauma*, illustrates this insistence as well.

3   S. Freud, *Beyond the Pleasure Principle*, S.E., 18: pp. 44–61. London: The Hogarth Press (particularly pp. 59–60), 1920. (See also my earlier reflections on this text: "L'insistance d'Éros" in *Esquisses psychanalytiques*, No. 10, Paris, autumn 1988, 143–171.)

4   Freud, ibid., pp. 57–58.

5   The difficulty of using the biological paradigm as a metaphor to represent the human is obvious. Freud did not underestimate it and took an apparently contradictory stand in regard to it. On the one hand, he continued to use the biological model as an illustration and, on the other hand, he demonstrated its lack of usefulness for elucidating his concepts.

   One example is his attempt to discuss psychic economy as linked to sadism. He states that he always recognised that the sexual impulse has a sadistic component. But when he postulates the existence of a primary masochism presumed to be anterior to sadism, his argument follows no phenomenological thread. Conceptualisation precedes experience and serves to interpret it.

   The theory of primary masochism remained unclear to me for a long time. I believe that the difficulty associated with understanding this theory stems from the fact that Freud introduced it as part of his discussion of sexual instincts. For me, the theory becomes clear if we associate it with the question of energy of the protective shield (in this regard, see Note 8). In this perspective, what Freud calls primary masochism is the manner in which the psychic apparatus constructs its negativity within the framework of its functioning based on repetition compulsion, since the psychic apparatus cannot exist without this negativity. Here, we are not in the sphere of representations produced at the level of the primary. We are speaking, rather, of phenomena which concern the period when the mother is subject to this "illness" that allows her to identify completely with her baby. This is why the term "life-supportive masochism seems better suited to this function.

   What I would like us to keep in mind is this important aspect of Freud's reflection: *[E]xperience is not what informs Freud on the instinctual connection between sadism and libido, between the death drive and the life drive, nor on the prior existence of the death drive. On the contrary, such an interpretation of experience is made possible by the theory of instinctual interconnectedness. Freud recognised the need to invent a new theoretical framework to deal with the new problems we encounter in practice.*

6   "Our consciousness communicates to us feelings from within not only of pleasure and unpleasure but also of a peculiar tension which in its turn can be either pleasure or unpleasure. Should the difference between these feelings enable us to distinguish between bound and unbound processes of energy? Or is the feeling of tension to be related to the absolute magnitude, or perhaps the level, of the cathexis, while the pleasure and unpleasure series indicates a change in magnitude of the cathexis *within a given unit of time?* Another striking fact is that the life instincts have so much more contact with our internal perception – emerging *as breakers of the peace* and *constantly* producing *tensions* whose *release* is felt as pleasure…" (My emphasis.) Freud, *Beyond the Pleasure Principle*. S.E., 18: p. 63.

7   The idea of the *insistence of Eros* is borrowed from Benedict de Spinoza; this mode of functioning finds its roots in what Spinoza called *the third kind of knowledge*. See Letter 36, *Freud and Spinoza*.

8   *The protective shield, the negative and resistance*: Taking the Kantian concept of time and space as his point of departure, Freud draws attention to the atemporal nature of the unconscious, emphasising that our abstract representation of time is derived from the preconscious/conscious system, that is, from consciousness. Such a representation acts as a *protection against instinctual stimuli*. Defining our conscious conception of time as a protective shield against internal stimuli is very useful and

makes it possible to distinguish, on the one hand, the amount of time necessary to elaborate unconscious constructions and, on the other hand, the conditions necessary for emergence of the unconscious. This distinction plays a fundamental role in our practice. The abstract representation of time does not constitute a resistance at the conscious level of the ego system; it is a corollary of its existence. In the same way, the prevalence of sensitivity to external stimuli is a constituent element of this level. Therefore, from this point of view, Freud considers *the ego a protective shield at the conscious/preconscious level, protecting the entire psychic apparatus.* "Protection against stimuli is an almost more important function for the living organism than reception of stimuli. *The protective shield is supplied with its own store of energy* and above all endeavours to preserve the special modes of transformation of energy operating in it against the effects threatened by the enormous energies at work in the external world – effects which tend towards destruction." (My emphasis.) Freud, *Beyond the Pleasure Principle*, op. cit., p. 27.

It is surprising that analysts focusing on the functioning of the ego have not paid greater attention to these observations concerning the protective shield's own energy. Had they done so, they would have had a better understanding of the *negation*, and even negativism, we encounter in the course of some analyses, and they would have been able to assess more accurately the problem raised by patients locked in this position. This neglect is so surprising that we are tempted to believe that the resistance shown by these analysts to *Beyond the Pleasure Principle* is rooted in the reflections on negativity Freud makes in this text. In effect, this series of observations regarding the protective shield and its own energy provides a valuable clinical lesson: not all negativity is resistance. Sometimes, what appears to be negativism may be simply the sign of the *negation needed to allow the functioning of the psychic apparatus.* To illustrate, a psychotic patient who had been presented to psychiatric students for years due to his total mutism, declared on one of these occasions: "I don't speak because I don't want to speak." What did his silence protect? Probably the fragment of a real person that this silence succeeded in saving from a massacre.

In psychosomatic patients, maternal failure in the carrying out of the function of protective shield results in primacy of thing-presentations overt word-presentations. Because there are no neurotic constructions to counter the archaic, which is itself the result of an absence of internal maternal environment, these patients are forced to create a space between themselves and the external world, as well as between themselves and their internal world. (See Letter 17, *Perversion and somatisation: the work of Joyce McDougall.*)

In practice, in most cases the word "resistance" is associated with the adjective "aggressive". This is because it is easier to say that all lasting resistance is aggressive than to recognise the ignorance of the psychoanalyst and the difficulty he faces. And yet – and this is my point – it is precisely this ignorance that can serve as a starting point for the construction of a true analytic practice; it is from this point that the analyst can pick up the thread of his psychic work in order to repossess the non-analysable remnants of his own analysis. *Not to* recognise negativity in the patient as the limit where the incomprehensible and non-representation begin is to avoid acknowledging that this negativity is at work in himself, as it is in everyone. This avoidance produces more or less intense aggressiveness in both the analyst and the patient; of course, this aggressiveness is rationalised as a manifestation of countertransference, taken in its literal sense, that is, as a reaction "against" transference.

You will note that what precedes is an example of the way in which the analytic process can become a production line of obsessional mechanisms. In fact, when the analyst does not acknowledge this fundamental negativity essential to the life of the subject, the patient reaches an impasse.

Another hypothesis is that, sometimes, when the analyst repeatedly interprets what should not be interpreted, he forces the patient to withdraw, or to take refuge in psychosis. What was not tolerated by the Other whom the analyst represents is the reality of the protective shield, considered by Freud as *more important than the reception of stimuli*.

Thus, out of love for his analyst who makes the request, the patient may abandon this essential negation. The problem is that after such forfeiture, there is no ground on which the psychic structure can find support. There is no doubt that an inappropriately conducted analysis can lead to madness. Remember that psychoanalysis is a prime example of the catastrophic consequences of a human relation in which a subject assumes that he "knows" the desire of another. To deny this fact is the corollary of the irresponsible claim that psychoanalysis is not a therapy. In short, refusal of this essential negativity has unavoidable consequences on the conduct of an analysis, and *most particularly* on the theory concerning the end of an analysis. For, in effect, if the analyst rejects such negativity, what type of elaboration of his experience shall the patient be able to produce, other than one that validates his analyst's theoretical system?

The energy of the protective shield: You must be asking yourself: is it possible to change the organisation of this negativity essential to the functioning of the psychic apparatus as a whole? The answer is yes. This was, in fact, one of the questions on which Winnicott focused his research. His interest in this question is connected with his conception of the ego, or rather to the metapsychology governing the conditions needed so that the ego, this psychic agency, may emerge. His important conception of analysis as regression constitutes the theory of reorganisation of this essential negativity, which sometimes manifests itself as a false self. (As for Winnicott's metapsychology of the ego, it would be best to consult my book *De l'amour à la pensée*, where my description of it is – I believe – clear and carefully detailed.)

Thus, this negativity provides fundamental energy for the functioning of the psychic apparatus precisely because it is indispensable to the protective shield. But what is the place of the protective shield's energy in the theory of drives?

Freud reflected on this question. He summarised his conception of drives in *Beyond the Pleasure Principle*, op. cit., p. 52 *et seq.*

As you know, the original duality of instincts involved ego drives and sexual drives. Ego drives – a term Freud considered provisional – were presumed to be associated with self-preservative drives. This duality still contained the traditional distinction between hunger and love, which allowed the psychoanalysis of neurotic patients to establish its territory. The concepts of sexual drive and sexuality belonged to a sphere that had nothing to do with the reproductive function – and, as we know, this gave rise to an enormous scandal.

The concept of narcissism constituted a great step forward. Previously, the ego had been merely an agency. Repression served to define both its usefulness and the reason for its existence. With the advent of narcissism, the ego becomes a sexual object among others; better still, it is a prevalent sexual object. Narcissistic libido is a manifestation of sexual drives. This demonstrates the libidinal nature of self-preservative instincts.

Having recognised this, Freud goes no further. The fact that he stops here is of capital importance, given the various fates to which this text was destined, in the process of defining a new duality: ego drives and sexual drives, the latter composed of narcissistic libido and object-libido.

But let us be clear: this new duality *does not exclude* the previous duality. Transference neurosis continues to be a conflict between the ego and libidinal investment of the object. The only difference is that given this basic premise, we now have to recognise two types of drives in the sphere of the ego: libidinal drives and drives of the organism itself, that is, the protective shield's own impulses. At the same time, Freud asserts that self-preservative instincts are libidinal, and that is why we must call them "drives" rather than instincts.

Should we then accept Carl Jung's monism of psychic energy? Freud answers in the negative. What remains to be understood is the quality of this non-libidinal drive of the organism expressed in the spheres of the ego. According to Freud, this quality is the same as that encountered in the manifestations of repetition compulsion. In short, the ego includes drives other than self-preservative libidinal impulses.

"We suspect that [drives] other than those of self-preservation operate in the ego, and it ought to be possible for us to point to them. Unfortunately, however, the analysis of the ego has made so little headway that it is very difficult for us to do so. It is possible, indeed, that the libidinal instincts in the ego may be linked in a peculiar manner with the other [ego-drives] which are still strange to us" (Freud, *Beyond the Pleasure Principle*, op. cit., p. 53. We have replaced "instinct" with "drive" in Strachey's translation).

Freud's text is clear: he regretted that analysis of the ego had not made it possible to describe an impulse of a different nature, the one which insists in repetition, and which is also the one providing energy to the protective shield. As a result, at the time, certain analysts justifiably concluded that analysis of the ego had to be explored further. But when their investigations did not lead them beyond the limits of the libidinal, they concluded that Freud's hypothesis was mistaken. And yet, Freud had been very definite: "The difficulty remains that psycho-analysis has not enabled us hitherto to point to any [ego – drives] other than the libidinal ones. That, however, is no reason for our falling in with the conclusion that no others in fact exist" (Freud, *Beyond the Pleasure Principle,* op. cit., p. 53).

9 See Letter 28, *Loup Verlet: Psychoanalysis as a revolution of the conceptual framework.*

10 Freud, S. (1923), *Remarks on the Theory and Practice of Dream Interpretation*, S.E., 19: 109–121, London: Hogarth.

11 Freud, S. *Remarks on the Theory and Practice of Dream Interpretation*, op. cit., p. 117.

12 Freud, S. *Remarks on the Theory and Practice of Dream Interpretation*, ibid., p. 117.

13 I am grateful to the friend who pointed out this passage in Freud's text. It was particularly gratifying for me to know that my interpretation of *Beyond the Pleasure Principle* enabled him to understand at once that Freud was speaking of the compulsive nature of Eros.

14 In this regard, Aulagnier's pictogram can be of help. As a representation of the originary level of psychic functioning, the pictogram is present both in the primary and the secondary spaces (fantasy and consciousness) – and processes in its own fashion events occurring in both these spaces. Could we not imagine that what appeared frightening at the level governed by the pleasure principle might have been a pictographic representation, or something similar, that neither the primary or secondary level were able to process partially or entirely? (See Letter 16, *Freud, Michel Neyraut, Piera Aulagnier: anxiety between theory and practice.*)

Helio Pellegrino

Dear friend,

I hope your trip to Paris ended successfully, and that the possibility of working on the outskirts of the capital will soon materialise. I think it would be an enriching experience for you, and we would be able to meet every two weeks.

Thank you for your card. Your question was not at all indiscreet. I did not answer at once because I would have gone on too long and I preferred hearing you speak of your practice, something which is always a great pleasure for me.

In my office, the man in the photograph next to Freud is Helio Pellegrino, a Brazilian psychoanalyst. In a certain way, Helio is where everything started for me: my relation to psychoanalysis, of course, but above all my relationship with myself. He was a father to me.

The day I learned that Helio was dead was the day the book about the Latin American Psychoanalysis Meeting I had organised in his honour came out. He had died the previous day. It was his wife who called to tell me. The call came just as I was about to leave for the press conference. I could not stop crying.

The story of his death resembles one of those "fantastic tales" typical of Latin American literature that he liked so much. I do not know who invented this concept, whether it was Julio Cortazar or Alejo Carpentier. For me, it summarises the juxtaposition of the extreme contrasts typical of the continent: poverty and total generosity; the harshness of reality and complete confidence in what life may bring; the most refined intelligence and the most inane superstition; ancient traditions and advanced technology; the most savage violence on the one hand, and solidarity, tenderness and humour on the other.

Helio was hospitalised urgently due to a life-threatening heart problem. He was a very intense man, fought all battles, was capable of the greatest generosity, of the greatest passion, he made no compromises and enjoyed life fully. He had already had two heart attacks – probably caused by the tension he had endured during the military regime – and his friends were worried. But the clinic was excellent, the doctor, a world-class cardiologist and friend of Helio's, and Helio had been hospitalised at the earliest signs of danger. In fact, he was out of danger three days later, and everyone was relieved. It was then that it was decided, no one knows why, to remove intravenous support – a decision contrary to all treatment protocols in such cases – and Helio went into cardiac arrest and died. The absurdity, the stupidity of death! I agree with a friend who said that we were all included in the stupidity, because we had all decided, selfishly, that Helio would never die, since he was irreplaceable.

I was deeply depressed for weeks, until the day when the thought crossed my mind that one life was not long enough to pass on everything I had received from Helio, to honour my debt. This idea filled me with joy and my thirst for life returned. My joy was even greater when I realised that this idea could have been one of his. I was thinking, of course, of what I owed Helio personally, but alongside my own debt there was that of my whole generation, the first to be assassinated by the junta after the military coup d'état of 31 March 1964 in Brazil. All Brazilian intellectuals and artists of that era were indebted to Helio, whose courage and integrity were an inspiration and a source of hope. He had taught us all to combat dictatorship with the only weapons we had against brutality: reflection and indignation. He confronted the military regime using its own laws, he challenged it to demonstrate the truth of the official propaganda it was putting forth to fashion its image.

At the time of the coup d'état, Helio was already considered a guiding light as a teaching psychoanalyst admired by his colleagues, a poet, essay writer, editorial writer for national newspapers. A firm supporter of democracy, respectful of all freedoms and all differences – a respect rooted in a stimulating clinical practice, he would have agreed with Unamuno's statement to supporters of the Spanish Fascist Party: "I may disagree with what you have to say, but I shall defend, to the death, your right to say it."

A Leftist and a Christian, Helio respected certain right-wing intellectuals, who held him in high esteem as well. Therefore, although not untouchable – something no one can be in a totalitarian regime, his tolerance and impartiality made him a figure not to be disregarded. Thanks to his courage and energy, he was able to make the best possible use of his assets. And now we come to the story of the torturer.

At a symposium on psychoanalytic therapy organised by Helio and open to the public – which means that there must have been agents of the secret police in the audience, Helio was describing the activities of his Social Clinic of Psychoanalysis when a young man called out: "Helio, what would you do if you learned that one of the psychoanalysts who work with you is the physician at a military torture centre?"

"I would do everything in my power to see that he is punished," replied Helio.

"In that case, I am telling you that he was present when I was tortured, and when my companions were tortured."

Helio: "You have just made a very serious public accusation."

"And you just made a solemn statement that fills me with hope," the young man replied.

Helio: "I stand by what I said." And that was the start of the Lobo affair.

Amilcar Lobo, psychoanalyst in training and torturer, was in analysis with the President of the Rio de Janeiro Psychoanalytic Society to which Helio belonged.

A right-wing man and excellent strategist, this President arranged for Helio to be expelled from the Society, on the pretext that his public statements and his articles were harming the image of the group.

Most members of the group did nothing. Others, who were close to Helio, supported him in his political battle, but had reservations about the tone he used, and went so far as to wonder if, before revealing the facts, it might not have been better to discuss the details within the Society, among analysts. It must be remembered that discussion of such matters took place in a context where denouncing the crimes of the military regime could cost you your life. In fact, Helio received death threats, which included both him and his family.

How was he able to resist? There was his family and the support of his friends. Helio had many courageous friends, but that is not enough. How then, is it possible to hold one's ground in such a situation? The answer lies in one's deep-seated ambition. According to Hannah Arendt, the Germans who opposed the Nazi regime did so simply because they did not want to live for the rest of their lives harbouring an assassin in their internal world. I think that a true ambition is something as simple and as crucial as that. Most often, what are considered extraordinary actions are, for those who perform them, an inescapable subjective requirement, without which they would lose all self-esteem and would feel unworthy of the respect of their children. In such circumstances, solitude is an inescapable and beneficial factor, because it is rooted in the strength of one's desire to live. The magnitude of the risk must also be measured against this subjective requirement. For some people, dying, losing one's work, being excluded from a social group, are lesser threats than a compromise that would repudiate a vital commitment or betray one's loyalty to a community. Experience confirms it: those who try to find a compromise between personal ethics and institutional violence have never had a personal commitment to defend.

Helio's brilliant idea was to bring a summary action before the military court. His reasoning was simple: since he was not accused of committing any errors in his analytic practice, and given that, on the contrary, the premises for exclusion reasserted his qualities as a clinician and teacher, the decision was based on reasons not falling under the competence of a professional society. Since a legal action had been brought and the competent military authorities were conducting an investigation to uncover the truth about allegations so serious that, were they to be true, they would constitute an attack on the honour of the armed forces, the professional society had to await the outcome of the proceedings, postpone the decision regarding exclusion and reinstate Helio fully. Helio won his case. At that time, anyone who brought an action before the military court was very likely to be discredited for life. But thanks to Helio's moral authority and his famous sense of humour, the legal decision discredited those who had tried to exclude him, making them subject to ridicule. The allegations against Amilcar Lobo proved to be true.

This was not the first time Helio confronted the military authorities without hesitation. In 1966, in Rio de Janeiro, still the cultural capital of the country then, a 100,000 people participated in a giant demonstration, the first one held after the coup d'état.

The army had sent troops against students who occupied a university restaurant to protest against the manner in which the restaurant operated. The soldiers opened fire and a student named Edson was killed. This aroused immense anger. And immense fear. Fear that the repression may become even more brutal – which was to be the case, but only two years later. As far as the demonstration was concerned, the fear was that undercover members of the civilian police could transform it into a massacre, that the tension hanging over our lives could find release in wanton violence.

But everything went well. The demonstration was a model of peaceful public action, largely thanks to Wladimir Palmeira, the student leader whose calm determination and humour set the tone. At the halfway point of the demonstrators' route, there was an unforgettable moment when Wladimir Palmeira addressed the crowd: "And now my friends, calmly and without frenzy, in Edson's honour, we are going to burn the flag of the United States." And the flag of the United States was burned calmly – the United States whose government had supported the military coup and the military regime, and whose successive governments had planned the overthrow and assassination of President Allende, and helped to bring to power terrorist regimes in Chile, Argentina and Uruguay.

The final destination of the demonstrators was the legislative assembly of Rio de Janeiro, located on a wide esplanade. Before the door, at the top of the stairs, a rather shaky podium had been set up. Helio was the first speaker. A talented orator, he found the right words to speak simply of the murdered youth, to speak to him.

You know, dear friend, even today, more than forty years later, what surprises me the most is how natural I found it, how natural all the intellectuals of that era found it, that the man universally recognised as the greatest psychoanalytic clinician should be the one delivering a major speech to the demonstrators taking part in the first act of resistance against the dictatorship. Nor was anyone surprised to read in the press, a few days later, articles by Helio on Bergman, or on a play, or about a book or a painting exhibition. It was a time when in Latin American societies there was no division between psychoanalysis, courage and the need to reflect, between a requirement for the greatest creativity and constant commitment to the world. There was no difference between psychoanalysis and life. A psychoanalyst was not someone who knew everything; on the contrary, he was simply an interpreter – like a musician, a poet, a politician, a painter, a film director, or a journalist. No one expected his interpretation of the world to be more significant than someone else's. His interpretation was irreplaceable, like all the others, because it reflected a specific practice of thinking and a specific practice of passion.

Helio was a tireless psychoanalytic interpreter of the world around him, of his historical period, of the city in which he lived. Although many Latin American artists and psychoanalysts of the 1960s could justifiably be called Sartrian intellectuals, Helio undoubtedly personified this figure in exemplary fashion. I was always amazed by his openness to requests of all sorts, like the fantastic proposal to work together made by a sixteen-year-old boy who barged in on him one evening. He agreed to the proposal on one condition: "That you start analysis with someone I recommend, so that your excessiveness remains life-giving."

Helio was interested in every form of reflection like a passionate lover, with the spontaneity of a poet analyst and the modesty of a craftsman who painstakingly invents the details that make the magic possible.

As a political interpreter, he initiated, with Glauber Rocha[1] and six other important Brazilian intellectuals, a conference in front of the Gloria Hotel in the centre of Rio, while foreign ministers of the Organization of American States were holding a meeting inside. National and international journalists heard, for about an hour and a half, about infringements of fundamental freedoms, about poverty and about the lack of a short and long term vision of the military regime. Of course, all eight of them were arrested by the State police and held in military barracks for eight days before being released. The affair caused a stir in the whole country – there were still courageous publications at the time, and received wide international coverage. But the most important thing was the lesson in resistance: if eight people could destabilise the regime, organising an active opposition was not a far-fetched idea.

The patience of the craftsman, the spontaneity of the poet and the passion of the lover all went into making the Social Clinic of Psychoanalysis a reality. Helio's intention was to bring knowledge about the unconscious to the community, to the citizens of the city, so that it may be included in social practices. He chose to set up the Clinic in a favela, a settlement of flimsy shacks in the *morros*, the "small" mountains of Rio, home to those who live on the margins of society, in conditions of precarity, poverty, misery and violence, but cherish the samba and cultivate hope. The team of analysts was composed of experienced clinicians; each one worked at the clinic four hours a week, without pay. At first, their main concern was to be accepted and to determine their role in relation to other caregivers already present, like the healers, with whom cooperation was established very quickly.[2] Some of the psychoanalysts were physicians; since there is no access to health care in developing countries, medical care had to take precedence over analytic treatment. But, in time, the roles became clearly defined and were recognised by the population of the favela: the place of the healer, the place of the physician, the place of the psychoanalyst. Michel Foucault, who visited the Social Clinic, considered it the most significant anthropological experiment of the twentieth century.

When I decided to organise a meeting in Paris to bring together psychoanalysts who had worked under terrorist regimes in Brazil, Argentina, Uruguay and Chile, my motive was twofold. First, I wanted the meeting to be a tribute to Helio Pellegrino, to the wonderful person he was, as a citizen-psychoanalyst, as a member of the resistance. I also wanted to pay tribute to him as the creator of the Social Clinic, a pioneer in the attempt to bring knowledge about the unconscious to the population, so as to widen the field of possibilities, to render the encounter with reality more creative and make the encounter with the Real a more humane experience.

My second motive had to do with my intention to publish a book that would record the theoretical experimentation on which these psychoanalysts based their work. My feeling was that these ideas had to be recorded quickly, before they faded from consciousness, before they were repressed.

Helio was enthusiastic about the project. The venture I envisioned was ambitious. I wanted these analysts to be welcomed in France in a manner worthy of the exceptional people they were. I wanted their travel fees to be covered, of course, and wanted them to receive a princely welcome. This all became possible thanks to Madame Danièle Mitterrand, who understood the importance of the event.

We decided together that for each country we would choose an analyst whose work was known, and who would suggest analysts they considered important.

The obvious choice for Argentina was Diego Garcia Reinoso. From their exile in Mexico, he and his wife returned to Buenos Aires, putting their lives at risk, to set up a support structure for the mothers of the *Plaza de Mayo*.[3] Like Helio, Diego contributed greatly to giving psychoanalysis a literary and political dimension. Both of them considered that the alliance between politics and psychoanalysis is not founded on a political project, but rather on clinical practice. They believed that what was needed was not to inject politics into psychoanalytic practice, but to introduce the human subject into reflections on power. For politics to recognise singularity could constitute an indirect but effective way of taking the unconscious into account when designing social projects.

Two examples best illustrate the effects of this perspective on a society. In Argentina, under the terrorist regime, if it was discovered that a political activist who was arrested was in analysis, his analyst was tortured in an attempt to obtain other names. An analyst who treated one activist must certainly treat others. In other words, the terrorist regime considered that a psychoanalyst who practiced his profession was as dangerous as an armed activist.[4]

Another example: during the so-called "demonstration of the hundred thousand" in Rio, to which I referred earlier, a friend who was a student leader gave a very moving speech. He had always been a talented speaker, but that day his words were pure inspiration. When he walked off the podium he was overwhelmed with emotion. I took him in my arms and told him he had been brilliant. He answered: "I know, I just killed my father" (who was a military man linked with the repression). From the singular to the universal...

Planning the Latin American Psychoanalysis Meeting took over three years. This event was of vital importance to me. I was overjoyed at the idea that Helio and Diego were going to meet. But they never did. Ten days before the start of the Meeting I received a call from Helio. Serious events in his private life made it impossible for him to leave Rio.

The Latin American Psychoanalysis Meeting turned out to be what we had all wished: a week-long festival of thought. Diego died a short time later. He had several heart attacks in succession, just after Alfonsin's government granted amnesty for the assassinations committed by the Generals of the dictatorship.

Helio liked the title I had given the book containing all the texts and discussions of the Meeting: *Le Psychanalyste sous la terreur* (The Psychoanalyst under Terror). He agreed that the book should be dedicated to Diego's memory. We were going to celebrate the publication of the book, with our wives and our friends, in Paris and in Rio. I had loved Helio for twenty-eight years.

Best regards,

Notes

1 Father of *Cinema Novo*, author of one of the greatest films in the history of the cinema, *Deus e o Diablo na Terra do Sol* (Black God, White Devil).
2 Letter 32, *Totalitarian regimes and psychosis*, describes the importance of the healers in greater detail.
3 The mothers of May Square (*las Madres de la Plaza de Mayo*), who called themselves "the mad women", gathered every Thursday in front of the presidential palace to demand the return of their children who had "disappeared" under the dictatorship.
4 For a description of the situation in Argentina during this period, see Letter 31, *Hallucination as a defence and Claude Lanzmann's triple knowledge*.

Humour

Dear friend,

I consider humour an inherent part of play. I like to play and I introduce play in my exchanges with patients as early as possible. Of course, this presupposes that we already have a strong bond, built on trust and tenderness.

Play is not to be used as a technique. Even though it could be one of the factors which structure the analytic relation, the presence of play confirms that the clinical exchange and the working through crucial to the patient take place in a friendly setting. It is the analyst's countertransference that introduces play.

As I said, humour is a component of play. The aggression inherent to humour must remain at a level similar to the level of anxiety in play. In other words, at a very low level. If the anxiety surpasses a certain level of intensity, humour no longer sustains the process through play, but breaks through and disorganises the setting. In the same way, when aggressiveness goes beyond a certain threshold, it no longer serves humour, becoming irony instead. Humour accompanies, while irony establishes, a particular quality of distance, a critical, mocking perspective. Irony is hurtful and mobilises the defences against persecution, slanting the relationship towards rigid and regressive positioning.

Since there is aggression in humour and anxiety in play, some patients do not tolerate either. They experience humour as an attack and any attempt at play as a trap. This in itself is enough to discourage those who might consider using humour or play as a technique. In addition, these clinical observations show that humour is also a matter of interpretation and that, as is the case with any interpretation, it can only be received favourably if specific psychic conditions are present. In this respect, an error in the use of humour provides differential information: when a patient, contrary to our expectations, is not receptive to humour he is informing us that the transference is taking place at a much more primary level than the level at which we believe the relationship to have developed.

Receptivity to play and humour presupposes participation of the mind, the capacity to distance oneself from emotions and affects, recognition of the other as different, and the ability to experience difference and externality as non-persecutory.

By contrast, those who do not tolerate this form of communication construct relationships on a foundation of deprivation and trauma so that the slightest blunder is experienced as rejection, and any divergence or lack of harmony arouses distrust in the child who was once mistreated, humiliated, and abandoned.

The space dedicated to humour and play authorises the kind of complicity that allows children to laugh at the seriousness of adults. It makes it possible to put defences in perspective, to see them for what they are: necessary psychic solutions, improvised and perhaps temporary.

As you can see, I have no objection to the possibility of mutual amusement in your work with your patients, to you making them laugh and enjoying their humour in turn. You are a woman with a zest for life, who is full of vitality; it would be surprising for this aspect of your personality not to be expressed in your practice. Have no fear: the idea that a psychoanalyst must remain as austere as a monk was no doubt born in the brain of a repentant priest!

To quote my friend Spinoza:

> I recognize a great difference between mockery... and laughter. For laughter and joking are pure joy. And so, provided they are not excessive, they are good through themselves. Nothing forbids our pleasure except a savage and sad superstition. For why is it more proper to relieve our hunger and thirst than to rid ourselves of melancholy?
>
> My account of the matter, the view I have arrived at, is this: no deity, nor anyone else, unless he is envious, takes pleasure in my lack of power and my misfortune; nor does he ascribe to virtue our tears, sighs, fear, and other things of this kind, which are signs of a weak mind. On the contrary, the greater the joy with which we are affected, the greater the perfection to which we pass, that is, the more we must participate in the divine nature. [Do you think this is a religious concept? Continue reading.]
>
> To use things, therefore, and take pleasure in them as far as possible – not, of course, to the point where we are disgusted with them, for there is no pleasure in that – this is the part of a wise man. It is the part of a wise man, I say, to refresh and restore himself in moderation with pleasant food and drink, with scents, with the beauty of green plants, with decoration, music, sports, the theater, and other things of this kind, which anyone can use without injury to another.[1]

(You see, for Spinoza the divine nature and human nature were one and the same.)

Please send me a description of the case you would like to discuss. In the meantime, I am going to recount two situations I had trouble remembering – an indication of how closely they are linked with the content of the countertransference.

The first concerns a patient who was usually quite reserved, but who, one day, started to cry as soon as she was on the couch. She said she felt irritated and angry with everyone. She claimed that she had no reason to feel this way, and enumerated all the good things in her life, of which we were both well aware. Speaking the way some adults speak to children, I said something like: "I know why she is out of sorts. If I let her guess, I am sure she will figure it out." Familiar with my way of doing things, she started to laugh at once. Continuing to speak in the same tone, I reminded her that we had only two sessions left before I went on vacation, saying she was upset that I was leaving at such a crucial moment in her life, and reminding her of her fear of abandonment. To my surprise, she said she was crying because she was very touched: she was happy and grateful that I had given her a telephone number where I could be reached while I was away, and she felt life was giving her more than she could have expected. She said all this laughing with joy, happy to have understood why she was crying, to be able to say it, to be able to distance herself from the symptom, thanks to humour.

The second example concerns a patient whose sessions were conducted face-to-face. As soon as she sat down, she said that she had had a very frightening dream. She was withdrawing money from a banking machine. Instead of the amount she asked for, the machine spewed out millions of bills. "You deserve them," I said, interrupting her account of the dream. She smiled and relaxed. When she went on, she paid greater attention to an aspect of the latent content of the dream: the difficulty she had recognising good internal objects (and recognising her own value, her beauty, her sensuality, her intelligence).

You notice that in both cases I commented very early, at the start of the session. Both women had been in analysis with me for a long time, and the transferential relation had already uncovered the central difficulties with which they struggled. You also notice, no doubt, that both women found it very hard to allow themselves to experience pleasure.

Your friend,

Note

1 Spinoza, B. (1996), *Ethics*. Translated by Edwin Curley, London: Penguin Classics, 1996; Part IV, Scholium of Proposition 45, p. 140.

Paranoia as seen by Philippe Réfabert

Dear friend,

It was a lovely spring day. I was on my way home, where I intended to review my notes on the work of Philippe Réfabert, and start to write you this letter, in order to answer your questions about your paranoid patient. I was enjoying the balmy weather and was feeling happy about my life. I had already written the outline for my text, and was looking forward to rereading the last letter of *From Freud to Kafka*.[1] I remembered the effect that this letter had had on me, and was curious to see if a second reading would confirm my original impression. In short, I was experiencing one of those moments of absolute trust in the benevolence of life, without which living would not be possible.

A few metres from my building, a man I passed made a peculiar impression on me; he was tall, bald, about forty, with a strange face. As I continued walking, I heard someone speak loudly behind me. I turned around and saw that the man was talking, and was apparently addressing himself to me. "Are you talking to me?" – "Yes, to you. Don't you think I saw that suspicious look you gave me?"

I walked back to where he was standing. When I was next to him, I had the impression that the giant was very, very frightened. I said right away: "Excuse me, Sir. I did not look at you suspiciously. But it is true that I was startled by the strength of your face" – and as I was speaking, I realised that what had shocked me was the brutality of his features. When he heard what I said, his face took on the expression of a baby. The baby said: "Please excuse me, Sir."

Afterwards, the first thing I thought about was the extraordinary, infinite complexity of a gaze – and I will come back to this. Then I thought about Freud. I told myself that the pain-filled Goliath must have glimpsed my scandalous joy and well-being, this inner intimate universe that sometimes spills out into the reality of the world. At first, he must have wanted to swallow this well-being, but very quickly he was hurt by it and he had to attack it. That is when he projected onto me the hate that overwhelmed him.

My recourse to Freud was combined with other methods of deciphering, worth examining more closely. I was referring back to Freud when I supposed that the giant wanted to swallow my well-being. Why? Because I am presuming that his desire to situate himself in relation to this other who is observing him and whom he is observing originates in a libidinal impulse. But very soon this processing of the encounter slipped away, became inadequate as a frame of reference. You noticed that I did not say that the stranger wanted to swallow the other, and certainly not his penis. I presumed that he wanted to swallow a state of well-being, and consequently a certain relation to the world. Here I was thinking of envy, the twin sister of hate, and of Melanie Klein's theory concerning hate. And I was coming back to Freud when I referred to the projection of hate. But whose hate is being projected?

According to Philippe Réfabert in his book *From Freud to Kafka*, it is the hate of the parents, or one parent of the giant, "relieved to find in him a container in which to expulse the monster (he carries)", who transformed the baby he once was into "the troublesome witness of the murder of the witness".

In his book, Réfabert throws a new light on hate, inviting us to reflect on the matter. The type of subject he describes, like those I once called the "sons of dinosaurs",[2] illustrated by the giant or by *Schreber*, the paranoid patient analysed by Freud, "[does] not possess the warp yarn: hate, around which a coherent pattern could be woven…" Like the giant, "Schreber has no knowledge of hate, because both his parents transferred their hate into him innocently, unknowingly."[3]

I am tempted to add that he has no knowledge of this psychic-foreign-body-hate he is trying, powerlessly and in vain, to eliminate – possibly by throwing it onto another who happens to be present.[4]

Contrary to Freud, who attributes the paranoid delusion to the rejection of a homosexual impulse, Philippe Réfabert postulates that Schreber's delusions are caused by his lack of knowledge of hate. But, Réfabert specifies, "Schreber loses his head not only because he is unable to perceive the hostile signs directed towards him […] In Schreber's case, objective, external hate has no subjective, internal support. As a result, his image faces a highly alarming scenario. Instantly, he loses countenance and is banished from reality. He is no longer participating in an exchange with someone else, he is radically alone" and, I would like to add, alone like Franz Kafka…

> Not only is Schreber unable to name hostility and silence, he is unable to turn to his colleagues and ask for help. He cannot formulate a plea, he cannot ask for support. Schreber does not know that asking is possible […] [He] has to sustain an image of himself alone, and this is why he can never relax his vigil […] Like Narcissus, he cannot detach himself from his image because no one sees him […] [His image has not been held in any gaze.] The so-called narcissistic personality corresponds to a situation where the "I" is in charge of the ego […] To compensate for the absence of an image in the mirror held out to him by his mother… Schreber sets in place the will to destroy… His parents worked at killing the witness in him and passed their crimes off as a pedagogical procedure.

The letter I am quoting is at the end of the book and thus provides an exemplary conclusion. Exemplary because it illustrates the attention and respect with which

Réfabert treats the subject, without any attempt to rely on psychopathology. He writes: "Schreber's healing is catastrophic [...] As soon as he is transformed into a woman, suicide is no longer the only means [he] has for finding his place in life [...] Thanks to this feat [...] he is able to perceive the same images and sounds as other human beings, and can dispense with mediation through a persecutor. Not having received from his parents the gift of an image, Schreber constructed a vicarious paradox he could use as support.

"His parents worked at killing the witness [to their crime] in him and passed their crime off as a pedagogical procedure..." Philippe Réfabert has been studying the question of the witness for some time: "I propose that we consider psychoanalytic treatment from the perspective of testimony. This idea occurred to me while I was expanding on the concept of 'soul murder', which Daniel Paul Schreber borrowed from Germanic literature. It seemed to me that this perspective could be extended to the whole range of psychotherapies, and that it would be beneficial to see psychotherapy as an experience where the analyst creates conditions in which the analysand's ability to testify, for himself and on behalf of the other, can be repaired and recovered [...] The person who has learned to ignore his sensations and his pain, who no longer knows how to ask for help, cannot avoid leading the other to subject him to the same crime, a crime that was never prosecuted. The same is true in analysis, where, as Sándor Ferenczi maintained, the analyst always repeats the crime."[5] The characters in the life of the patient – the living, the dead and the phantoms – enter the analytic stage, like Pirandello's characters, and force the therapist to play the role of the ancestors.[6]

But what do I mean by a witness? For me, the witness is someone with a point of view; a point of view is what allows exteriority. Therefore, when I meet the witness, I necessarily encounter externality, the other. The witness's perspective, exterior to me, makes me aware of my solitude, not as isolation, but as something open, changeable, a bridge to the world. The witness meets me and throws me off centre, solicits me and defines my limits. The witness invites me to speak and forces me to acknowledge a point of view, my own. The witness is not a spectator; he accompanies me. The ground we tread is not the known, but that which is emerging. He manifests his agreement, of course, and – above all – his difference. Thus, the witness is also a friend. It could be said that I am using Philippe Réfabert's writing to support my point of view. I am. For me, the ethics of psychoanalysis and the ethics of friendship are one and the same. And I think you will agree that the letters we exchange are proof that friendship stimulates reflection more than anything else can.

Philippe Réfabert says that he wrote this book to testify to the fact that, just as Kafka did, anyone can relinquish the ties with the worst, constructed in a panic in order to survive; and that a psychoanalyst can help with this task on certain conditions, the first of which is the ability to put Oedipus in his proper place. But to do so, we must define "normality".

Réfabert notes that the normal man, the man-from-the-country as Kafka calls him, does not automatically possess the ability to turn around, nor the capacity to initiate the play between the "I" and the ego, so that the "I", following the rhythm that punctuates his encounter with the world, a rhythm set by the mother, can retreat or find support in the space of the ego. For this to happen, the mother must identify with her child and endow him with the paradoxical system love/hate – the negative. Réfabert considers the negative to be the trace of death, and he rightly adds: "Without a trace of death the subject lacks support for his life…" It is a matter of transmitting what Réfabert calls the paradoxical system required to make life possible. "The destruction of the paradoxical system causes madness, death, or the creation of a new Subject." (The capital of "Subject" indicates catastrophic healing, like that illustrated by Schreber.)

To illustrate the destruction of the paradoxical system – which makes it impossible to turn around and recognise one's own thoughts and feelings – Philippe Réfabert suggests that we imagine a situation where parents who are out for a stroll with their child suddenly hide from him. The child, now alone and lost, dumbfounded, is shaking with fear. "The parents come out of hiding. – It was a game, you big silly." Using one of Schreber's descriptive terms as a theoretical concept, Réfabert calls this diabolical game, in which the parents enjoyed the child's terror, soul murder. "The parents who hid without saying a word broke the paradoxical system of a protective shield, where all things have a shadow [...] [The child] has received a deadly blow which has no psychic inscription [...] The trace of death has been erased [...] The destruction of the paradoxical system always involves complicity between two parents.[7] Because of this complicity in not knowing…, in affective non-involvement, the child's agonising experience has no witness [...]." The parents carry inside them an unnameable thing, which is often "a far-off echo of historical events intersecting with an event in their personal history".[8] The child's bodily experience of panic, his trembling, "acquired no psychic existence [...] Soul murder engenders a new subject who creates otherness in a panic"[9] (pp. 55–63).

Réfabert points out that Freud, who assumed that the self-reflective capacity is *naturally inherited*, did not develop a concept of an alternative, paradoxical psychic system, and proposed closure in its place (first letter of *From Freud to Kafka*).

He goes on to explain how this closure is founded in natural philosophy, given that Freud constructed his theoretical edifice on the scientific doctrines of his era. The statement that "every child is a budding Oedipus constitutes a break with all materialist or spiritual determinism [governing] psychic life." By introducing the Oedipian myth, Freud "audaciously intends to found a new scientific field on a fiction, a daring initiative that takes into account the ability to conceive death, and awareness of the discontinuity between generations [...] But this attempt… is only partially successful [...] Freud sees Oedipus as representing the incestuous posture, a posture Freud takes for granted as natural [...] Up until 1897, the child was seen as the possible object of a seducer." But once trauma theory is abandoned, Oedipal theory "transforms the child from the passive victim of an assault into the subject and object of psychic disturbances provoked by this assault, seen as internal. The patient becomes the subject of his drama, participates in writing… it

[...] Seduction is internal before being external [...] Now, the theory is founded on the idea that sexuality is traumatic in itself, and that psychic life develops along the lines of the legend of Oedipus and of the primal fantasies this legend organises" (p. 21).

This paragraph deals with several questions, several stages in the history of psychoanalysis. We can review them together.

When Freud discovered the Oedipus complex, he repudiated his previous etiology of trauma. Until 1897, his seduction theory held that trauma resulted from the seduction of the child by a perverse adult, usually the father. But theorising that every case of emotional disorder can be linked to the presence of a perverse agent in childhood is a very "naturalist" concept of human suffering.

With the advent of Oedipus, sexuality is still traumatic, but the cause is *internal*: fantasy is the agent. Of course, this discovery humanises trauma and modifies prognosis. What remains to be done is for the subject to change his interpretation of his own incestuous sexual fantasy, since it is this interpretation that can produce a traumatic effect. It is a question of bringing the patient to accept that although it is not possible to do everything, one has the right *to think, to desire and to feel everything*.

Philippe Réfabert recognises that such a hypothesis is a great leap forward for humanity. Like Ferenczi, he points out that we must not forget the existence of the child's parents, that we must not forget the other, who is also part of the internal world. In fact, the way in which this parental other was present to the child will create a more or less happy internal world, or a damaged world. Réfabert reminds us that all of this is not determined in advance, it is not automatically given, and that not every child had a good-enough mother like little Sigmund's mother.

Réfabert notes:

> When the child harbours, from birth, an incestuous and parricidal desire, the discontinuity Freud postulated for humans is erased. Oedipus' ability to reflect on his image as an incestuous and parricidal criminal without going mad or killing himself is not naturally given. The ability to see oneself, to look back at one's image in order to step away form it, is not inborn. Rather, it is linked to the capacity of the maternal environment to encourage the development of a primary paradoxical system in the child [...] A self-image implies that a paradoxical system formed by the trace of death and the objection to death is in place.
>
> (p. 18)

Philippe Réfabert examines other consequences of setting trauma theory aside. If the other no longer plays a symbolic role in the genesis of the psychic apparatus, Freud must look for the cause of any new psychic organisation in the closed psychic monad (the Freudian monad). Réfabert points out, for example, the absurdity of the concept that a distinction between the inside and outside can be established based *solely* on muscular efficiency when dealing with excitations. When speaking of Schreber, and therefore of psychosis, Réfabert has to refer back to the theory of drives, if only to point out the limitations of Freud's hypothesis, with which you are doubtless familiar, that Schreber's paranoia is the result of a struggle against homosexual libidinal impulses.[10] Réfabert's remark "Basing the definition of instinct on the notion of need constitutes the weak link in the theory, the door left ajar for naturalism to enter" fills us with admiration. As does his statement that "practice has stayed ahead of theory because the concept of the sexual was never fully humanised" (p. 20). At the same time, we are vexed because before reading this we had contented ourselves with mentally correcting this type of epistemological impasse in Freud's writing – with the help of Ferenczi and other authors. But this critique had to be made *explicitly*, and Réfabert was one of the first to make it. (Winnicott himself had not made it, although his work clearly indicates that he was aware of Freud's impasse.)

I agree with Philippe Réfabert about the need to humanise sexuality – on the condition that we assume it is still savage. Man speaks and has sexual intercourse. This is the paradox inherent to humans, always at work in their lives. (Réfabert agrees when he says: "The particularity [of man] in the animal kingdom consists in the fact that agreement between these natural instincts and his reflection is never acquired once and for all, and must always be reinvented.") Of course, at times man makes love – but this is a victory, a victory which does not abolish the paradox. I can still see sexuality as being, at the same time, animal, savage and traumatic. Love, which includes sexuality, is always an opening onto the Real. This is why every true encounter has a catastrophic dimension, why every true encounter is always traumatic.[11]

For me, the problem with abandoning the theory of trauma is not related to the traumatic nature of sexuality – a concept with which I agree. Rather, the problem is that from that point forward Freud bypasses the other as the one who conveys humanity to the child. Seduction theory portrayed the other as a perverse agent of trauma, but at least an agent who was present. The primacy of fantasy excludes the other and imposes recourse to a naturally good and ideal mother, whose only function is to provide closure of the monad and, subsequently, to ensure its self-engendering functioning.

I am convinced by Réfabert's argument that Freudian dualism cannot be the foundation of a paradoxical system, but I prefer this dualism to Lacanian monism, which frightens both Réfabert and me. What I mean by monism is an absence of heterogeneity between the object of the theory and the tools used to understand it. (In Lacanian theory, heterogeneity is created by the signifier and excludes the body.) But I am equally wary of a monism of the other – caricatured by the clinical practice of proponents of the "strong ego/weak ego" theory, which has wreaked havoc through a use of transference that considers the relation to the analyst to be the sole agent of a change of position in the subject.

Like Winnicott, I think that the concept of a paradox is compatible with Freudian dualism. I do not mind that Freud does not perceive the "*economy of psychosexual life to originate in the site of death*". I no doubt correct the concept myself, because I am convinced that this economy will be transmitted by the mother (or not transmitted, in which case it remains to be inscribed in the working through made possible by transference). What bothers me is that Freud *does not emphasise* that the functioning of the psychic apparatus based on a compulsion to repeat also applies to sexual drives. The concept of Eros covers a wider field than the concept of the libido, and includes sexual or sensory irrepresentability.[12] And, at the risk of shocking moralists, I want to confirm that "*the experience of pleasure*", by a victim of soul murder, is a "*creation of the human in the face of aggression, and not the sign of a return to animality*".

Philippe Réfabert and I both believe that this economy of enjoyment cannot be changed by remaining within a libidinal frame of reference. Changing this economy requires throwing open the doors of the closets, dealing with the dead, identifying the soul murderers, the living and the phantoms that crowd the psychic stage.

In his exploration of the limits of Freudian theory in treating psychosis, Réfabert converses with Kafka. He acknowledges Kafka as:

> the writer who describes most accurately, and in the most colourful terms, the feat that has to be performed by a person who must maintain the symptom serving as a vicarious paradoxical foundation, a foundation he himself constructed without knowing it.

If we adopt a hypothesis positing Freudian closure, we speak of a narcissistic disorder. But Kafka's hero does not suffer from a narcissistic disorder or any hereditary constitutional disorder, or from any fragility of the ego. What we are dealing with are always the effects of a frightening relationship between a child and a parent who has not expelled him at the start, making it problematic for him from then on to turn around (to reflect on his image or on his feelings).[13]

How can transference be of use in dealing with this impossibility, even this prohibition of any self-reflection? Where can the psychoanalyst look for allies? I will let Philippe Réfabert answer:

> No child, even the child of a zombie, can do without the ability to turn around, something he can only do at the expense of the parent. Without the ability to turn around, even at the expense of a zombie parent, the child will be unwell. When a person has to rely on his own support, he does not do well; he uses himself up, he kills himself working, he drinks or, like Schreber, he creates his own scenario with a God and a Schreber skull; or, like some poets, he is eventually killed as he strives to turn around and look for support in his own internal world. But I think that when a person is alive, it means that he had support. Being alive means that there was support, and it is the psychoanalyst's function to help the patient rediscover it. In every case, there was someone who gave you credence, who believed in you, trusted in you, had faith in you, in short, made you the object of the three theological virtues, and who expelled you at the right time. Sometimes, this other was an animal. Yes, sometimes it is an animal, perhaps a dog in a kennel. Often, it is a servant, a maid. A maid who was quickly sent away. Because there are parents who

are very happy that their children are loved, but who, at the same time, cannot tolerate it. They are happy but envious at the same time, and one day they suddenly send this person away, brutally interrupting a love/hate sequence in progress. From then on, the child waits. He does not know what he waits for. He does not know that he expects something from another human being. In any case, he would never think that he is expecting something from this maid, whom he had completely forgotten.

I hope, dear friend, that Réfabert's reflections will provide you with support for working through your own ideas.

Sincerely yours,

Notes

1 The extracts from *From Freud To Kafka: The Paradoxical Foundation of the Life-and-Death Instinct* by Philippe Réfabert (Karnac Books, 2014) featured in this letter are reprinted with the kind permission of both Philippe Réfabert and Karnac Books.
2 Réfabert, P. (2014), *From Freud to Kafka*, London: Karnac Books; and "Les enfants de dinosaures", Topique, No. 28, 1982; reprinted in *De l'Amour à la Pensée*, op. cit.
3 The text in italics is quoted from Réfabert's book, ibid. (trans. A. Jacob).
4 Freud, S. (1911), *Psychoanalytic Notes on an Autobiographical Account of Paranoia*. S.E., 12. London: Hogarth, 1911.
5 Réfabert, P. "Le témoin, sujet de la psychanalyse", *Le Coq Héron*, No. 171, December 2002.
6 Réfabert, P. "Un personnage, un auteur, un acteur", *Pratiques*, No. 41, third trimester 1995.
7 I came to the same conclusion. I proposed the term *deadly pact* to designate this parental complicity. See "Les enfants de dinosaures", art. cit.
8 This concept is in agreement with that of Françoise Davoine and Jean-Max Gaudillière. See Letter 23, *Françoise Davoine and Jean-Max Gaudillière: history beyond trauma*.
9 Among the figures representing the results of this catastrophic construction, Philippe Réfabert sees Don Juan neither as a repressed homosexual, nor a hysteric, but rather as a psychopath who has become, in his turn, a soul murderer – an irrefutable view, in my opinion. A superb analysis of the short story *The Judgment*, in *From Freud to Kafka*, presents the birth of Kafka, the artist, as a paradigm of the birth of a subject in the aftermath of the massacre perpetrated by his parents.
10 On this subject, see Herbert Rosenfeld (1949) "Remarks on the relation of male homosexuality to paranoia", *International Journal of Psychoanalysis*, 30: 36–47. Reprinted in *Psychotic States*, London: Hogarth Press, 1965.
11 I must mention that I am puzzled by Philippe Réfabert's disagreement with Freud's use of Broussais' principle – formulated by Auguste Compte – who had known madness – a principle asserting that there is only a difference of degree between the normal and the pathological. I have always thought – and I still do – that by reinstating this principle Freud prevented psychic suffering from being viewed as a medical problem, and invited instead an anthropological, and sometimes archeological perspective. August Comte, who had personally experienced the psychiatric approach, knew what he was talking about. I kept asking myself why Réfabert insisted on reintroducing a discontinuity between the normal and the pathological. And one day, a trait of Philippe's character came to my mind. Philippe is a man who can get angry. The two of us have

this in common. In fact, it is one of the things which cement our friendship. But when someone is angry, he does not have time to explain. When one is angry, one is caught up in the urgent need to think and, as you surely know, urgency is a form of truth. When I pictured Philippe angry, I was finally able to understand what he wanted to say. He was saying that a battered child knows nothing about the normal child. Libidinal economy does not provide the tools needed to apprehend the massacre. Since what takes place here is topical destruction – destruction of a place in the subject – sexuality, like everything else, runs amok, tries to repair the destroyed zones.

See letter 33, *True love*.

These quotes are paraphrased by H. de Macedo from content in P. Réfabert's book From Freud to Kafka, London: Karnac Books, 2014; they are presented in this form on the site Quatrième Groupe, June 2004, under the title "Le Témoin" (The Witness).

12   See Letter 11, *Reading* Beyond the Pleasure Principle: *the insistence of Eros*.

13   "Un personnage, un auteur, un acteur", art. cit.

Letter 15

The player

Dear friend,

You paint a very interesting picture of the "middle-aged woman" whose problems seem to be of a psychotic nature.

Let me offer some suggestions. You feel responsible for all the ills that befall her because you are too close to everything she tells you. She complains that you give her too little time, and you respond by having her stay an hour and a half instead of an hour. She says that Sundays are her worst days and you arrange to see her on Sundays, and so on. I am not saying that you are wrong to do this; after all, you are the one who is working with her, you are the object of the transference. What seems problematic is the fact that you are surprised she is becoming more and more demanding. So I say: be careful!

Severely disturbed patients suffer terribly, but the intensity of their pain does not prevent them from being intelligent. Your patient tyrannises you and she knows it. But the tyranny of the psychotic is matched by equally great guilt. For you, the problem is to avoid becoming irreplaceable to such an extent that she cannot separate from you. It is important to keep in mind that with emotionally deprived patients it is impossible not to hold this place and, at the same time, it is essential to make it possible for them to eventually leave us. Not an easy feat!

You are baffled to see her in such a state of discomfiture again, after several sessions in which a structuring process was taking place. I think that she is right and that this proves that the two of you are doing good work together. If you understand what she experiences at a certain level, why shouldn't she solicit your help at a more complex level, where the work is more difficult? The unconscious script must be something like this: if she understood this, I can certainly go further with her.

You seem discouraged to see almost no signs of recognition on her part for everything you have given her. In fact, dear friend, anything else would be surprising. If she could recognise everything you did for her, it would mean that she is already able to contain all the pain that will be caused by the realisation of everything she did not receive from her parents. Right now, she is testing you, and this is to be expected. She will only grant you her trust and recognise your loyalty much later, after you've worked together a long time.

Your discouragement is due to your idealisation of the function of the analyst. It would be too easy if all we had to do is love our patients and give them what we think they need, for them to be able to enjoy life.

Do not forget that repetition in psychic functioning always includes the attempt to reduce any new relationship to the conditions that were present in childhood. The more traumatic the childhood relationships, the stronger this constraint will be – the unconscious is lazy, it resists the unexpected. As a result, we should not be surprised that the patient places us in the role played by all those who prevented him or her from living, from desiring. It's fair and square. We must accept this role, fill it – and then speak the lines of another, unprecedented character, without expecting the patient to notice the difference at once.

One last thing. You apologise for your naïvety. Yes, you are naïve, but this is a good quality. Those who have seen it all are not made for this work, or should no longer do it. But because the psychoanalyst's function is an exercise of power, it is essential that you practise foreseeing, anticipating transferential reactions, the traps that your patients will unconsciously set at different levels of their relationship with you, so that nothing changes, so that the old scenario continues to repeat itself.

Practise cheating at poker!

Your friend,

Freud, Michel Neyraut, Piera Aulagnier

Anxiety between theory and practice

Dear friend,

Your last letter gave me a lot to think about. You are asking me in what essential way the conception of a HUMAN being was modified by Freud's discovery of the unconscious.

I know that you do not expect a long, learned discourse, which I would be unable to deliver, but rather that I tell you what, in my opinion, has changed radically since Freud, in man's relation to himself and to the world.

Roughly, I would say that before Freud, man was defined either by his relation to thinking, or by his relation to the senses. In our civilisation, where religion provided the frame of reference for centuries, the world of the senses was a negligible aspect of life, because real life was eternal life, which starts after death. Freud rejected this notion of transcendence and proposed a definition of man based on two characteristics: man speaks; and man makes love. In Freudian theory, not only is there no difference between sexuality and thought process, but there is a stated certainty that the rejection of this identity is at the root of all pathologies. The refusal of the notion that thought transcends the senses had already been formulated by Spinoza, and Freud admits being in his debt.

Of course, this Freudian conception of the human comes at a high price. If we stop considering the world of the senses, and above all sexuality, a negative thing compared to real life, we place conflict at the centre of human life. At the same time, the nature of truth changes, since truth is no longer rooted solely in the world of ideas, but must also be rooted, from then on, in bodily experience, and must become embodied truth. But the conflict inherent in the double purpose of human existence: to love and to think, inevitably creates anxiety. Therefore, we can say that when Freud united thought and sexual desire, making conflict an inevitable part of this perspective, he made anxiety the crucial agent of all human accomplishment.

This, then, is what I see as the Freudian revolution: the idea that thought is rooted in sexual desire; the acknowledgement that conflict is central to human reality; and the use of anxiety as a paradigm for all affects.

But it was not easy for Freud to assign this fundamental place to anxiety in his theory. In the beginning, in respect to the infant, Freud had to define a place where bodily experiences, that he considered sexual pleasures, could become memory and material for thought. This place is the psyche. The psyche, the psychic apparatus, receives the trace of bodily experience with the affective impression of this experience, that is, a pleasant or unpleasant affect. Freud created the concept of *drive*, a concept designating this merger between bodily, erogenous pleasure and the trace of the experience that produced it. Thus, the drive is composed of three elements: the trace of experience; its *representation*; and the affect.

The first Freudian theory of anxiety, which is also Freud's theory of affect, was developed in relation to repression – that is, material which is denied entry into the sphere of the ego. (For our present purposes, we will set aside the question of the constitution of the ego in an infant.) Freud posits that what is rejected by the ego, what is repressed, is the representation of experience. The affect is not repressed, and does not inhibit sexual energy, the *libido*, which, when separated from the representation of its origin, turns into anxiety. From this perspective, affects are pleasant or unpleasant depending on whether or not they are in tune with the ego. Therefore, no matter how frightening, the anxiety felt by the subject is simply the result of its separation from the representation of the repressed experience.

In effect, what is played out on the psychic stage insistently (the attempted return of the repressed) is merely the re-presentation of what once was already there, the work of the psychoanalyst being to persuade the ego to accept the initial harmony between the pleasurable affect of desire and its representation. This conception presents the psychic apparatus as autonomous, self-sufficient, seemingly self-generated – allowing Freud to use the image of a monad to describe it. But in *Formulations on the Two Principles of Mental Functioning*,[1] he points out that such an organisation, which ignores the reality of the external world, cannot survive; but he adds: "The employment of a fiction like this is, however, justified when one considers that the infant – provided that one includes with it the care it receives from its mother, does almost realize a psychical system of this kind."[2]

Now, Ferenczi enters the stage and takes a particular interest in this mother who provides the care, and in the clinical configurations resulting from a relation to a mother who is unable to identify with the psychic needs of her infant. And although Freud might have been annoyed by the need that arose to review his reflection on the reality of trauma, he was also realistic enough to admit that not all mothers were as exceptional as his own had been – particularly since his friend was speaking from personal experience. (This, despite the fact that Freud was unable to play the role of the mother Ferenczi was assigning to him in the transference.)[3]

Although Ferenczi had no descendants of his own, in the context of Freudian realism it can be said that he left a theoretical inheritance to Klein, Balint and Winnicott, who all focused their research on the earliest stages of the relation of the infant to the world.

Lacan's remarkable reading of these stages determines a major turning point: the other is a constitutive element of the child's psychic apparatus. Desire for the other, pre-existence of the other, even before birth, through the process of imagining the unborn child, through the symbolic meaning of the world into which he is born. But Lacan is fond of order: although Ferenczi's texts convince him of the importance of the mother, he refers at once to the Other, in order to give priority to this Other (with a capital "O") over the other (with a small "o"), the nurturing mother who is the primary connection to the universal. When all is said and done, Lacan's incursion into the world of Ferenczi and his descendants is a courtesy call paid to talented but marginal colleagues. (His relation to Winnicott is much more complex, but I will not repeat here what I already stated in my book *De l'amour à la pensée*.)

Lacan refers immediately to the universal and the symbolic, from the start, saying about Klein: "She jams the symbolic into little Dick." And then there are the texts of his disciples, bordering on the caricatural, in which the hierarchy of the symbolic and the imaginary is just as rough-hewn as the fundamental hierarchy of the libidinal stages proposed by Abraham in the early days of the history of psychoanalysis.

In fact, if the symbolic is what dominates, we can forget about anxiety, and therefore about affect; man is on a par with the gods – or with the machine – and the only question left is how to insert death into this system since, despite the signifier, death is inevitable. In the meantime, there is "lack of being", "I've got news for you", and "in one ear and out the other", that is to say, scorn. It was at this point that Wladimir Granoff, the ally who appreciated Ferenczi and was not afraid, brought back the child in the adult. Lacan was annoyed. The differences between the two men were to deepen over time.[4]

In France, Piera Aulagnier's interest in the treatment of psychosis led her to follow closely the work of the so-called British School. In addition to the concept of originary process, she was to elaborate a metapsychology of this practice based on hypotheses regarding the infant/nurturing mother relation. Undeniably, Lacan introduced otherness into the psychic apparatus – a turning point – but Aulagnier instituted the theoretical, metapsychological rule of the affect of the Other, placing it at the centre of what is at stake in the work of the psyche – a revolution![5]

Freud considered affect to be suppressed and displaced, and considered repression to apply only to representations. Therefore, affect is not part of the unconscious, making it very difficult for the therapeutic process to unfold towards its objective: connecting the setting of the analysis with its object, the unconscious. Although transference is the tool that makes possible the restructuring of representational configurations, in other words, the tool allowing access to and working through of unconscious material, rigorous application of the theory requires that all affective manifestations between the two subjects be ignored. Yet, many types of anxiety and affect arise in the relation between the analyst and his patient; they are intense and essential for the working through that occurs in the analytic elaboration.

This hiatus between the metapsychology of the therapeutic process and its intended result has created, for some, an obsession with the purity of the setting and with the neutrality of the analyst, who is required to be less than a shadow and forbidden to express any type of feeling. Others, whom the former considers deviants and heretics, try to follow the Freudian precept – theory is all very well, but we work with clinical reality – by affirming, more or less awkwardly, that the actual reality relation between transference and countertransference plays a role in the emergence of representations and changes the unconscious position of the subject in analysis. Despite objections, these deviants are tolerated in Freudian circles. They are called "clinicians" and no one suspects that the "innovative" character of this term was already contained in the conceptual incommunicability between the clinical domain and the theory underlying and justifying this practice. As you can see, the question of affect is not simple.

Michel Neyraut tried to formulate the difficulty that arises when we attempt to connect the transference/countertransference dialectic with the metapsychological monad, in these terms:

> While, on the one hand, transference is described as the driving force, the innermost heart of analysis, the source of psychic creation, the stumbling block of neuroses and psychoses, the very principle of analysability, this powerful phenomenon and its psychic impact have no metapsychological status...
>
> On one side, there is the metapsychological monad, on the other, an accident, a complication, almost a regrettable epiphenomenon that nevertheless allows resistance to manifest itself...
>
> There are, no doubt, several reasons for this, the first of which is that transference appeared unexpectedly in the corpus of an already-constituted theory, in *Project for a Scientific Psychology*, and later in Chapter VII of *The Interpretation of Dreams*; that it was presented as a troublesome phenomenon, an inevitable but permanent obstacle best dealt with separately, as a particular technical difficulty against which neophytes had to be warned sooner or later.

According to Michel Neyraut, Freud reduces affect to its level of energy, that is, to its intensity, in order to avoid the question of quality in favour of quantity. This could explain the fact that Freudian metapsychology could not integrate or account for transference.

If affect is not part of the unconscious, if instead of taking into account its quality – pleasant or unpleasant – the theory focuses on its intensity, we can understand why there is "a discontinuity between metapsychology and the study of transference [...] The monadic system of the psyche, which constitutes the metapsychology, is opposed through this monadic character to the analytic situation which is essentially dualistic, and even essentially dialectical according to some."[6]

Lacan resolved this paradox by executing a pirouette: he reduced clinical practice to metapsychology, overlooking transference. The catastrophic effects of this metapsychological logic are well known. The masterpiece illustrating the disaster was an article by Jacques-Alain Miller, published in *Le Monde*, in which we learn that the analyst no longer needs to speak, since we now know what was not yet known in Freud's era: namely that the unconscious interprets itself.

This is how things stood when Piera Aulagnier arrived on the scene. A clever epistemologist, she did not oppose the Freudian unconscious. She simply postulated that it is preceded by a level of psychic functioning – the *originary* process – that the unconscious has to take into account, and in which the product of representation, the *pictogram*, is both a representation of affect and the affect of the representation. The originary level of functioning is short-lived as an exclusive process in the psychic life of the infant, and very soon psychic life comes to require the work of repression and the creation of fantasy. Throughout life the originary level continues to process, based on its own rules, that which will appear in the sphere of two other levels of functioning: the sphere of fantasy (primary level); and the sphere of consciousness (secondary level).

Although in the very first paragraphs of *The Violence of Interpretation*[7] Aulagnier reminds the reader that her practice with psychotic patients served as the backdrop of her theories, she soon admits that her research is also a way to question the usual definition of the psyche – in other words, the theoretical model serving to understand neurosis, which leaves aside experiences prior to language, experiences we have all shared, before the establishment of certainties and commonly held perspectives certified by the discourse of a given culture.

Aulagnier's ideas constitute a return to Freud as well, since she considers that maintaining the heterogeneity of the maternal psychic space and the limited possibilities of representation of the infant's psychic functioning means refusing both a biologisation of the advent of the subject, and a theory of a chain of signifiers that overlooks Freud's insistence on the role of the body and of the sensorial and somatic model that the body provides to the psyche.

Thus, in her view just as in Freud's, the primary condition for the representability of encounter is connected to the body, and specifically to its sensorial activity. The second condition is that representational activity be linked with a pleasure *bonus*.

According to Piera Aulagnier, the pictogram is the first self-representation produced by psychic life. But what does the pictogram represent? It represents the relation between an object, for instance the breast, and what Piera Aulagnier calls its complementary zone-object, in this case, the mouth. She describes two originary representations: that of originary pleasure – the fusion pictogram; and that of originary unpleasure – the rejection pictogram.

Aulagnier maintains that, very early, there is perception by the psyche of *an excess of pleasure* experienced through representation during a situation of real satisfaction – such as breast-feeding. But she emphasises that in order for the psyche to experience this *excess of pleasure*, the satisfaction must bring actual pleasure, beyond constituting need satisfaction. For this to happen, an essential condition must exist: the experience must be represented as bringing pleasure to the two entities that constitute the object and the complementary zone; in other words, the mouth – the infant, and the breast – the mother, must experience pleasure simultaneously.

I want to draw your attention to the pleasure, or lack of pleasure, experienced by the mother during breast-feeding and the care she dispenses to her baby. If she experiences pleasure, we can foresee that the primal process – the baby's imagination and his fantasies will be grounded in love and tenderness. This allows us to postulate that *excess of pleasure* in originary representational activity is linked with shared pleasure in the real situation. Piera Aulagnier asserts that psychic activity always has an affective dimension, and therefore all experiences in the psychic space are also metabolised by the originary processes. In my opinion, what is crucial is the emphasis placed by Aulagnier on the affective quality of the other in representational activity and its psychic destiny – that is, in the encounter between the subject and the world, between the subject and his own self.

(As I stated earlier, Aulagnier proposes something Freud believed to be impossible: that an affect can have a representation.)

Here, we find obvious parallels between Aulagnier's reflection and that of Winnicott (as well as Bion, with whom I am not familiar enough). If the mother's affectivity is crucial for the way in which the child creates a representation of his relation to the world, we can conclude that the mother's invasive anxiety prevents the child from representing his experience as other than distressing.

I have just come to understand the radical consequences of this formulation concerning the metabolisation of thought processes by the originary. It was clear to me that each thought – or to be more exact, the investment of a thought by the "I" – has an inscription at the originary level, where the affect of the "I" is rooted: joy, sadness, anger, etc.

What I had not yet understood perfectly is that this inscription is represented by the image of a physical sensation, which is the material serving to construct the representation of the original experience – that is, the pictogram. The fact that the "I" has no access to this representational background does not prevent its effects on the "I" from manifesting themselves outside the sphere of psychopathology. This is illustrated perfectly by expressions referring to states of the body, such as: "to feel comfortable in your own skin", "to walk on air" or "these people make me sick".

To say that each thought corresponds, at the originary level, to the image of a physical sensation redefines the theoretical and clinical possibilities that existed before Piera Aulagnier's theories established an unprecedented course for navigating in the universe of psychosis. Metabolisation of thought into corporal hieroglyphics makes certain transferential encounters, not necessarily located in the sphere of psychosis, much clearer and more plausible, that is to say, more acceptable.

At the originary level, the activity of thinking coincides with a "partial function zone"; therefore, as is the case for all partial zones, it can be the source of authorised pleasure, or be a zone that the Other is likely to destroy, or a zone whose activity is forbidden by the judgment imposed by the desire of an Other filled with anxiety.

Thus, Aulagnier postulates that all psychic events are simultaneously processed by three modes of psychic functioning: on the one hand by the two modes of the Freudian unconscious, the level where fantasy is generated (primary stage), and the level of consciousness (secondary stage); on the other hand, by the mode she proposes, the originary level, where the representation of affect is associated with the sensory experience. But, as I said at the beginning of this letter, Freud did not consider affect to be part of the unconscious, since it is a qualitative component of drives, and quality has no representation in Freudian theory. In other words, to postulate a simultaneous translation of all primary and secondary activity into the affective and sensory language of the originary, resulting in the re-presentation at both levels of pictographic processing involving their productions, means postulating the *circulation of a message between two heterogenous systems*: on the one hand, the originary mode which represents the quality of affect; and on the other, the Freudian unconscious primary and secondary modes.

I hope that you appreciate the importance of Aulagnier's project. Imagining the possibility of a dialectic circularity of information between two heterogenous systems immediately changes the conception of the domain of transference, defined by Piera Aulagnier as the space in which, in certain circumstances, the most important thing is that which is not repeated, the never-before-seen moments of encounter with the other that can be instituted in the therapeutic space, a space in which the subject will experience what he did not experience as a child in his relationship with his mother: being a novelty; a beginning; a surprise. Piera Aulagnier's metapsychology, which in the final analysis proposes the model of circulation of a message between two heterogenous systems, no longer opposes the dialectics of the therapeutic process, because her metapsychology is a reflection on encounter. Her contribution has equipped us metapsychologically to consider, at times, the psychoanalyst's psychic activity the essential element of the analytic process – just as we consider that the mother's relation to her infant is crucial for the development of his psyche.

Yours as always,

Notes

1 Freud, S. (1911b), *Formulations on the Two Principles of Mental Functioning*, S.E., 12: 218–226.
2 Freud, S. *Formulations*, ibid., p. 220.
3 See Letter 7, *The Ferenczi predicament*.
4 See Letter 7, *The Ferenczi predicament*.
5 In all fairness, we have to mention that Ferenczi had already spoken of repression of affect.
6 Neyraut, M. *Le Transfert*, op. cit., Chapter II.
7 Aulagnier, P. (2001), *The Violence of Interpretation: From Pictogram to Statement*, Philadelphia, PA: Brunner-Routledge.

Perversion and somatisation

The work of Joyce McDougall

Dear friend,

I am happy to hear that you attended Joyce McDougall's conference. Your impressions confirm my feeling that she is an altogether exceptional woman. Joyce also considers that the analyst can constitute an environment from which an intimate space will emerge, a space of solitude for the patient.

This is what she writes in *Theaters of the Body*:[1] "A second analysis is a little like a second marriage which Samuel Johnson, the famous British critic and lexicographer of the seventeenth century described as the triumph of hope over experience. Like a second marriage, the second analysis is not as deeply rooted in illusion, and sometimes aims at making the second partner pay for the shortcomings of the first, while seeking reparation for the injury he inflicted."

This quote illustrates McDougall's style and her most characteristic trait – present in all her books: the awareness that living thought has priority over knowledge. Living thought is humour, courage, rigour, amorality. She expresses her thoughts simply and clearly. The reader has the impression that what she says is obvious, an impression characteristic of great texts, resulting from McDougall's enormous work of reflection and her attention to the choice of words.

In her practice and in the elaboration of her theory, she sheds light on three concepts articulated in admirable fashion: libidinal economy (that is, the psychic economy of affect); narcissism (love of self); and the subject (the inner world). What is surprising is the matter-of-fact presentation of the need to take into account their interrelation in the analytic process. At the time when her first book was published (*Dialogue avec Sammy* [Dialogue with Sammy]),[2] she was already moving freely between libidinal economy and the structuring of narcissism, or the question of identity (the subject) – thanks to a happy balance between her British training and the French School, where the attention given to the subject does not obscure the question of pregenitality and does not diminish the consideration given to the imaginary.[3]

Today, the connection between these three concepts seems even more problematic. This is the result of the Lacanian conception of the unconscious, which admits of no heterogeneity between his linguistic premises – the theory of signifiers, and the object of his research – the unconscious constituted by signifiers. This lack of differentiation between the elements of the theory and those of the object the theory aims to elucidate has eliminated the body and its sensations, that is, the place where affect is rooted.

Affect holds an essential place in McDougall's work, particularly in its connection to countertransference and the psychic work of the analyst. She considers countertransference – that is, the analyst's feelings in the course of his work with the patient – a terrain where it is possible to elaborate the means of resolving therapeutic stalemates – and she speaks of the neurotic and psychotic sectors of the personality. It is refreshing and helpful for defensive structures to be given recognition, instead of remaining loyal to a perspective that classifies the psyche base on "structures", a perspective which introduces academic psychiatric nosography into the sphere of psychoanalysis. Freud, who never lost sight of defensive structures, considered them permeable and did not hesitate to speak, for instance, of the hysterical core of obsessional neurosis.

McDougall's idea that all defences are creations is exciting. First, because it discourages all psychopathologisation of the analytic process. Second, because it is a reminder of the enigmatic nature of every singular human existence, and attributes the best role to the psychoanalyst: that of a researcher who must find – sometimes conjecture – the bridges that tie the defence created to the need that prompted its invention.

Her theory of perversion and of psychosomatic response is revolutionary. She considers these two defensive structures the consequence of the exclusion from the psyche of an early childhood trauma. To fill the void left in the psyche by this exclusion, the subject builds, not a delusion, but a perverse "illusion" or somatisation. This concept is extremely rich in possibilities. First of all, it raises the question of the reversibility of this exclusion. McDougall's answer, validated by her clinical work, is: yes, the exclusion is reversible… provided that the psychoanalyst is willing to pay a price – the necessary psychic price.[4] In addition, this perspective makes it possible to reflect on the fragments of the Real which we all carry and which originate in more or less serious traumas – without compromising in any serious way a creativity that accommodates both anguish and lack.

Joyce McDougall's other theories of perversion are just as exciting. The clinical concept of a "perverse" structure was the focus of her earliest work. Her first two articles – "The Anonymous Spectator" and "Primal Scene and Sexual Perversion" – began to change the existing views on perversion. According to Joyce, the perverse scenario is a desperate attempt by the subject to work out his relation to parental figures and to parental sexuality – what Freud calls the primal scene – in such a way as to include two temporalities: the Oedipal stage; and the archetypes of the pregenital stage. McDougall's genius consists of her focus on this attempt, which brings to the forefront the method used by the subject to create a psychic framework that can contain the immense pain of the wounded child he carries inside him. In terms of the dynamics of the analytic process, whose complexity Joyce McDougall describes well, the analyst's role consists of abandoning the position of an anonymous spectator and becoming the *witness*[5] who will help the patient recognise that the perverse scenario is the construction of a truncated primal scene through which he *protects* (her emphasis) his mother and father against his fantasised destructiveness. This destructiveness is deflected by denial of the parent's psychic reality; instead, the patient *attacks a function of his own ego* (my emphasis). At the same time, the analyst helps the patient recognise the incredible fact that, in his psychic functioning, "castration (that is to say, our limits) is not painful, […] better yet, it is the very condition allowing enjoyment".[6]

Joyce McDougall sees perversion as an identificatory caricature which presents bisexuality as anxiety-provoking and forbidden. Perverse organisations are characterised by depression "that invariably comes to light in the analyses of these patients [and] is frequently linked with the father's nonrecognition of their sexual identity, […] of their intrinsic value as human beings…"

The person who chooses perverse sexuality as a solution had parents whose cultural discourse was deviant. Clinical experience often reveals a mother who forbids introjection (that is, a mother who cannot bear for her infant to tolerate not being in her actual presence), as well as a belief on the part of the patient that his energy is bad or dangerous (belief that he has a bad internal penis), and a lack of masturbatory activity.

Perversion is the "positive print" of neurosis, and the "negative image" of psychosis. What differentiates perversion from neurosis is that there is "expression in action instead of psychic elaboration" and that "this action is openly eroticised". "One of the triumphs of perversion may consist in the erotisation (of the deadly character) of primal sadism."[7]

The economy of perversion involves avoidance of castration anxiety and of the depressive position. In fact, for the pervert, castration becomes the condition required for sexual enjoyment. The addictive sexuality associated with perversion is counterphobic sexuality, resulting from a failure of "the vital attempt to render absence significant" (counterphobic = anti-anxiety). Although perverse sexuality is, undeniably, false, manic reparation, it is also a creative act, the triumph of Eros over death (see *Theaters of the Mind*).

In certain borderline personalities, sexuality plays a different role. McDougall's proposal of "archaic hysteria" is most pertinent. By this she means "a defense against pregenital libidinal wishes that have remained blocked and encapsulated rather than … repressed." The patient has no access to "some portion of his psychic reality […] and his symptom conceals a repressed meaning linked to narcissistic castration". The mobilisation of "feelings [and images] that do not fit in with his own ideal image" is excluded from the psyche, predisposing him to "a high psychosomatic vulnerability…"

At the same time, archaic hysteria is associated with "operant phenomena… with their inexplicable outbursts of uncontrollable anxiety… of which the individual is unaware because [it has] been foreclosed from consciousness." Neurotic hysteria involves the imaginary body, while archaic hysteria refers to a situation where the real body has gone mad. "Neurotic hysteria is predominantly dependent on language links, while [archaic hysteria] is concerned with protecting not only the sexual organs or the sexuality of the subject, but his whole body, life itself, and is constructed through preverbal somatopsychic connections."[8]

Joyce McDougall sees grave psychosomatic phenomena as resulting from a radical heterogeneity of body and psyche. She does not consider somatisation (an ulcer, for example) as a bridge to representation – diverging on this point from the "École Psychosomatique de Paris" – but rather as proof of the subject's inability to identify and represent inner conflict. McDougall sees somatisation as a manic defence, a defence that "throws out" of the psyche anything that can arouse anxiety or pain.[9]

She asks herself: "By what economic and dynamic means is the psyche able to manipulate the perception of external reality? What enables the "I" of the (psychosomatic) subject to submit to hallucinatory experience? Why has repression not worked… in times of… inner conflict?" She adds: "The capacity of the ego to attack its own apparatus and functions is pertinent to our reflection on psychosomatic phenomena" (see *Theaters of the Mind*).

To answer her own questions, Joyce McDougall developed a well-structured theory. She started with the clinical observation that psychosomatic subjects have difficulty distinguishing their internal reality from external reality, and are unable to integrate the split representations of a good and a bad mother. This inability is the result of the failure of maternal care to perform its protective function, to act as a protective shield, leaving it to the analyst to perform this function in the course of the therapy. The absence of an internalised mother can be due to the excessive distance or the excessive closeness the mother imposes on the child. This absence will be the source of unfathomable anxiety that will oblige the child to invent massive defences in order to survive. Maternal failure to provide a protective shield, this absence of the introjected mother, is one of the factors which explain why affects are more likely to achieve representation as body-things rather than verbal messages. The lack of neurotic construction in the face of the archaic forces the psychosomatic subject into creating a sterile space between himself and the external world, between himself and his internal world.[10] If, in order to communicate, the body must use "the language of affect", in psychosomatic subjects in whom affect has been destroyed, foreclosed from consciousness, a part of the body is left "to talk in the mind's place". This is why Joyce McDougall does not consider psychosomatic symptoms metaphors, but rather "obscure reflections of the mute, biological body […] an emotional stalemate in which the economy of affect, as well as the work of representation, are blocked" (see *Theaters of the Mind*). As for patients who have opted for somatisation as their privileged defence mechanism against pain, in *Plea for a Measure of Abnormality*, McDougall describes their plight as follows: "Faced with an infantile I, the psyche refuses to recognise suffering, while the soma defends itself as though threatened by a biological danger." Brilliant.

Given that in sleep one "merges with the trace of the internal object", these subjects whose internal object is rather sketchy often suffer from insomnia. As to the limited ability of psychosomatic subjects to dream, McDougall offers a keenly insightful explanation related to the day's residues. (The day's residues are traces of the day's events replayed in the scenario of our dreams.) She says that the day's residues are constructed from "perceptions that are likely to represent the objects of drives", which are repressed and transformed into the material constituting nocturnal dreams.

The psychosomatic subject, who is unable to repress, treats these perceptions as if they were hallucinations. If an internal maternal environment is absent, any encounter with reality is traumatic: be it external reality; what is left of internal reality; or instinctual drives.[11]

If language does not function as a filter separating the thing from its representation, the subject could, for example, like Tim in *Theaters of the Body*, smoke frantically to be reunited with a father whose death was caused by heavy smoking – something Tim remembered only after several years of psychoanalysis, and after a near fatal heart attack. Similarly, Georgette, discussed in the same book, needed several years to remember that her father loved seafood; when she ate seafood, she was unconsciously swallowing something of her father, sometimes his penis. McDougall shows that the working through of the paternal function, or of the importance of the paternal penis or the symbolic extensions that confer the phallus its place as a fundamental agency, can only occur – if at all, once the stalemates rooted in the relation to a terrifying archaic mother have been resolved.

Of course, Joyce McDougall acknowledges that her patients suffered very serious early deprivation. She even goes so far as to say that deprivation is the fabric of the psyche in psychosomatic subjects, whose relation to the world is governed by actual psychosis (a term modelled on Freud's "actual neurosis"). She writes: "When certain mental representations [are expelled] from the psyche, an affect can be denied psychic expression, without any compensation for the loss of the experience and of the representation of the event associated with it. This means that this *exclusion from the psyche* [my emphasis] is not compensated by the creation of neurotic symptoms or by the transformation of fantasies and perceptions excluded from the psyche into delusions [what Freud described, for instance, in the Schreber case, in 1911]. In such a situation, we can say that the psyche is in a state of deprivation." Here, McDougall makes a theoretical choice whose relevance is demonstrated by her work, and which I hold to be one of her decisive contributions to a critical review of psychoanalysis.

She writes: "The entanglement between the narcissistic libido (self-love) and investment in object relations (interest in the outside world) is not only extremely complex, but inescapable." This point of view required her to take a clear stance on conducting the analysis which she described as follows: the narcissistic transference relation "only becomes analysable after identification of instinctual roots (potentially objectionable) dispersed throughout [the analysand's] life, just as they are in the analysand's discourse." This approach deepened the rift between her and the "École psychosomatique de Paris", which did not admit the possibility that object relations could exist for these patients. Nevertheless, she acknowledged her debt to this School in these terms: "Studying the work of psychosomaticists dealing with the psychosomatic ills of babyhood enabled me to understand that my adult patients were at certain times functioning psychically like infants who, [unable to] use words with which to think ... respond to emotional pain only psychosomatically."[12]

Joyce McDougall is also known as one of the few psychoanalysts who examined closely the psychic work of the analyst during the analytic process. This is particularly important when working with psychosomatic and borderline patients.

Subjects whose defence mechanism consists of repudiating from consciousness, excluding intolerable representations and affects, obliging the analyst to feel, in their place, what they refuse to feel or to think. The analyst is therefore burdened by these affects and representations – probably in the same way the patient was invaded and burdened as a child by the psychic reality of his parents, which they deposited in him. In these borderline situations, the analyst's psychic reality is filled with objects, affects and representations by the patient. The psychoanalyst needs time to identify and name these affects and representations, to understand their role in the transferential relation, before attempting to make them thinkable by the patient.[13]

The idea of creation is central to McDougall's thought. Defences are a creation of the child, symptoms are a creation, analytic work is a creation. Joyce McDougall is the illustration par excellence of the fact that the ethics of psychoanalysis places the analyst at the crossroads of science and poetry, where the poet celebrates all aspects of life.

Your friend,

Notes

1 McDougall, J. (1989), *Theaters of the Body*. New York: W. W. Norton.
2 McDougall, J and Lebovici, S. (1989), *Dialogue with Sammy: A Psychoanalytic Contribution to the Understanding of Child Psychosis.* London: Free Association Books.
3 Aside from *Dialogue avec Sammy*, published by Payot, all of Joyce McDougall's books in French are published by Gallimard in the collection *Connaissance de l'inconscient.*
4 I do not like the term "illusion" to designate what is constructed by the pervert where the psychotic would construct a delusion. I believe the positive connotation of the term ought to be preserved, the meaning originating in the infant's experience of illusion – the forerunner of transitional object and space – instead of illusion as it is understood in the ego function. The term I would rather use is "drifting"
5 Concerning the importance of the witness, see Letter 14, *Paranoia as seen by Philippe Réfabert.*
6 McDougall, M. (2015), *Plea for a Measure of Abnormality*. New York: Routledge.
7 McDougall, J. (1989), *Theaters of the Body*. New York: W. W. Norton.
8 The clinical case presented in Letter 20, *Hysteria*, illustrates some characteristics of what McDougall calls "archaic hysteria" and Pankow calls "hysterical psychosis".
9 The term "drifting" that I am proposing for perverse construction takes into account the manic character of the defence. Drifting, unlike daydreaming, produces no

pleasure. Drifting is an unsuccessful attempt to fill the void of a fantasy that could not be constructed.

10   The mother's inability to identify with her infant, to perform her ego-support function, forces the subject to turn his soma into a protective shield.

11   When Winnicott presents the mother as an ego-support function that protects from impingements upon the space in which the subject can emerge, he highlights the possibility of trauma at the earliest stages of life, and the fact that any experience of the world in that early period is potentially traumatic. See Letter 10, *Winnicott's concept of* continuity of being: *transference and the treatment of trauma.*

12   McDougall, J. *Theaters of the Body*, op. cit. In other words, it is the skin that becomes the protective shield of the psyche. Psychosomatic patients find it difficult to abandon this functioning because they are afraid of giving up this protective negativity.

13   In Letter 6, *Transference*, see reference to the time it took me to tell the patient what she did not dare to think in her childhood: "I hate your mother, I hate your brother, I hate your stepfather." In these borderline clinical situations, repetition compulsion dominates, in both its aspects, Eros and Thanatos. Piera Aulagnier considers that excessive suffering in a subject in whom the libido *is no longer supported by representations* forces him to choose between death and recourse to a delusional causative agent – that is, the construction of a persecutor. Michel Artières has proposed the existence of "depression of the void" (*la dépression du vide*), understood as immobilisation of psychic life, as a third alternative (Michel Artières, "*Silence, discours inhibé, discours anecdotique*" (Silence, Inhibited Discourse, Anecdotal Discourse), *Topique*, No. 24; and "*La dépression du vide*" (Depression of the Void), *Topique*, No. 30). This depressive alternative involves the cessation of introjection, so that henceforth the other is no longer recognised as separate.

Michel makes two very astute fundamental remarks: what the patient manifests in these analyses is essentially affect, affect that cannot be tied to any process of fantasy elaboration. Therefore, the analyst must be able to put his all into his work with these patients. Because their psyche is saturated with affects related to the primal instinctual conflict between Eros and Thanatos, their words are the equivalent of bodily objects. This saturation of the psyche by affects serves to maintain psychic life; in addition, this saturation is neutralised by dependence on an external object. The analyst, to whom the patient provides no fantasies, is at a loss, even though these patients are particularly attentive to the person of the analyst and to the setting. According to Michel Artières, this awareness of the analyst's reality, which provides a counterbalance for the massive transference, is what differentiates these analyses from those of psychotics. And yet, depression does not provide the same stability as neurotic or psychotic defences; between life and death, on the edge, the subject will choose pain over deprivation, which is a way to avoid encountering a primal affect that would sweep everything away on its path.

In direct contact with the primal affects of the patient – as witnessed by the analyst's incapacity to fantasise or to intellectualise – unprotected and obliged to control the positive and negative reactions aroused in him by the conflict between Eros and Thanatos in its most violent form, the analyst is a real subject who must be able to receive *that which, for the patient, has never been formulated in words, but merely felt or acted out.*

Here, we are dealing with an extreme degree of breakdown of the subject, with the crucial event of an initial separation not yet completely realised and in the face of which the patient is all the more helpless given that the possibility of investing thought as a source of pleasure was denied him by the mediator, the maternal environment. These patients are asking something of the psychoanalyst. But what?

Michel answers that he allows these patients to experience something they never have before – which, as you see, is my conception of the transference/ countertransference relation as the space where what is important is that which does not repeat itself. The analysis then becomes the space of an experience of a state of narcissistic unity in a relationship, a state which is a prerequisite with these patients before gaining access to their drive structure. Michel thinks there is no need to conceive of *a disconnection between ego structuring and its foundation as a drive*, and he forewarns those who would be tempted to speak of a narcissistic state in this context – which would, moreover, suggest that the transference is not organised as described earlier. We conclude that interpretations are designed to help the patient recognise *his* own *differentiated psychic space,* within another space, that of the analysts, which contains and protects him.

Michel Artières points out that, from the standpoint of traditional analytic practice, these patients do not communicate. It is this lack of communication, this primitive communication, that was of interest to Joyce McDougall as well (McDougall, J. (1992), "Countertransference and Primitive Communication" in *Plea for a Measure of Abnormality*. New York: Brunner/Mazel).

Joyce McDougall, like Michel Artières, invites us to reflect on these patients whose trauma occurred before language acquisition, at the stage where the infant – mother relation renders the mother's unconscious the first reality for the child and for his thinking apparatus. At this stage, the child can only catch hold of affect in order to "*react* to the mother's emotional experience"; this capacity precedes language acquisition. Joyce also pointed out that for these subjects speech does not serve to communicate, but rather to cause the analyst to feel something; this language has no relation to the repressed; it is intensely charged with affect rooted in the body, it is full of rage, it smashes thought to smithereens, it is garbage speech, fusion speech, "throwing out of oneself of everything that threatens to be a source of psychic pain", speech *through* which, not *thanks* to which emerges "the debris of as catastrophic experience, which took place in an early relationship".

Joyce also described this primal transference she called "fundamental", in which the patient treats the analyst like a part of himself, "while at the same time fearing a deadly fusion". That which needs to be heard, says Joyce, is excluded from discourse and from the Freudian unconscious; the analyst is "affected" by signs he must interpret. "Although the analogy cannot be extended too far, the analyst is placed in the role of the mother who becomes able to hear the cries and distress signals of her child and to translate them into language, acting as his *thinking apparatus*."

Both Michel and Joyce point out the importance of shame in these subjects. My own experience confirms this.

I think that, at the initial stage of elaboration, shame reflects an absence of self-esteem, which is itself a result of the impossibility for these patients to create an internal world – an impossibility caused by the suspension of the introjection process. At a subsequent stage, what always emerges is immense distress at having been neglected, abandoned by the maternal environment.

We can understand how this affect of shame prevented these subjects from sinking into psychosis. This is so because in a situation where a psychotic would have seen hate as the cause of psychic functioning, they found the strength to remember their pain at having been forsaken, abandoned by the maternal environment. This memory involves a recognition of which the psychotic is incapable: that of an expectation of love, a need for love which was not met by the maternal environment. Contrary to the psychotic, who would have interpreted this lack of response as a refusal, an act of hate, these subjects interpret this lack as an inadequacy of the maternal and paternal environment. And they feel ashamed for these parents, for their incompetence. In these patients, the affect of shame – an affect which protects them from psychosis

– is the primal affect of shame of the inadequate mother. Paradoxically, it is this unspeakable suffering that makes an investment possible – no matter how tenuous – of the relation with the analyst: the hope that, this time, the other will be able to respond to this request which is vital for the psychic life of the subject – and that the response will reveal the secret (and inaccessible) content of shame.

In the organisation of the transference/countertransference sphere understood as *a subject composed of two people*, the analyst is asked to place himself in the opening of the passage allowing the primary system to process the productions of the primal sphere, a breach into which is engulfed, returning to its source, most of the material which, mixed once again with aggression not yet integrated into the libido, threatens to break through into the space of fantasy, sinking the subject into the hate of the spokesperson. Thus, what the analyst is asked to do is to lend the patient his psychic apparatus so that primal affects may be named and fantasies constructed, when the patient cannot recognise these affects, nor construct these fantasies.

Money

My dear friend,

Thank you for your letter so full of intelligence, humour and sensitivity. You are right to point out that money is an essential element to take into account when reflecting on the dissymmetry of the analytic relation.

Why, then, is an analyst paid? From the patient's point of view, the analyst is paid to continue living after having been devoured by love. He is paid to be chewed, crushed, pulverised, torn to pieces and swallowed out of love. He is paid to be bored, not to seek revenge for aggression or hate, to endure and to bear anguish. In short, money is intimately linked with transference, with the extreme limits of transference.

From the analyst's point of view, money, like humour in analysis or orgasm in bed, is connected to the deepest roots of personality, of temperament.

Money serves to keep the psychoanalyst alive. This presupposes that the money he earns gives him access to that without which life would be bland and his work impossible: the superfluous. This means that he has to be well-paid.

Paying for missed sessions is part of this reasoning. Freud's conclusions on this subject are clear. The patient's reality must not penalise the analyst's reality. Our practice requires a limited number of patients who cannot be replaced at the moment's notice and for a short time. More generally speaking, reality should not influence the analytic setting – given that one of the functions of this setting is to interpret what the patient considers reality. Finally, in terms of the transferential relation, paying for missed sessions allows the two protagonists to avoid the unconscious resentment of the psychoanalyst.

The question of money must also be considered in connection with the possibility of conducting analysis in public mental health institutions. I agree with those who think that this is possible, because I presume that an analyst who works in such institutions has already resolved the question of money at a personal level, and that due to ideological reasons – that is, political convictions, the modest salary or no salary at all that he earns there suits him perfectly. (I am not minimising the difficulties that not paying for the analysis creates for Social Security patients. But I am convinced that this secondary question can only be resolved once we have answered the first.)

I have no sympathy for psychoanalysts who try to make an exact determination of the financial means of those who ask to be in analysis with them, before deciding whether to accept them or not. These penny-pinching calculations brimming with good will and Christian charity are really very violent. What good is all this "personal attention" if in the end the answer is no, unfortunately twenty euros is not enough, I cannot work for less than… a much higher amount. Pure sadism.

I prefer the method of a friend who scandalises some of his colleagues by saying that he keeps three places (and in his case this means nine sessions) for those who can pay between ten and fifteen euros, and charges the others the full fee. This way of doing things is based on a radical epistemological choice: although money is the indicator of reality *par excellence* – the universal common denominator, as Marx called it – in the analytic process it should be considered, above all, an element of psychic reality. As such, it is worthy of respect. From this perspective, requesting a fee of ten euros after painstaking calculations is not the same thing as proposing this amount as a result of an internal agreement to which the analyst arrives with himself. In fact, I think that after one or two preliminary interviews an analyst acquires a rather precise idea of the patient's social and financial status – with no need for penny-pinching calculations. Accepting a new patient is an analytic choice; this implies that the aspect related to money becomes a dimension of the setting in which the work will take place, and therefore an element lending itself to analytic reflection – that is, an element which is interpretable and can have an interpretive function.

At the level of a social commitment, what is the analyst paid for? His time? I do not think so. The session can lead him to certain discoveries, for him or for the person to whom he is listening, in which case this intense psychic activity is enjoyable; or he spends the session waiting, or being bored. Whatever the case, there is no social price to be paid.

Furthermore, I do not think that the analyst is paid for his competence or skill – even if it is hoped that he brings these to his practice. In addition, he cannot be called a "professional", even though he works in a professional manner. I do not think that it would be appropriate either to say that he is paid for his clinical intuition, even when this intuition is considered remarkable. Clinical intuition, like love, cannot be commissioned; there is no guarantee that it will be there in any given situation. Why is it that something so quickly understood with one patient took years to understand with another? Could it be that one was a better analyst with the first patient? It is not at all certain. Being an analyst is not perfectly objectifiable: two clinical situations, like two encounters, are never identical – and the transference paradigm reveals the differences.

I think that the psychoanalyst is paid to be a psychoanalyst during the period he spends with the subject, in the course of each session and for the entire duration of that patient's treatment. This involves something that is not easy: the analyst makes a commitment to *focus primarily* on the person to whom he is listening during the entire session, and to be there for him. Instead of thinking about the night he just spent with the woman he loves, or about the article he is writing, or about his next dinner with friends, his attention will focus, and will be available to hear what is being said to him during these thirty or forty minutes. He will listen to what is being said, and will try to connect this with what he has already heard in the unfolding of this particular story. He will also try to link what is being said with his understanding of the "story" of previous generations, while trying to guess, based on Freud's teachings and on his work with other patients, or based on his own analysis or his life experience, what is not being said, what causes a stalemate, what are the roots of repetition. This can lead, for instance, to the discovery that enuresis in a forty-year-old man has its roots in the attempted rape of the patient's mother by the grandfather. In terms of trauma, the psychoanalyst is paid to invent a new answer to parts of the other's story that were violent or destructive, an answer than can put an end to the repetition of the massacre.

But is it not true that the psychoanalyst enjoys his work? Of course he does, but his pleasure is *circumstantial*, since he could enjoy thinking about other things just as much, or more.

In terms of the dynamics of the transference, since in the case of perverse and neurotic patients money is part of the setting, once the conditions are agreed upon by the two protagonists, any difficulty refers, broadly speaking, to a problem with the law, with the difference the other represents, as well as to the guilt related to taking care of oneself and/or letting someone else provide this care. Things are more complex when children, adolescents and psychotic patients are involved, and someone else pays the analyst. In this situation, where the analyst is often asked to be "effective", it is important that he have a clear understanding of that for which he is being remunerated.

The idea that patients pay off a debt by paying for their sessions seems absurd to me. No monetary value can be assigned to the care, the suffering, the boredom, the anguish, the hate or the desire felt by the analyst. I am willing to say that they pay for *contingent reflection*, but unless the notion of paying a debt is reduced to a purely imaginary transaction – so much money given for so much psychic availability – it is impossible, fortunately, for the money exchanged in analysis to "pay" for the carrying over of the effects of this work done by two people in the reality of the world. Our debts to friends, to lovers, to analysts and to patients cannot be erased; these debts are constitutive of our being, they give our lives depth and fuel our desire to transmit.

I will finish my letter by recounting a joke told to me by a friend.

A psychoanalyst hears the sound of an explosion in his apartment. He investigates and finds that the bathroom is flooded. He shuts off the water supply, cancels his appointments with patients and finds a plumber who arrives quickly, works expertly and solves the problem. The analyst is impressed and compliments the plumber for the speed and efficiency of his work.

"How much do I owe you?"

"A thousand euros."

"A thousand euros! That's very expensive!"

"The problem is solved and you are pleased. The price is what I charge."

The analyst pays.

As the plumber is leaving, the analyst stops him:

"Can I ask you a question? How do you manage to announce so calmly the fee you consider to be suitable for your work? I am asking because I find it very hard to tell my patients how much they owe me for their sessions."

"I quite understand. I had the same problem when I was a psychoanalyst."

My very best regards,

Transference and friendship

Dear friend,

You write me that your objective is no longer to cure your patients, but that, as a result, you feel somewhat lost. Now that you do not consider your patients research subjects similar to those participating in laboratory experiments, you ask yourself what is the nature of the relationship between the analyst and the patient and, more specifically, what grounds the analyst in his listening and in his commitment.

I do not think that we should abandon the idea of a cure altogether. I know that this idea does not have the approval of certain psychoanalytic circles where protocol is more important than the meaning of our work. Young psychoanalysts are told over and over that they should not focus on a cure, but remember that a cure is always a bonus in the psychoanalytic process, and so on. You will agree with me that, if we consider psychoanalysis a therapeutic practice – and I know that this is a crucial factor for you – it becomes awkward to engage in this practice without wanting our patients to be "cured". The question is, what is a psychoanalytic cure, and we have Freud's answer: at the end of the therapy, he says, our patients should be able to love *and* work, that is, sexuality and reflection, no longer dissociated, have become integrated as the two life forces they in fact are.

Freud did not consider this attitude to be in contradiction with the scientific status of psychoanalysis, a status whose legitimacy is not founded on the natural sciences. From his perspective, our theories play a crucial role in our work with patients; these theories are part of the psychic environment – ours – into which they are received. It is this theoretical background which allows distance when distance is needed, makes it possible to wait for the right moment to offer an interpretation... It is also thanks to our theories that we venture to make our inventions and digressions, and that we surpass ourselves. Even when we weave the fabric needed to tie the psychoanalyst to his analysands from nought, we know that we can refer to our theories in discussions with our colleagues, in order to clarify the meaning of our practice and... theorise it.[1]

But your question concerns the quality of this relation, the foundation on which the analytic process is built, and without which the encounter would not be possible. To answer your question, I think that when an analytic process is established – and I make no distinction here between psychoanalysis and psychotherapy – it is a relation of friendship that unites the two protagonists and makes it possible for the therapeutic or analytic process to unfold. In this regard, in *Analysis Terminable and Interminable*, Freud writes: "Not every good relation between an analyst and his subject during and after analysis was to be regarded as transference; there were also friendly relations which were based on reality and which proved to be viable."[2]

But what is friendship? This is what Spinoza tells us: "Apart from men, we know no singular thing in Nature whose mind we can enjoy, and which we can join to ourselves in friendship..."[3]

As for Donald Winnicott, this is what he has to say on the subject:

> In this way I am trying to justify the paradox that the capacity to be alone is based on the experience of being alone in the presence of someone, and that without a sufficiency of this experience the capacity to be alone cannot develop.

Now, if I am right in the matter of this paradox, it is interesting to examine the nature of the relationship of the infant to the mother, that which... I have called ego-relatedness. It will be seen that I attach a great importance to this relationship, as *I consider that it is the stuff out of which friendship is made* [my emphasis]. It may turn out to be the *matrix of transference* [Winnicott's emphasis and mine]."[4]

The principle is clearly stated: the matrix of friendship and that of transference are one and the same; this matrix is a relation making it possible to experience solitude as a space of well-being.

Although transference can be seen as founded on friendship, it is more limited than friendship: it is a powerful instrument, circumscribed by its function, which facilitates a new awareness of the relationship of a subject with himself and with the world. *Experience has, in fact, shown that in certain transferential settings it is the friendship we feel for the patient that enables us to sustain the analytic process. We hope that at the end of the analysis he will be able to meet us at the place where we sustained both him and the transference.*[5] Let us remember as well that friendship was at the origin of psychoanalysis: friendship between Freud and Wilhelm Fliess; between Freud and Karl Abraham; Freud and Carl Jung; Freud and Sándor Ferenczi – origin and friendships documented by their correspondence.

This possibility raises a serious epistemological problem. How can we suggest that friendship is the source and support of transference when analysis is based on a crucial *asymmetry* while friendship presupposes *reciprocity*? If we take this objection into account – as we must – we need to identify the reciprocity involved in analysis, and establish to what extent it opposed the asymmetry required by the process.

Let us consider a patient who imagines himself to be seriously ill and who takes his analyst for the most learned and healthiest man on earth. Even in a situation such as this, the two protagonists have in common the *desire to reflect on* the psychic cause of this pain, this suffering, this repetition which drove the patient to seek therapy. In addition, as experience clearly shows, any reflection on this cause, no matter how painful or unpleasant, brings pleasure and joy in its wake. What produces pleasures and joy is the victory over the process of destruction (Thanatos) gained every time a thought can be formulated regarding the psychic cause of suffering. This is why I am convinced that a tragic portrayal of analysis, which disregards this triumph of thought, leads to a doloristic, sentimental and religious view of psychoanalysis.

The desire to think provides the setting for reciprocity of the desire to think, and is a prerequisite for the existence of an analytic process, just as asymmetry is the foundation of the psychoanalytic dialogue. The fact that each protagonist draws strength from this desire while playing his particular role forces us to recognise the power of this shared desire. Of course, this communality of desire implies a *circularity and reversibility* of subjective positions – as Freud, Winnicott and every psychoanalyst worthy of the name have always acknowledged. Without this acknowledgment, it would not be possible to maintain, as every Freudian analyst maintains, that the analysis is the central element of training, making it possible for today's analysand to occupy the place of the analyst tomorrow. This reversibility of roles is also the foundation of the circulation and transmission of the unconscious as an object of reflection. In fact, I wonder how those who refuse to admit this obvious truth let their patients leave at the end of an analysis, presuming that transmission of the unconscious as an object of reflection has taken place. We are clearly not in agreement on this subject. Undeniably, the acceptance of the notion of circularity and reversibility establishes unequivocally a certain conception regarding the ethics of a psychoanalytic practice based on friendship.[6]

But what is the source of this powerful desire to think, to experience the pleasure and joy of reflection? I mentioned earlier that if we accept the Freudian theory that the psychic apparatus functions in accordance with a compulsion to repeat, we must constantly oppose to the undoing operated by Thanatos the insistence of Eros to represent and to link representations together.[7] And since receptivity to the imperatives of this requirement – which sometimes demands enormous psychic effort on the part of the patient as well as the analyst – is a source of joy, there is a leap that I do not hesitate to make, consisting of the hypothesis that *any desire to think is in fact a desire to experience joy.* This hypothesis most closely reflects the method characteristic of the analytic process, without excluding the use of other methods. It is a formulation akin to Spinoza's notion of the third kind of knowledge. And since it attributes meaning to psychoanalytic work, it also provides a theory regarding the end of analysis.

I will leave you with this thought borrowed from Spinoza once again:

A desire which arises from joy is stronger, other things equal, than one which arises from sadness. Desire is the very essence of man, that is, a striving by which a man strives to persevere in his being. So a desire which arises from joy is aided or increased by the affect of joy itself, whereas one which arises from sadness is diminished or restrained by the affect of sadness. And so the force of a desire which arises from joy *must be defined both by human power and the power of the external cause* [my emphasis], whereas the force of a desire which arises from sadness must be defined by human power alone. The former, [a desire which arises from joy] therefore, is stronger than the latter.[8]

Warmest regards,

Notes

1   Michel Neyraut wrote that the psychoanalyst's theory is part of his countertransference. See Neyraut, M. *Le Transfert*, op. cit.
2   Freud, S. (1937), *Analysis Terminable and Interminable*. S.E., 23: p. 222. James Strachey, English translator and editor of Freud's work, has identified six occurrences of the word "friendship" in Freud's writings. The first is in *Psychopathology of Everyday Life*, in the *Index of Parapraxes*, under the heading "Lost and Mislaid Objects" (S.E., 6: p. 293). The second occurrence is in Chapter III of *Psychoanalytic Notes on an Autobiographical Account of Paranoia* (op. cit.), in the fourth paragraph, where Freud notes that homosexual instincts attach to ego-instincts, conferring erotic overtones to friendship. In paragraph 11 of *The Dynamics of the Transference* (1912), he points out that friendship is rooted in sexuality. It is from this same perspective that he refers to friendship in Chapter VI of *Group Psychology and Analysis of the Ego* (1921), in the sixth paragraph (S.E., 18: p. 91). In the postscript of the same text, under Section C, Freud emphasises the ease with which erotic desires can arise from relations of friendship (p. 139). Finally, in the 1922 article "The Libido Theory", he spoke of "feelings of friendship" emerging from repressed sexual instincts (S.E., 18: p. 235). Strangely, Strachey does not mention the reference to "friendly relations" I found in *Analysis Terminable and Interminable* (op. cit.).
3   Spinoza, B. (1996), *Ethics*. Translated by Edwin Curley, London: Penguin Classics, Part IV, Appendix XXVI, p. 158.
4   Winnicott, D. W. "The Capacity to Be Alone", *International Journal of Psycho-Analysis*, No. 39, 1958, 416–420.
5   Some readers may object, saying that in certain analyses the transferential stakes appear immediately, before there is time for friendly feelings, and even less for feelings of friendship, to develop. But let us remember that the ego ideal is a great reservoir of friendship.
6   Letter 27, *The divine part of man*, examines the question of the relation between asymmetry and reciprocity in analysis and in friendship.
7   See Letter 11, *Reading* Beyond the Pleasure Principle: *the insistence of Eros*.
8   Spinoza, B. (1996), *Ethics*. Translated by Edwin Curley, London: Penguin Classics, Part IV, Proposition 18, p. 124.

Hysteria

My dear friend,

I shall try to do as you ask. Today's task will be to try to define how the psychic activity of the analyst comes to constitute a psychic environment that the patient can use to start building a space of intimacy, a place of solitude in which, as I was telling you earlier, he can be at ease. To do this, I will talk about hysteria.

I will start by reproducing a portion of a session with a patient. She says:

I made myself beautiful. I wanted him to look at me. I like that. It makes me feel good when he looks at me. I feel radiant. And I want to take him in my arms, I want him to make love to me. When I think of him I see pictures in my head. I see myself sitting on top of him, his face against my chest, the two of us locked together. So we go to his place. And suddenly, when he starts to undress me, I become frightened. I am afraid that he will touch me. As if my body was an abscess filled with pus that would burst at the slightest contact. But if he stops, if he speaks to me, tells me stories and talks about his love for me, I want him again. I hold him very tight, I unbutton his shirt, I caress his chest. He kisses me, he is a real man, not a ghost. I take his penis in my mouth, I like that, we undress quickly, we kiss, I want to devour him and want him to swallow me, I am happy, I am not a little girl any more. And, again, suddenly something goes wrong. Suddenly I find him old, I find myself disgusting and everything seems too heavy. I tell myself that I am in a bed rubbing myself against a man who is rubbing himself against me. I feel clammy. I stink. I forgot to put on make-up. I am afraid that my blemishes will show.

I think: he finds me beautiful. I try to concentrate on this idea so that the rubbing will stop and the magic will come back. But nothing works. I think: he finds me beautiful because he's stupid. He is fucking me. I pretend and I wait for it to be over. I am dead.

This story illustrates the feminine stumbling blocks of the characteristic of hysteria; but before explaining exactly what I mean by this, let us look more closely at the way language expresses these contradictory psychic tendencies. First, to come back to what we mean by stumbling blocks, we must admit that the mapping provided by theories of repression are insufficient to explain the psychic jolts in the account I just reproduced. The specificity here is that, although sexual desire and the obstacles standing in its way are described accurately, the subject has no space available in which to conceptualise the rift between the world of desire and the world of love. And it would be unfortunate for the analyst to favour one world rather than the other. (I suggest that you read Chapter VIII, of my book *De l'amour à la pensée* – "Winnicott: From Love to Reflection" – which discusses in detail these impasses in female hysteria.)

The analysis offers to be the space that can contain the effects of these discontinuities, and in which a reflection on their causes can emerge.

The hysteric experiences all sexual phenomena in the mode of infantile sexuality. The woman whose words I quoted is well aware of this. She is also well aware of the link associating pus and damaged skin with the libidinal investment of excrement, which occupies a dominant place in her psychic life. The crucial question the theory of repression leaves unanswered is why the hysteric reduces everything to sexuality, why everything becomes sexual for her, although no satisfactory outcome is reached either in terms of pleasure or in terms of reflection. It is clear to see that she makes love like she eats (or vice versa), that she thinks like she defecates (or vice versa), without anything shifting, being disrupted, going beyond the scope of what might be called psychoanalytic psychology.

A hysterical woman is a false virgin dreaming of being a false whore (or vice versa). And reaching back to the little girl who dreamed of being both virgin and whore is of no help, since even at that early stage sexuality had the function it would subsequently keep: a fruitless attempt to escape anxiety. Unfathomable anxiety. In other words, if sexuality has a function so precise that it excludes any extension of sexual experience, it is hopeless to look for a meaning that might put an end to this libidinal digression. The hysteric recognises her digression, her anguish and the uselessness of her constant recourse to sexuality. On this subject, we have nothing new to teach her. And yet, like the scorpion in the story with the frog, she keeps on doing what she does.[1]

Winnicott formulated a totally new approach to hysterical organisation. But aside from his concept of transitional space – to which we shall return – the theoretical and clinical potential of the notions of dissociation and integration has not been sufficiently explored.

Winnicott focused his reflection on the *constitution* of the ego. He believed that the concept of a weak ego is inaccurate. From his point of view, the ego is constituted of the integration of several ego-nuclei that always give rise to intense sensory experiences: the salivary nucleus; the oral nucleus; the epidermal nucleus; the anal nucleus; etc. Each nucleus is strong; what can be weak is their mutual integration.

In the infant's early life, the good-enough mother, who provides adequate mothering, who is not too persecutory, brings about this integration. If, as I suggest, the first identification is identification to a psychic space in the other who is the mother – that which constitutes the self, the most intimate part of ourselves – the unconscious ego of the infant unfolds and internalises the *support, the handling and other techniques of maternal care*. The primary function of the unconscious ego, like that of the good-enough mother, is to protect the self. From this perspective, the origin of the ego is not associated with an image, but with the need for a system of protection. The ego is primarily a protective shield. Let me explain. There is an intermediary space between the mother and her baby, a real and distinct space, but one which the baby is unable to recognise as separate from him. Winnicott calls this intermediary space a *transitional space*, and calls the objects present in this space *transitional objects*; a transition between two stages, from the stage of undifferentiation of the stage where the other and the world can be recognised as external to the self. This is illustrated by the baby's relation to a stuffed animal or a blanket. The baby knows very well that his stuffed animal or his blanket exist outside himself and, at the same time, he needs these objects so much to maintain a sense of security (thanks to their smell, texture, etc.) that their absence can cause the most profound distress. Winnicott understood that these objects are part of the internal reality of the baby, but that it is crucial that they exist in *external reality* as well, and he asked that we accept this paradox. He used another term to designate these transitional objects, calling them *subjective objects*.

For maternal care to be contained in the transitional space for the required duration, the mother and her way of caring for the baby must be both objective realities external to the space of the infant *and* subjective objects for the infant. As subjective objects, they cannot be recognised as distinct. A subjective object is not a fantasy; it requires the real existence of an external object. A subjective object is located between external reality and internal reality, it is part of the psychic skin of the subject, it is the material and the envelope of his dreams. Winnicott once said that "there is no such thing as a baby [outside a] nursing couple".

Maternal care techniques are constantly imaginarised, and these imaginarisations will later serve to build a fantasy life. But they will also be used by the baby just as they are, to protect his innermost self and to compensate for deficiencies appearing gradually in the environment. Thus, these techniques will become an integral part of the ego, the part entrusted with protection, functioning as a protective shield. *The constitution of the self, the integration of the ego nuclei and the continuity of being* are Winnicott's key themes reflecting his particular concern with ensuring that an event in the life of a subject be experienced as real, that is, likely to enrich and strengthen his confidence in his connection to the world and the others.

Just as the self needs a good-enough environment to constitute itself, in the case of certain experiences it is preferable – sometimes indispensable – that a degree of organisation of the psychic apparatus already exist, to make it possible for these experiences to be integrated. For example, aggression – which is initially ruthless and without guilt – must first serve to develop motor skills, and therefore the relation to reality, before serving sexuality. If, for various defensive reasons, sexuality uses aggression before the latter exists as a real experience in its integration to motricity, the subject will have difficulty experiencing his sexuality as a reality belonging to his body and to his psychic world.

In more general terms, in order for the energy of instinctual life not to frighten the subject but rather enrich him, this energy must arise in a space capable of taking possession of it both as energy and as reality. At the start, this is the work of the environment, in other words, the mother. But if the mother does not fulfil her maternal function, if she is too anxious or perverse, then the subject may use his auto-erotic sexuality as a defence against the impingements of maternal affect. *In that case, sexuality will be dissociated from the space of the ego, a space which protects the most innermost part of the subject, the self. In the hysteric, sexuality, which has not been integrated into the ego, faces two pitfalls. Attempts to integrate it could destroy it, because the subject is too familiar with its use as an active defence. But an attempt to eliminate it altogether renders existence unreal, and the possibility of suicide arises at once.* Trapped between these two pitfalls, the hysteric is always disappointed. This is the source of the recurrent "disappointment of the hysteric".

Therefore, the theory of a dissociation between sexuality and the ego in the hysteric involves three different premises the analyst must take into account: that of the ego, applying to ego-related psychic needs (for the ego, sexuality is a psychic need); that of the pleasure principle – concerning repression and conflict between drives and identification phenomena – and that which concerns impingements of the environment, which are very closely linked with sexuality in the hysteric. This is a far cry from the notion of narcissistic injury, with the "orthopaedic" correction it implies.

With these subjects, the analyst must take into account both ego needs and a sexuality mixed with destructive impulses, and look after the ego until favourable conditions allow sexuality to be integrated in a manner beneficial to the subject. So that it can be good for him. Looking after the psychic needs of the ego means taking care of love-related injuries and, for this reason, very often looking after the ego is tantamount to looking after the subject.

As I said earlier, the theory of integration does not involve corrective measures. Their futility is demonstrated by the partner of the hysterical woman. What does this woman want? She wants the man to be the good archaic mother she never had. And if the loving partner accepts the injuries to his pride that this desire on her part involves, she loses all interest in him as a sexual object.

The paradox is as follows: if a man refuses to play the maternal role that the woman assigns him, she finds him hateful but rewards him with passionate sexual desire. If he accepts a maternal function, she loves him with boundless gratitude but cannot turn to him for sexual fulfilment. And yet, it is in the relationship with this type of maternal man that this woman will discover her femininity. This useless lover, presenting no risk at the sexual level, will allow the woman access to a sexuality with no strings attached, that serves no function and remains unused. An ideal of femininity, so to speak, which she will try to use elsewhere, most often rather unsuccessfully.[2]

It is precisely because the hysteric uses sexuality to protect herself from the sexual passions of an invasive mother that she can never abandon herself to the man who loves her. To do so would amount to being violated by her mother once again. On the other hand, if the man she loves accepts a relationship based primarily on love rather than sexuality, he will internalise, in her place – without any working through on her part – some dissociated aspects of the ego. It is for this reason that, during this period, she will be able to experience her femininity.

Through transference, the psychoanalyst can play the role of the good archaic mother. If he contents himself with this, he can maintain the dissociation between love and sexuality indefinitely. This is because, as Granoff and Perrier have pointed out – with little attention being paid by clinicians – the girl is "infinitely more dependent than the boy on the libidinal organisation of the parental relationship".[3]

In other words, an invasive archaic mother – meaning a poor primal environment – signifies a father who does not play his role, who does not know his limits or the law, and is therefore unable to transmit them.

The outrageous erotisation in which the hysteric engages with men is rooted in this impossibility and is – in addition – an attempt to repair the father's masculinity. The same process is at work in the organisation of transference as passionate love.

Thus, *the analyst offers to be a space* that can contain the consequences of breaks in continuity, *in order to conceptualise their causes*; in other words, in order to integrate a dissociated sexuality into the ego. Therefore, his first task will be to separate the subject's psychic space from those who invaded it or impinged upon it.

The analyst must keep in mind that the person before him either considers life with his parents as a Universality, or feels profoundly guilty and hurt to have discovered that they represent a mere Particular. To separate spaces, to respect the parents, means treating them as particular individuals who deserve, like all subjects, to be granted the same respect and the same rights that universality guarantees everyone. From this point of view, the analyst is a messenger of the universal: he places permission where the particular had inscribed the forbidden; and he introduces a ban on the trauma produced by the particular.

The parameters that circumscribe the analyst's interpretation include the following notions: *messenger of the universal – which includes sexuality; guarantor of an unprecedented symbolic exchange; director creating a new performance space, a space of illusion, creativity and reflection; rearranger of the real and actual superego; therapist of the psychic environment.* To add a technical comment, it is not a matter of simply interpreting that which is repeated, but rather of providing access to that which parental pathology had unduly kept unknown up until that point. In this role, the analyst is the author of new scenes, the playwright who animates characters who had been secondary or absent, like a great-grandfather, a nanny or a distant cousin, who constituted crucial psychic spaces in the child's history, spaces in which the authentic part of the subject is alive.[4] Here, the best interpretation consists of a rereading, of a re-presentation of the parental narrative, of its reinterpretation. This way of doing things is based on Freud's definition of the function of construction in psychoanalysis, which he considered identical to interpretation. The only difference is that in the case of hysterics what is involved is not simply reconstruction in retrospect of the relation to the environment, such as that accompanying or following the working through in transference of that which is repeated.

Here, *what is involved is helping the subject to actually construct an intermediary symbolic space between him and his parents, between him and the world.*

Applying this method has at least two unorthodox consequences relative to what is usually defined as standard psychoanalysis – forgetting that the only standard attribute of any analysis worthy of the name is to be an exception to the rules that attempt to normalise the particular. These consequences concern the *clinical treatment of reality* and the clinical treatment of the other individuals in the current history of the subject.

According to an established convention, the psychoanalyst should not concern himself with the current *reality of his patients*. This recommendation is based on Freud's request that his clients make no changes in their lives during the analysis. But it is easy to see that today such a rigorous rule would be disloyal to Freud's principles. In Freud's time, an analysis rarely lasted over a year – which seemed a reasonable period to leave one's life unchanged. But today, the excessive duration of psychoanalysis – a subject to which we must sooner or later give some serious thought – would turn this recommendation into a request to stop living, to exclude chance from the field of existence, which would mean going back to a religious conception of the world.

Of course, today no analyst would presume to make such an absurd request for abstinence. But surprisingly, this decision rarely leads analysts to draw a logical conclusion, that is, to formulate a theory on the processing of the reality experienced by a subject in the course of the analysis. On the contrary, analysts place the subject in a position resembling the double bind theorised by Bateson in regard to psychotic patients. If the analyst does not request that the patient leave his reality unchanged, he acts as if this reality does not exist. In situations where I was the second or third analyst of a subject, I was faced with intricate entanglements created in the previous analyses.

Is reality something too serious to be entrusted to psychoanalysts? A hysteric might address such a pleasantry to his analyst. Although the handling of reality by a hysteric is not necessarily an acting-out, if the analyst treats reality like a neutral or absent dimension, based on an inappropriate premise of opposition between fantasy and the reality of trauma, the hysteric will need to prove him wrong. And no matter how well he recognises and identifies fantasmal equivalents of these realistic scenes, he will never be done with the traumatic effects of certain situations where he had (or chose to have) the position of anonymous spectator defined by Joyce McDougall in a well-known text. The psychoanalyst's difficulty to settle the score with the traumatic character of these realistic enactments is increased by the fact that this traumatic character is a sign of the dysfunction, the lack of integration of the ego he is attempting to treat.

When discussing archaic hysteria to illustrate how the psychoanalytic process creates an ego-support environment into which the real person (the subject) can emerge, I stressed the fact that at this stage of the work the analyst leaves repression aside almost entirely. If he must take it into account, it will be secondary in relation to the issues it creates in transference.

The analyst supports the patient and provides a setting that he adjusts tactfully to the psychic needs of the subject. In this context, the support and particular attention given to the subject are *integrative functions and, as such, they facilitate the emergence of the new ego-support environment in which the real person, the true self, the innermost self can be strengthened.* This support, this careful adaptation to particular psychic needs, and the desire not to impinge on the space of the true self, are all unprecedented experiences for the subject. This novel nature of the experience indicates that the same factors that serve to build a new ego-support environment also determine the *type of interpretation* needed at this stage of the analytic work. Since in these analyses the most important element is that which is not repeated, each time the patient can identify a new form of encounter with the other – an identification which is neither obvious or easy – the degree of distortion of the original ego, the distortion that imprisoned the subject in an alienating relationship with another whom he needed, and who was deadly, decreases. Thus, each time that the analyst, by the quality of his presence, is encountered as another (capital or small "a") as yet unknown, the degree of alienation diminishes or disappears, even if it is for a few moments, and *new spaces* are experienced as possibilities of the Real: a new space for the ego; a new space of encounter; a new space between the subject and the world. And this is also why these interpretations designate and build an intermediary space between the patient and the analyst, a space that the patient will hopefully be able to transfer one day to his relation with the world. This transitional space and the analytic space overlap completely for a certain period of time.

When Winnicott spoke of the analyses he conducted, he often used expressions that showed the *pleasure* he took in working with his patients. No doubt pleasure, humour and tenderness are important elements of play, of the playful setting that allows the expansion – and sometimes the establishment – of transitional spaces and phenomena in the course of the analysis. But I believe that the sharing of joy and of an interest in the work – for instance, when the analyst and the patient look for the appropriate interpretation together – must be given special attention, precisely because it is something that is closely related to the question of friendship.

You notice that I always come back to the question of friendship.

Till next time,

Notes

1 A scorpion asked a frog to carry him across a wide river.
   The frog objected: "You are going to sting me and I will die."
   The scorpion: "But if I sting you, you will sink and I will die too!"
   Convinced by this reasoning, the frog accepts. In the middle of the river the scorpion stings him.
   The frog: "But you stung me!"
   The scorpion: "Well, yes."
   The frog: "But I am going to die."

The scorpion: "Well, yes."
The frog: "And you too."
The scorpion: "Well, yes."
The frog: "But you are a fool."
The scorpion: "No, I am a scorpion."

2 Ingmar Bergman described better than anyone the role the hysteric assigns to a man.
3 Wladimir Granoff and François Perrier, *Le Désir et le Féminin*. Paris: Aubier Montaigne, 1979.
4 Philippe Réfabert discusses this as well. See the last paragraph of Letter 14, *Paranoia as seen by Philippe Réfabert.*

Letter 21

The therapist

Dear friend,

Last Friday I went to hear a conference given by the Italian therapist you told me about, who was in Paris for a few days.

I wanted to acquaint myself with his thinking, knowing that it orients you in your work with patients. In any case, I have always preferred to hear an author expose his ideas in person, whenever I can, before I go on to read his texts.

I found this man likable, warm. It is always moving to listen to someone whose words testify to fifty years of experience. A lifetime. His familiarity with psychosis allows him to describe the strangeness of the psychotic's universe simply and clearly.

I found that his clinical examples illustrated a courageous manner of encountering psychosis and an inventive way of treating the material emerging in the sessions, not unlike your way of doing things – like the time you told a woman analysand to go and get the only photograph left of her mother from her aunt, at the other end of the world.

But unlike you, I found that this man was unable to render psychosis familiar, and therefore thinkable. When you speak of your work, your starting point is always your astonishment – which confirms the radical strangeness of this type of encounter. At the same time, what you say contains something else, something that reveals your psychic reaction to this absolute difference, and your attempt to formulate *in your own terms* the unthinkable which organises the psychotic's way of being in the world.

On the contrary, our Italian colleague seems to have opted for stupefaction as a method, a position that deserves admiration but unnecessarily complicates an already difficult task. At times it seems as if his compassionate way of formulating the problem requires more energy than the energy he spends in his work with the psychotic.

Harold Searles, a brilliant American psychoanalyst whom he quotes often, speaks of the mystical aspect of psychoanalytic work with schizophrenics – an aspect we actually encounter in our practice. But the Italian therapist is more inclined towards religion than mysticism.

To come back to his perspective, and so to his theory, I must admit that most of the time I found it very confusing. When I read what he had written, this impression became even stronger. Out of consideration for you, I tried to find in his texts a clearly defined conception of his relation to psychosis. But my efforts were scantily rewarded. Beyond a fanciful hypothesis presented as a completely novel, revolutionary understanding of the universe of the psychotic, what he proposed consisted of two prosaic notions based on common sense, which have long been advanced by all those who have tried to conceptualise insanity: that the schizophrenic has no ego; and that the aim of therapy is to invent the means of providing him with one. (But at times he speaks of hypertrophy of the ego ideal. He does not explain how he reconciles these two contradictory hypotheses.)

It is always surprising to note that two accurate ideas suffice to make it possible to obtain therapeutic results in such an arduous and unpredictable clinical field. But there is also so much wasted generosity and lost time, frequently seen in psychopathological domains where there was massive early deprivation. For instance, in the field of drug addiction, therapists with strong personalities have accomplished miracles in cases where the efforts of the best trained teams remained fruitless.

As far as this particular therapist is concerned, I wonder if his disagreements with the leading psychoanalytic institutions have not resulted in isolating him in terms of the elaboration of his ideas, so that I cannot determine if his refusal to acknowledge any indebtedness is a primary or secondary factor in his theorising.

As for the technical aspect of his work, I have trouble agreeing with him when he recommends that the therapist act as a mirror for the schizophrenic, or when he makes it a requirement that the therapist enter the psychotic's delusion. Given that psychosis is characterised by the subject's inability to differentiate himself from his mother – more specifically, from his primal environment – I can imagine the anxiety he creates in his patients by reflecting back to them, like in a mirror, their psychic disorganisation, their despair, their insanity. As I was telling you recently, I feel that, on the contrary, our work consists of trying to insert an intermediary space between the psychotic and his therapist, a distance allowing the psychotic to feel less threatened of being invaded by the other, so that they can both work more comfortably.[1]

I will not discuss the importance he attaches to the dual relationship that he considers the foundation of all possible change; my reservations are related, *grosso modo*, to what I said above about a necessary distance.

Nor will I repeat what I said about passionate involvement in the transference, the condition required for the advent of what he calls "interpretation from the inside". I will only comment on his choice of an object for therapeutic work: affect.

While there is universal recognition of the importance of the therapist's feelings in any analytic process, and particularly in therapeutic work with a psychotic – what in our jargon we call the appropriate use of countertransference – it is also understood that the affective disorganisation of the psychotic is of secondary importance. It is a consequence of an absence of ego, and of the fact that the psychotic does not inhabit his body – the body which is the centre of all emotions, of all affect. This makes it difficult for me to understand how one can focus on affect before dealing with the psychotic's relationship with his body, before examining the relation of this body to space. This is why I believe that, despite the great subtlety required, focusing on the status of the body in psychosis, on bodily experience and its representations, is a more constructive and therefore more fruitful, as well as more therapeutic and therefore "simpler", approach to working with psychotics.

Till next time, with warm regards,

Note

1 See Letter 8, *Psychosis: the encounter with Gisela Pankow* and Letter 9, *Gisela Pankow and her teaching.*

Victor Smirnoff

An example to follow

My dear friend,

Victor Smirnoff exerted a great influence on my particular manner of being a psychoanalyst, through something he passed on to me or allowed me to acquire – and I believe the two go together. First, there was the man himself, with his humour, his vivacity, his intelligence and his elegance, his interest in literature, film, theatre, music, painting, politics and the ordinary affairs of the world. It was easy to guess that he enjoyed fine food, loved women and was truly a man of the world, but also that he could give way to anger and show great intransigence. His passion for psychoanalysis, his commitment to the work, his ethical sense and his openness to various theories – all this was always present, contributing to a continuous invention of the encounter and constituting the particularity of his personality. But there was also his contagious joy, providing both stimulation and support. To be with him, to think in his company, was comfortable, warm, cosy and intense.

I am making this inventory in an attempt to help you grasp that which escapes classification, to give you a glimpse of the way Smirnoff was at ease in his body, the way he looked at people, the way he smiled. I know my efforts are in vain, and that to describe the indescribable I will have to recount some stories in greater detail.

First, let me give you some background. When I met Smirnoff, I was going through a rough time. Gisela Pankow had suddenly put an end to the work we had been doing together for almost three years. She did not want me to live with the woman I loved at that time.

At first, I took her opposition for friendly concern, or even maternal concern, exaggerated of course; then I took it for a joke in poor taste, and finally for an intrusion. I did not get angry, but I tried to make her see that she was crossing the limits associated with my training, that she was going too far. She refused to listen and she put an end to the supervision.

When I met Smirnoff, I had much to discover and was far from feeling very confident.

I don't remember how I came to know him. Perhaps I had heard of him before. From Françoise Dolto? Not likely, since in that case I would have known that he worked with children, and in fact I did not. From Pankow? Perhaps, but I do not remember. It was a time when too many things in my life were changing at once, when many things needed urgent attention. I am almost certain that I had never seen him before I went to the address on Rue Duguay-Trouin, because otherwise his image would not have remained so sharply etched in my memory.

Rue Duguay-Trouin, then. A beautiful building, ground floor, on the right. His consulting room was large, akin to a drawing room, and sunny. I remember being pleasantly surprised that it was so bright despite being on the ground floor. In my memory, this room was always bathed in light, which cannot be true, since I sometimes went there in the evening. The force of this impression speaks volumes.

I was on time, as I always am, and he showed me in right away. Smiling, jovial, warm. Victor Smirnoff was a short, bald man with light blue eyes, a little overweight and elegantly dressed. I was struck by the bow tie; I think it was the first time I met someone who wore one. The bow tie and the bald head went well together. He wore a dark green jacket over a light blue shirt (the bow tie was of a shade that matched the jacket); he wore venetian red trousers and matching shoes. The shades complemented each other. But the combination of a bald head with a bow tie, worn with a jacket of the same colour, called to mind a clownish appearance. Did he look ridiculous? Not at all. On the contrary, his appearance suggested a generous harmony, a solidity that inspired confidence. The clownish appearance, combined with the large, sunlit room, appealed to the Brazilian in me; all this seemed to welcome childhood with open arms.

I talked to him about my problems with Pankow and about the other upheavals in my life. I asked him to see me in analysis. He saw me a second time and, after a long meeting, he told me he felt that what I really needed was to speak as an analyst to another analyst. He could not offer me a specific time slot, but he understood that my need was urgent. So, if I agreed, we could see each other whenever his schedule allowed, for a while. He took out a little card – he had no appointment book – and gave me a first appointment in two days.

We had only been working together a few months when Smirnoff told me that he was writing an article for the *Nouvelle Revue de Psychanalyse*. I questioned him about the issue and, after explaining briefly, he asked me if I would mind if he quoted my conceptualisation concerning a patient we had been discussing together. Of course, I was deeply touched. And I was very proud, when the issue was published, to receive an autographed off-print. Such was Smirnoff's generosity.

Another time, much later, he said he had a favour to ask me. After our session together, he was scheduled to see a patient who worried him and he had not had time to think since their last meeting. Would I mind if we used our time together to discuss this patient? It was not the first time he spoke to me about his patients. Instead of intervening directly in the analyses I described, he preferred to use examples from his practice, to refer to the methods he used to solve similar problems. But this time he was doing something else. Of course, we discussed the patient, but the important thing was the way in which he had presented things to me. When he made his request, Smirnoff had a mischievous smile and twisted his nose a little to the left, he made a little grimace when he was pleased with himself, as if he had played a good joke on someone. His suggestion was like that of a ringleader who asks one of the young members of his band to take part in a dangerous heist. He knows he is bestowing a great honour on the boy, and at the same time he is amused and curious: how will the lad manage? Will he dare see the whole thing through?

On another occasion I was speaking to him about a patient, knowing that we disagreed about her predominant defensive organisation. I saw it as hysterical, he saw it as psychotic. I recounted my last session with her, during which she said that she cut the face of a man who was bothering her in a nightclub, with the cap of a can of beer. Smirnoff exclaimed: "You were right about her hysteria." To my surprise, he asked me: "Do you like beer?" – "Yes" –"Would you like to have one?" He came back with a can and a glass, removed the cap and handed it to me. I still did not understand. And he, brimming with joy, took the little piece of metal between two fingers saying: "It is the symbol of bisexuality!" Of course, what we have here is a good illustration of his clinical sense, his presence of mind, his awareness. But there is also something else: he could show that he was pleased with himself, like a gifted child conscious of his talents, usually modest but happy to share with his playmate his pride in the feat he just accomplished.

For a while, my meetings with him took place in the early afternoon. He would nod off often. I found this upsetting and finally spoke to him about it. We decided to meet in the morning. But once, before this change, he had greeted me by saying: "I had a little too much wine at lunch. What do you say to a walk in the Luxembourg Gardens?" As he spoke, he was picking up his keys and putting on his coat. It is obvious that he enjoyed the prospect and was eager to get going. No doubt the unorthodox character of the project contributed to his glee; he was delighted to show the young fledgling that he was thumbing his nose at laziness and tiresome conventions; he displayed the audacity of an older playmate pulling a younger one into the hazardous adventure of building a hut in the neighbour's woods. As we walked, Smirnoff was telling me about the way Freud analysed Ferenczi while they took walks together. I told myself that he would no doubt have liked to be in Ferenczi's place.

At a certain point, I started to suffer from constant fatigue. Smirnoff, who was an excellent physician and liked to prove it, advised me to have a series of tests. I did and the results were normal. He advised additional investigations. The results were normal again.

To be more precise, what I experienced was this: after the weekend break, I felt very well on Monday. The fatigue set in Tuesday morning and lasted until Friday evening. Saturday, Sunday and Monday I felt fine. Then the cycle repeated itself. This situation worried me, it interfered with my work; I felt like I was dragging myself. Smirnoff took this problem seriously and we discussed it often. Once, the day before I was to work with him, he telephoned to ask that I bring my weekly schedule with me the next day. We studied it together and noticed that I had many patients whom I saw only once a week. Smirnoff, who was well versed in these matters, commented (he was not really asking): "The ones with the most serious problems, and who can't pay?" I acquiesced. He went on: "If you continue like this, you are inviting a heart attack; you have little time to elaborate the transference, you are carrying the weight of these analyses alone by serving as the memory of your patients. They have to be more involved. At the rate you are seeing them, you are doing more construction work than interpretation. The danger is that the process of intellectualisation replaces true psychic elaboration, in which case all your efforts are in vain."

I went home and decided to take a vacation. I resigned from the *Centre médico-psycho-pédagogique* and I informed all my patients that, when I was going to come back, I was going to change my work schedule. I would work three weeks and take one week off. During the weeks when I would work, patients who used to come once a week were going to come twice, those who used to come twice would come three times, and those who used to come three time would come four times. It was this or nothing at all. Everyone agreed to my terms, including the children from the CMPP (Centre médico-psycho-pédagogique), whom I now saw at home free of charge. There was only one exception: a perverse patient who found it unbearable to imagine me doing nothing for a week. And the fatigue disappeared.

The following week, when I saw Smirnoff, I told him about the arrangements I had made. He looked at me in silence, with a serious expression on his face – which was unusual for him. "I am very happy to hear it and I congratulate you. I always knew that you were a decisive man, but I am impressed by the speed with which you acted. You must be careful not to expect that your patients or the women in your life show the same type of spontaneous generosity you are able to have towards yourself. Most people react more slowly, because of their neurosis or their laziness." I said that it was thanks to him that I had been able to do what I did. "Maybe," he said, "but you are the one who did it, not me, and you should remember that as well. Whatever you do for your patients, they are the ones who have to invent their lives. But we both have reason to be proud, we have done good work." I have not forgotten. In terms of limiting my expectations, I am able to do so with my patients, with those close to me, I am afraid I might be incurable.

We spent a lot of time considering the case of a patient who truly puzzled me. I was recounting my frustration for the hundredth time, when Smirnoff interrupted me: "You could solve the problem by throwing him out the window. But since you can't do that, accept the fact that you will have to see him for the rest of your life. At least he doesn't bother you during the sessions. But he bothers me. Why don't you tell me about someone else?"[1]

When he read my first published book – the manuscript that I had submitted to Pankow – he invited me to lunch. What a reader! He had especially liked the chapter in which I described various modalities of lying in the context of transference, and was surprised that I was not aware of Winnicott's notion of false self, and even more surprised that I did not know Winnicott. He guided me in my reading of Winnicott's works and he spoke to me of the man, whom he had known well.

There is no doubt that Winnicott entered my life thanks to Smirnoff, who followed his example: in his ability to provide a holding environment; to identify with the other; to enjoy work; to include play in his manner of working; and to be delighted to play – as well as in the practice of psychoanalysis as therapy. But the essential factor, as you have certainly guessed, is something of a different nature. The essential thing is the central place Smirnoff gave to the child in him. He was living proof that boredom is antithetical to thinking, that the means needed for making clinical discoveries in psychoanalysis depend on attributes of childhood: living in the moment; being open to surprises; to what might emerge; to the joyful thrill of adventure; to the risks associated with the unknown. Before I met Smirnoff, I had already understood that transference was a tool for guessing the Real. What I owe him, thanks to the work we did with patients, is the conviction that gaining access to this repressed or excluded reality can be as exciting as the joy felt by a child in the pursuit of his adventures.

Helio Pellegrino's genius taught me that life and the courage to live it are tied to psychoanalysis, Françoise Dolto's genius gave me a glimpse of infinite possibilities, and Pankow's intransigence taught me how to practise psychoanalysis. As for Victor Smirnoff, he taught me by example to resuscitate the joyful, daredevil child I once was thanks to the uncle who saved my life. In the course of my own psychoanalyses, I had described an unhappy child obliged to be his parents' therapist. Smirnoff, who had not stopped being a child, convinced me that it was the joyful child in me who would complete my growing up and help me become a man, and that this gleeful child would turn me into the analyst I was able to be. And it is in fact this child who made me the psychoanalyst that I am.

With warm regards,

Note

1   I discuss this patient in Letter 28, *Loup Verlet: psychoanalysis as a revolution of the conceptual framework.*

Françoise Davoine and Jean-Max Gaudillière

History beyond trauma

Dear friend,

I would like to talk to you about a much-needed book that we all welcomed, because it combines psychoanalysis and psychiatry with political theory. The two authors are French, but the book, entitled *History Beyond Trauma*, was first published in English by Other Press, New York, in 2004. The French version, *Histoire et trauma, la folie des guerres*, was published by Stock in the collection under the direction of Anne Dufourmantelle.

This book that was lacking, and which will hopefully generate many others, teaches us that a book is a living being, alterity in its optimal guise. Not only because in this case the book is the inscription of two lives dedicated to research at the frontiers of thought, but also through the use Davoine and Gaudillière make of the writers who allowed them to progress on this path. Their adventure, like all adventures worthy of the name, makes fascinating reading.

The way in which Cervantes, Barrois, Descartes, Homer, Faulkner, Guimaraes Rosa, Musil, Fromm-Reichmann, Sullivan, Wittgenstein – as well as Bion, Freud, Winnicott and many others – are invoked brings to mind a gathering of friends seated around a table, discussing the things essential to living and the courage needed to be ready for the unexpected, for suffering, for joy – in short, for the Real. As Guimaraes Rosa says, "Living is dangerous". And the psychoanalyst is a person presumed to be fully engaged with life; but I will come back to this later.

I am presenting the book in these terms first – not an aspect of it, but its very nature – in order to show the direct and simple manner in which these authors – a couple – discuss the unbearable, unbelievable question of truth.

A couple. A detail worth noting. Obviously, these are two researchers who have been conducting a weekly seminar together at the "École des hautes études en sciences sociales". But also two people who are actually a couple – a fact mentioned in the book, with its implications for clinical work with trauma patients and psychotics. But what is a couple, in actual fact today? A couple is a hybrid psychic entity, threatened with extinction, which, when it exists, creates a space in which two individuals can rest, affirm their differences, nurture their solitude; it is also a place where desire can encounter joy, and a refuge from vulgarity and envy – these products of hate exacerbated by the standardisation of individuals in our developed societies.

Françoise Davoine and Jean-Max Gaudillière work as psychoanalysts. But each of them came from a background of a different nature: literature. Today, when the tendency is to start psychoanalytic training practically in kindergarten, the exercise of psychoanalysis as a second life, as a place of exile, creates a distance which no doubt explains in large measure the feeling of freedom imparted to us by these authors. In their psychoanalytic explorations, Davoine and Gaudillière like to use tools of reflection acquired elsewhere. Recourse to this otherness testifies to their lack of religiosity; but it is clear that they understand the meaning of the sacred perfectly well.

Who is the intended audience of the book? Psychoanalysts, of course, and all those who try to comprehend the woundings of memory passed down to us by history for generations, including those of the past century, whose sources are now far enough away to allow acknowledgement with less resistance. (Françoise Davoine and Jean-Max Gaudillière speak of a necessary lapse of fifty years.) It is from this perspective that they invoke the authors mentioned earlier, as well as Hannah Arendt, a pioneer in this field whose political analyses ground their own reflections.

In France, authors like Robert Antelme and David Rousset have testified to the wounds inflicted by history, a number of researchers have revealed the horrors of the Vichy regime, and Claude Lanzmann created his monumental work, *Shoah*, whose effect, when it was shown in Israel, was to allow survivors of death camps to break the silence surrounding this reality, and begin to relate their own stories to their children.

The all-encompassing consequences of the events described in the book transform the reader into a co-searcher who draws on echoes of the past in himself while engaging in the pursuit of immobilised time which houses the horror of frozen words.

Co-searcher: Françoise Davoine and Jean-Max Gaudillière like to use this term to designate the psychotic patient; they make use of it constantly in their seminar entitled "*Folie et lien social*" (Madness and the Social Link). From their perspective, the word "madness" does not refer to the structure of an individual; rather, it describes a type of social relation existing in an extreme situation... The madman shows us how to survive in the extreme circumstances of war. Madness bears the scars of the breakdown of time and the abolition of the limits of language. This is why they believe that an analyst working in the domain of madness must dream history. By means of these dreams, the psychoanalyst can name the images that have not been erased in the other, these thing-images so ever-present that they are invisible and remain unrecognised: immobilised time and the traces of horror blurred by familiarity born of habit, even the habit of suffering. The historisation of transference produces undeniable improvements in the individual, improvements which then permeate throughout the social milieu.

Davoine and Gaudillière believe that the absence of limits between inside and outside characteristics of psychotics has a positive aspect. This absence is the origin of the ability to testify to the disasters that have been erased from history. The madman reveals the disaster at the cost of his identity. *Thus, insanity is memory that does not forget.* Harry Stack Sullivan asserts the need for a bridge between mental illness and social sciences, since war and madness are strangely related. War can dwell in the sphere of transference – and not only metaphorically.

Davoine and Gaudillière consider the setting for clinical work with trauma patients and the mentally ill to be based on the principles of wartime psychiatry, which found a way to process the segments of the frozen time transmitted from one generation to another. They use the four principles defined by Thomas W. Salmon (1917) as the organising elements of their clinical work: immediacy; proximity; expectancy; simplicity – which I call time; space; affect; and manner.

Françoise Davoine and Jean-Max Gaudillière insist on the urgent need, for the psychoanalyst, to recognise that the removed segments of History are actualised in the present time of the analytic work. Each session is a battle against the absence of sense; each session is the last session. To treat mental illness, they say, the approach to the symptoms must reveal a break in transmission along the fault lines of social ties. Moreover, we must remember what madmen teach us: that which cannot be said must be shown.

The authors of *History Beyond Trauma* refer to medieval "fools" and their proclamation of the truth: what everyone thinks secretly is what they say out loud when they talk to themselves. This is what constitutes the political and therapeutic nature of "madness". Davoine and Gaudillière maintain that today the analytic space is the only place where the knowledge contained in madness is taken seriously. The analyst speaks to insanity, instead of speaking about insanity.

Another key element: psychoanalytic work with psychotics is related to the oral tradition, which exceeds the realm of history prior to writing, and is not confined to so-called peoples "without history"; madness juggles, gesticulates and resists within the space of this temporality.

Working through transference with psychotics requires enough time to go from the symptom that befalls you and causes you to fall, to the historical narrative in which the analyst is an actor who plays opposite the protagonist. The psychoanalyst's work of transference is an attempt to exist in the non-existence of the patient. Madness which speaks to itself or to everyone – that is, to no one – *shows*, outside the limits of temporality, and therefore within a space, what no one wants to know, that which is not yet inscribed as the past.

Each psychosis requires that the analyst respond to the remainder, the residue of the simplifying discourse of social sciences, including psychoanalysis. This is why Davoine and Gaudillière counter Wittgenstein's proposition –"Whereof one cannot speak, thereof one must be silent", by saying: "whereof one cannot speak, thereof one cannot remain silent".

Thus, madness is a means, not a destiny. It is a tool serving to escape from hell, not an inescapable repetition. In the *research process* undertaken with psychotics, the analyst is the assistant who follows the lead of the patient. Insanity opens the fields of the Real; this is why, in the elaboration of transference, the distinction between cognitive knowledge and unconscious knowledge is unclear. This awareness allows the book to combine the political with the unconscious.

The domain of the transference, defined in these terms, makes it possible to escape the uncanny relation to the Real. The analyst working with insanity and trauma is constantly confronted with fragments of the Real because the lack of meaningful language prevented the inscription of the event in the unconscious. Therefore, the usual tools of psychoanalytic treatment become ineffectual; in these spheres where temporality is suspended, in these lifeless spheres, there is no subject of language, not even of repressed language. Indeed, in the lifeless spheres, the subject is not yet constituted. What is at stake in these cases is, in fact, the emergence of the subject, the subject of a story. Not of a censured story. What occurs is the emergence of the subject of a story that has been erased, reduced to nothing – and which, nevertheless, exists. (Galileo comes to mind: "And, still, it turns.")

The one who has suffered a catastrophe – and Davoine and Gaudillière demonstrate that in all catastrophes there is betrayal by those one trusted, those one loved – transforms the other. The other, who is the guarantor of the symbolic order, becomes a surface of signs and forms that must be deciphered against the background of a world where words have no value. In this deadlocked position, the analyst attempts to internalise the patient's suffering, while looking for a way to allow the patient to internalise his (the analyst's) words. It is in the space between these two attempted feats that a *subjective subject* can be born, a subject with the characteristics of Winnicott's transitional object. If this transitional subject can be created, he allows the analyst and the patient to proceed, bound together, in an encounter located at the frontiers of the Real, where loose forms and images unfold.[1]

The creation of the subjective subject depends in great measure on the therapist. With psychotics, it is the analyst who sets the unconscious in motion. To do so, he recounts the dreams he has on behalf of the patient, or the details of his own history which coincide with that of the patient. If we concede that psychosis is a means for the subject to attempt existing by inscribing the Real that is not communicable, the stories and dreams narrated by the analyst are a means, like fiction, to circumscribe this Real. The therapist's desire to find, beyond madness, the subject who has left the ground of his search, the ground his symptoms are left to explore, is a necessary condition – but never sufficient – for him to be accepted for a time as a companion in the hunt for the Thing. This is so because, prior to the encounter with the psychoanalyst, no one else was able to respond to the subject's experience of the Real. Now, for this transitional being, the subjective subject, to be able to emerge, it is preferable – as I have often said – that the analyst be a living subject. But, as Davoine and Gaudillère constantly emphasise, a living subject who has also survived disasters. The authors call on Claude Barrois to confirm this perspective. Psychoanalysis is the only process that can exert an action on trauma, that can find a trace of the point of fracture, of a previous time when fantasies and dreams had their place. These subjects have encountered death, their own death, but this death they met face-to-face has no representation. Davoine and Gaudillière add: this death has no representation, except, on occasion, through another horrified subject.

Resonances and exchanges. These observations elucidate a number of clinical and epistemological situations. What I understand is this:

- the usual psychoanalytic method is inadequate in a context of psychosis because this method relies on representations, and the psychotic's experience has no representation inscribed in the repressed unconscious. The repressed unconscious of the subject does not hold a representation of death, specifically of his own death, despite the fact that this death has occurred;
- this is why time has stood still, has become frozen: it is impossible to speak of one's own death as something that has already taken place, when one continues to exist. At most, one can emulate Bion who, after having fought in the First World War, declared: "I died in the Ardennes" (Bion is a British psychoanalyst to whom Françoise and Jean-Max dedicated their seminar for several years);
- since there are no representation communicable in words, the subject can only show his experience;
- but since showing an experience that has no representation is also impossible, what the subject shows is the affect of terror associated with the experience, an affect still present, which completely invades his relation to the world and to the other. The therapist is asked to accept and share this affect. Without this, no encounter is possible. But another condition is also required: that the therapist meet this horror from the place of his own experiences of terror, whether they occurred in his personal history and/or in terrifying socio-historical events which marked his life or by which he was marked. If these psychic regions are not mobilised, in the absence of this quality of commitment, the patient will be unable to leave the death zone;
- initially, what makes possible the encounter between the madman and the psychoanalyst serving as his interlocutor is not any interpretation made by the latter, but simply his presence, or his attempted presence to this pain that he acknowledges as unnameable. The fabric of this attempted presence is woven from the catastrophic experiences of the analyst, which he is willing to share in the domain of the transference. In other words, the shared creation, by the analyst and the patient, of a subjective subject is built on the analysts' own experience of trauma. And, as Davoine and Gaudillière have the courage to say, on the tact the analyst has show *since childhood* in dealing with this type of situation.

Based on their long clinical experience, Davoine and Gaudillière insist on this logical requirement for the psychoanalyst to encounter madness with his traumatic experience, and with a trauma inscribed in a specific historical temporality; observations gathered by other researchers serve as the theoretical basis of their claim. For instance, the similarity of symptoms seen in soldiers, civilians and children in wartime, and the absence of discontinuity between trauma and psychosis. Davoine and Gaudillière's conception of transference in the context of therapy with psychotics and traumatised patients is also confirmed by research on the importance of telling a child traumatised by a catastrophic event what we know about the event and how we are affected by it. By doing so, the therapist unburdens the child by removing the weight of his knowledge: he is *no longer the only one to bear it*. This opens the possibility for the child to be a witness (not merely a carrier or container) to a fragment of the Real that is looking for a way to enter the play of language.[2]

Coincidences, coincidences… The three of us share an interest in epic narration, and agree on the importance of friendship as a most valuable tool for taking hold of the Real. If we agree that madness is an epic narrative, that the patient is a hero, that friendship is the only space in which something can be said about a trauma, we can easily understand the immense significance of the concept of *therapon* developed by Homer.

The *therapon* is the companion in arms, the ritual substitute. He is the one entrusted with the body and the soul of the other, in life and after death. The *therapon* inherits the warrior's arms, and is in charge of funeral rites. He is also the one who will be visited in his dreams by the soul of the deceased. In other words, the psychoanalyst working with psychotics is a *therapon* – that is, as I understand it, an *epic analyst*, able to transform the banalisation of trauma into a founding myth for the life of the subject, able to help him bury his dead, honour them and, if necessary, hate them and banish them.[3] Françoise Davoine and Jean-Max Gaudillière point out that the subject produced by the analytic process connected to the Real is the subject of a historical reality *cut away* from History. They advance the idea that psychotic patients and their psychoanalysts can serve as memorial plaques for the inscription of the disasters of an era, which will become myths and stories for the generations that follow.

Davoine and Gaudillière discuss the question of perversion late in the book. This is justified, since the entire book deals with the need for transference to take into account the ravages of traumas that are always the consequences of perversion – familial, social, historical. They point out that a society that requires of its survivors the sacrifice of their knowledge in exchange for membership is a morally and spiritually bankrupt society. The question of perversion is associated with the demonic as well: the analyst encounters the demonic in the spaces where time stands still; on those occasions, like it or not, he enters the universe of boredom and hate, beyond desire and memory, where the impersonal assassin of bodies and souls wields his savage power. This raises a crucial clinical question: is the use of cruel means necessary to effect the return of the subject exiled by a totalitarian discourse?[4]

Question, questions… In their book, Davoine and Gaudillière never speak of certainties. This choice reflects their position that the analyst must always be in search of an encounter that remains uncertain. In contrast, when an analyst takes a baby in her arms and tells him in a firm tone, while massaging its belly, that he is not responsible for that which struggles to be recognised in his parents, with the result that the constipation that has lasted for days disappears, we can assume that this analyst has a certainty. The same is true when she tells a patient a dream *she knows* she had for him, or when in her first session with a patient, before the patient says anything, she starts telling him a story which serves to contain his restlessness, to calm him and make it possible for him to speak. All this underscores the fact that the analyst's familiarity with this zone at the boundary of the Real allows him to access this dimension of certainty seen in paranoia. (I will not quote any more extraordinary, extremely moving clinical examples given in the book to illustrate analysis with psychotic patients. Since I would have to quote them fully, it is best to read them in the book.)

Question, questions... The Real is full, there is no void. It is frightening to think about this. Because to think of it implies no longer being in it, and it is frightening to remember having been in it. The horror of the Real can only be known by *remembering* the period spent in hell. This remembrance can constitute the past, but it is not a memory that can be repressed. The one who has spent time in the Real can never forget this experience. All this brings up a fundamental theoretical concept vis-à-vis which one must take a stand: the concept of primal repression. If psychoanalysis with psychotics and traumatised patients can be successful, it means that this therapy performs an act of primal repression that allows the subject to pull himself out of the grip of the Real which holds him captive. In my view, this repression concerns aspects at the border of experience, aspects that, once repressed, make it possible for the first time for borders to exist; thanks to these borders, experience can be circumscribed, there is an inside and an outside, a before and after the experience. But this repression does not concern the experience of the Real as such. The memory of the experience will always exist – no forgetting of an experience of horror is possible. The difference is that, from this point on, the experience enriches the subject's relation to the world, giving it resonances it never had before. The experience of the Real cannot be reduced to representations, and is therefore inexhaustible, unforgettable. If this is so, what can be forgotten once repression is achieved? What will constitute a border? All the perverse mechanisms used to keep the subject imprisoned in the Real. I feel that Françoise Davoine and Jean-Max Gaudillière share this point of view. I shall come back to this question.

I have thus outlined, very briefly, some of the points I would like to develop based on this book which will accompany our work from now on, and to which we are indebted.

Although Auschwitz was the death of poetry, which had already been assassinated a thousand times throughout history, Françoise Davoine and Jean-Max Gaudillière remind us that only through the poem can the incurable wounds of history be thought.[5]

Your friend,

Notes

1 For the concept of subjective object and subject, see the Winnicottian theory presented in Letter 20, *Hysteria*.

2 Regarding the importance and meaning of the place of the witness, see Letter 14, *Paranoia as seen by Philippe Réfabert.*

3 The question of the treatment of the dead is examined in Letter 32, *Totalitarian regimes and psychosis.*

4 For a detailed discussion of the concept of the demonic as outlined by Freud, see Letter 11, *Reading* Beyond the Pleasure Principle: *the insistence of Eros.*

5 Attentive readers no doubt noticed the difference between the precautions Gisela Pankow takes in her encounters with psychotics, and the hand-to-hand psychic combat with madness described by Davoine and Gaudillière. I would say that Pankow presents a method, while the other two authors present a style. This style presupposes the integration of Pankow's method, which deals with the conditions of proximity to the massacred zones in the subject.

Winnicott's contemporaneity and psychoanalytic societies

My dear friend,

The myth that Winnicott was a naïve man unconcerned with the real world is just that: a myth. You can judge for yourself from what follows.

Excerpt from Winnicott's letter to the Editor of *The Times*, 6 November 1946:

> Already a Minister of Health has been the one to decide not to include osteopathy and faith-healing in the state medical service. From the doctor's point of view this is exactly as bad as if he had decided the other way. That such decisions should rest with whomever the parliamentary majority happens to give charge of [...] health [...], is a depressing thought. [...] A body of people, untrained in scientific method but elected because of the complexion of their political views, had finally destroyed a good thing out of ignorance.[1]

Excerpt from a letter to Melanie Klein, dated 17 November 1952:

> Dear Melanie,
>
> I want to write to you about last Friday evening's meeting, in order to try to turn it into something constructive.
>
> There is no doubt that my criticism of Mrs. Rivière was not only a straightforward criticism based on objective observation but also it was coloured by the fact that it was exactly here that her analysis failed me [...]
>
> I personally think that it is very important that your work should be restated by people discovering in their own way and presenting what they discover in their own language. It is only in this way that the language will be kept alive. If you make the stipulation that in future only your language shall be used for the statement of other people's discoveries then the language becomes a dead language, as it has already become in the Society [...] The worst example, perhaps, was C's paper, in which he simply bandied about a lot of that which has now come to be known as Kleinian stuff without giving any impression of having an appreciation of the processes personal to the patient. Your ideas will only live in so far as they are rediscovered and reformulated by original people in the psychoanalytical movement and outside it. Every

original worker requires a coterie in which there can be a resting place from controversy and in which one can feel cosy. The danger is, however, that the coterie develops a system based on the defence of the position gained by the original worker, in this case yourself.[2]

This degree of awareness is doubtless related to working with children. How many of the psychoanalysts we know are capable of such honesty with themselves and their colleagues, while remaining concerned with public matters? Today we are confronted with the paradoxical situation where the harder a psychoanalyst tries to play a role in his cultural milieu, the more he blends into the societal environment. What exactly is this environment?

Today, we live in a world where we are constantly informed, by television, that there are ideal worlds, perfect and flawless, that are imagined for us while we live the reality of our actual lives with the joys, sufferings and troubles. As Serge Daney, French critic and essayist, put it: "I became aware that everything hateful about television sprung from a common source. Whether dispensing 'culture' or providing entertainment, all program animators have the same sickly sweet way of feeling sorry for us, since we have no one but them to compensate for the tragic emptiness of our supposedly insipid lives. They make us feel that without them we would be nothing."[3]

The world of television presents itself as a world beyond reproach; as for us, we must set aside the habitual modes of thinking that enable us to live, if we wish to gain any understanding of what is happening before our eyes, and which has a profound effect on our lives. First, we must hear the language used by the television to speak to us, the language of advertising – before we can interpret it. But such an interpretation will only interest a small number of select individuals, and has no chance of bringing into question the object of its focus. This impossibility of bringing something into question radically upsets the relation a person over fifty can have to reflection. Despite the fact that we witnessed the failure of a certain version of Marxism, the end of a polarised world, the proclaimed end of all ideologies, our reflexes and old habits persist. For instance, as we live through our experiences, the habit of building practical knowledge, building practice of knowledge that can exert an influence on the Real, that can have a certain hold on it; in short, thinking that can *also* be assessed by its effectiveness as a mode of thinking. But today this type of assessment has lost is relevance, and not only on television.

Television was believed to democratise information by rendering it immediately accessible. The most complex issues are flattened by images that, instead of making a place for the Real, transform it into melodrama. As a result, all topics acquire equal value.

Thus, the first thing to do is to acknowledge this situation which has assigned and is assigning a different place to reflection in the cultural edifice. We would need to imitate George Perec, the French novelist, who scrupulously noted each object he saw: its form; its location; the material of which it was made; its volume in space. While for Perec this was a method of apprehending and preserving the

Real, what we need to do now is find a means of understanding how the times we live in hide the Real and steal it from us.

But it is not always possible to recover from the elimination of a critical sense. This lack of recovery is the characteristic feature of postmodernism, the prized invention of its proponents. In this sense, some psychoanalysts were the first postmodernists.

Seen in this light, psychoanalysis is antiquated. Wladimir Granoff asked himself one day, nurturing no illusions, if psychoanalysis could still constitute a commitment to a mode of life. The work of the "elders" supports the possibility that the answer is yes for some individuals of your generation, who are now undertaking the practice of psychoanalysis. But what will psychoanalysts become when this work will no longer constitute a life commitment?

I am not going to comment on the petty and widespread project of acquiring social status or of having a deathly hold on others through transference, people have not waited for the advent of psychoanalysis to be contemptuous or to act like scoundrels. But I will acknowledge an undeniable fact: for some people, psychoanalysis has become an opportunity to "be an intellectual" with no need to think for oneself. The courage to have original ideas has been replaced by the brilliance of the model student loyal to the master's teachings. A passion for the unexpected has been replaced by flawless memorisation of a metaphysical system trusted to explain everything. As a result, it is not surprising that this obsessional guardianship of the dogma ends up turning knavery into an ideal. The petty bureaucrat of the analytic machine is fascinated by his perverse double, and when the latter brags about seeing a hundred patients a day, instead of calling such vaunting by its rightful name, that is, the flaunting of murder, the parrot will try hard to take it as proof of an industrial revolution in psychoanalysis.

This perversity is beginning to spread. More and more often one sees young people who call themselves psychoanalysts and who, despite their youth, are already disillusioned before having had any illusions. Not so long ago, most of us had another occupation before deciding to become psychoanalysts. Now, one can become a psychoanalyst while still a student in university, and what is there to prevent us from starting this training in nursery school, in the near future? The fact that more and more of those who are supposed to treat others say that patients bore them, and that they are bored with life, no longer shocks anyone. It has become an acceptable fact: there are so-called psychoanalysts who are tired of being analysts. Not only does this go unquestioned, it is now beginning to create a link, to be a sign of membership in an alleged community.

All this points to the fact that stupidity is the most obvious sign of the decadence that concerns us all. And if this ideology becomes generalised, it would not be surprising to see a Victims' Bureau or Public Hygiene Office prohibit the practice of psychoanalysis. Not surprising at all – on the contrary, it could be an opportunity to relegate Freudian psychoanalysis to clandestinity, in accordance with the wish expressed by Serge Leclaire[4] in 1981, just before he transformed psychoanalysis into the first reality show on French television.

In a field threatened with, if not actually in the process of, being abandoned, what can the example of Winnicott, a psychoanalyst working with children, contribute? Nothing overwhelming, of course, but rather little things, common sense details of an immoderate practice whose ethics remained precarious. Let us review them at random, like messages flung into the ocean with the energy and hope characteristic of despair.

First this: living is a craft, difficult, of course, but exciting. And this craft concerns psychoanalysis. Winnicott was also a paediatrician, and he worked with borderline patients and psychotics. This made him particularly qualified to hold highly responsible positions in the international psychoanalytic community. As a result, he was well placed to help us remember that psychoanalysts are fragile beings. We have all been prematurely ousted from childhood and were, to varying degrees, "wise babies" who had to be therapists to our unhappy parents. Later, after we had been in analysis, we established or joined psychoanalytic institutions in hopes that they would be kindergartens where we could play and continue to treat the children in distress we once were. The history of psychoanalysis in France and elsewhere is the story of the successes and failures of these kindergartens which we call, with great pretension – as children are wont to do – psychoanalytic societies.

Psychoanalytic institutions can only transmit a code of ethics if they are places where we can play and attempt to heal our incurable narcissistic wounds.

Winnicott gives the example of a psychoanalyst, who even though he is scholar, is never an intellectual, and makes it clear that he has everything to gain by living up to the expectations of a poet. Psychoanalysis is a therapeutic craft. In other words, it is not a matter of choosing between Freud and Ferenczi, but rather choosing Freud and Ferenczi. Nor is it a choice between Freud and Lacan, but a matter of choosing Freud and Lacan. And Granoff. And Perrier. And Pankow. And Aulagnier. And Dolto. And Neyraut. And McDougall, Davoine, Gaudillière, Réfabert. And Radmila Zygouris, Pierre Delaunay, Monique Schneider, Michel Tort, Pierre Kammerer,[5] and others as well. The aim is not to achieve some kind of theoretical eclecticism, but to reunite all the exceptional examples of those who testified and are testifying to the enormous psychic task of retaking possession of Freud's discovery and inventions.

Winnicott shows us that before acquiring the crucial ability to say no, that is, to separate from the other, the subject must be able to say yes, that is, to create long-lasting significant ties to another. He reminds us that although sexual desire is fundamental to all human beings, sexuality is frightening or functions as a manic defence against the absence of all hope, when the subject lacks an internal space where the experience of physical pleasure and orgasm can be integrated as an experience of excess and relaxation for the whole of the psychic apparatus. Since patients still seek the help of a psychoanalyst because they were unloved or because they are unable, or are no longer able, to love, it is time that psychoanalysts re-examine the question of love, this old question, from two perspectives inherited from Freud: a mother's love which includes the father and which leads to life, and a mother's love which leads to death. It is also time that psychoanalysts recognise the sudden arrival of love in someone's life for the salutary catastrophe that it is.

Winnicott reminds us that before a psychoanalyst can be regarded as "a subject who is supposed to know" (as Lacan puts it), the patient must consider him a subject who is alive. This mode of presence involves a willingness to participate in play. In Winnicott's view, to play is to think.

Winnicott also points out the real importance of pregenital sexuality. It is neither second-class sexuality, nor purely imaginary in nature. Instead, it is the source of all subsequent sublimation, after having been the kernel that concentrated the intensity of an Ego that emerges, in his perception, prior to the mirror stage.

Today, scandals linked to love and sexuality are still omitted from our cultural institution, although an attractive façade masks this omission. As a result, a psychoanalyst true to his vocation can identify with René Char's remark: "I practice an avant-garde profession."

Let us conclude. The history of tomorrow's psychoanalysis is being written today. But it is at least partly up to us, psychoanalysts, to see to it that it continues to be non-degradable: that is, a practice of the ephemeral. More specifically, that it remains a human enterprise that makes possible and brings into existence the *instant* that assembles the conditions needed for the emergence of the ephemeral that makes encounters possible, this fleeting instant without which no encounter can take place.

Warmest regards,

Notes

1 Winnicott, D. W. (1987), *The Spontaneous Gesture: Selected Letters of D. W. Winnicott* (ed. Rodman, F. R.). Cambridge, MA: Harvard University Press, p. 9.
2 Ibid, pp. 33–35.
3 Daney, S. (1988), *Le salaire du zappeur*. Paris: Ramsey-Poche Cinéma/Libération.
4 Serge Leclaire was a French psychoanalyst; a disciple of Lacan, he distanced himself from the latter by creating his own psychoanalytic theory.
5 Eminent French clinicians.

Psychic health

Dear friend,

What else could you have done? This woman was lucky to meet you, to meet someone who could distinguish between psychopathology and that which is simply human and which we all share.

Recently, I had a similar request from a patient, a man who had suddenly lost his beloved. He was in despair. He screamed with pain, lamented the uselessness of his love, the absurdity of life. I said I would try to help him. I did not say "help you go through this experience" because when one is experiencing such pain, it feels as if it will last forever. But I said right away: "The way you are reacting to your wife's death, the extent of your suffering, your anger with life, your breakdown – these are all signs of psychic health. You say that you are sick with pain. How could you not be when you just lost the person you loved most? You say that you don't want to go on living. How could you want to go on when the person who is your support in life suddenly disappears? If you were not sick with pain, if you did not want to die, the love you felt for your beloved would not have existed, would not have been real. Psychic health is what allows us to experience what we must experience. What would be unhealthy would be to block this pain, what would be pathological would be to deny the suffering and loss."

The man was both relieved and disappointed. I guessed the relief when I sensed the appeasement my words had produced. Appeasement and fatigue. A feeling of enormous fatigue was replacing unbearable emotional tension. I felt very relieved to know that this fatigue had come over him. Because fatigue is a sign that the body is reclaiming its rights, it is a brief pause in the present moment. A state of presence to the present moment, no matter how short-lived, offers respite.

Consciously, his predominant feeling was disappointment. He had hoped against hope that someone could cure him of this abandonment, of this void. In fact, his insane hope had been that he could be cured of life. At the same time, of course, he knew this to be impossible. But he must have said to himself, why not chance it, perhaps he would find a psychopathologist who would agree that all this suffering was harmful, that it must be removed, like a cyst, with antidepressants if need be, so that his good mood could return and things could be "fine" again. The advantage provided by such a dangerous therapist would be the inclusion of hate, or rather, a place where he could bring his abstract hate of destiny, where he could play it up. The unconscious never makes mistakes and our friend, who recognised that what he felt was something he had to go through, would have been aware of the trickery – which perhaps would not have prevented him from using it for a time, like a reprieve, a placebo against solitude, to give himself the illusion of being less lonely.

For an analyst, the common sense attitude, therefore the simplest and, as a result, the most difficult, the most complex, is that suggested by Winnicott: the promise to be there, the categorical statement that it is possible to be alone in the presence of another, to be alone with another. From this perspective, seeking a psychoanalyst – especially following the loss of a loved one – is particularly well advised. (Of course, loss does not always mean death.)

So he took his time, settled into time. He asked if he could smoke a cigarette. I had the impression that his mouth was dry, as it would be after some great effort. I said yes and offered him a glass of water, which he accepted. I had brought the whole bottle and he drank half of it. Afterwards, he lit his cigarette. I waited. I knew he appreciated my waiting, in all senses of the word. Then I thought that he would cry, and fall asleep afterwards. Finally, I understood that, on the contrary, he was awakening, coming out of a trance, emerging from a strange space between dream and hallucination. Through the pleasure he took in the cigarette, probably the first he was smoking "just for himself", for no reason, in a long time, he was allowing himself to have some respite.

Now solidly settled in his body, he was testing one final strategy: "So, if I kill myself, in your opinion that would be proof of my excellent psychic health?"

I liked the tone he used to say this because it revealed the subtlety of his intelligence. He was deeply sad, exhausted, but one could glimpse the humour that would underlay his question in other circumstances. A question that was only half serious. He was trying to trap me, but half hoping he would not succeed. It was also his way of checking if I was telling the truth, of evaluating if everything I had said – and which had touched him – was not merely patter coming from an experienced psychoanalyst who knows some tricks.

I liked this aggressiveness which testified to his presence in the moment, and to a return to narcissistic foundations. He was placing his chips into the pot, which meant that he still had chips of his own. It was as if he was telling me: "Very well, you succeeded in comforting me, I feel better right now, here. But I don't think that's enough reason for me to trust you. Great suffering does not prevent one from thinking. So I am thinking and I ask myself if I can take you at face value."

As I write this, dear friend, I am surprised, once again, at the enormous quantity of things that can be thought of without being put into words, and at the intensity of unnamed feelings we witness in such short spaces of time.

I replied: "Psychic health makes it possible to consider suicide, to not have to avoid it." I could also have said: "I don't know you, and so I don't know if you can survive this loss." That would have been true. But true and violent. And the difference between a psychoanalyst and an ordinary trustworthy interlocutor is that, theoretically, a psychoanalyst knows that one cannot say just anything to anyone, at any moment.

Everything I have been discussing is crucial to the ethics of psychoanalysis; and in these types of situations in which the suffering of the subject is nothing other than his participation in the human condition, our attempt to treat his experience as non-pathological is only the beginning of a series of other difficulties. Difficulties of a theoretical and technical nature, which in turn lead to other ethical considerations.

To be continued.

Your friend,

Trust

Dear friend,

Let me continue where I left off in my last letter.

When the psychoanalyst succeeds in providing a setting that allows the subject to be alone in the presence of another, in time the subject will be able to speak, to conceptualise his pain.

I am thinking of Guimaraes Rosa, the Brazilian writer who insisted several times, in *Diadorim*, that: "Living is very dangerous." Moreover, a psychoanalyst is someone who knows that when a person speaks, he changes. Unavoidably, as he speaks, the subject discovers ties between the experience he is going through and his past experiences, including those of his childhood. How could it be otherwise?

Each of us has one life to live and it is inescapable that most of what concerns us in the present resonates with similar experiences in our past.

What the psychoanalyst does with these "resonances" is not a simple matter. The theoretical issues involved are intimately bound with the ethics of our work. I will try to describe, in the simplest way possible, all the paradoxes present in this situation.

I am thinking of the woman who came to see you, shattered, after the death of her son. Because it is true that the pain caused by the loss of a loved one is not a psychic illness, once we have said this to the person who comes to see us we cannot contradict ourselves by putting in place an analytical protocol consisting of at least three sessions a week, with the scheduling and financial commitments involved. Since psychoanalysis is a practice of the spoken word, specifically of the true weight of words, a practice which teaches that words are also a level of reality, we must give precedence to the logic of representations, a logic completely faithful to the manner in which the spoken is constructed. As long as the logic of representations has precedence, as long as we let the exchange of *words construct the frame*, all the circulating affects and emotions nourish the exchange and contribute to psychic elaboration. But if stupidity, weakness or a need for control causes us to overlook this principle in the name of feelings we might be experiencing, the entire sequence of exchanges breaks down, becoming nothing but chatter. The breakdown is caused by disappointment with the fact that the psychoanalyst did not fulfil his function – because he did not keep his word.

In short, as far as the woman you refer to is concerned, I believe that once you stated that she was not ill – which was true at the time – you could not engage in an analytic process with her.

I know that what I am saying may seem radical, excessive and rigid. But believe me when I say that this is not a question of will, be it ours or that of our patients. What is at stake is the inflexible nature of the unconscious, where the value of words holds undisputed sway.

Maintaining this position is no easy task. Particularly when, as in the case of the woman you describe, major psychic stumbling blocks emerge along the way and we know that the best method for dealing with them is analysis. It is even harder when we have the impression that we misinterpreted the initial request – which seems to be your predicament, due to a mistaken diagnosis that might, for example, have obscured the pathological aspect of the mourning process. But even in these extreme situations, it is important not to compromise.

Remaining true to what one has said even if that commitment was based on an error, is what makes it possible to continue a process, analytic or not, in which thought will be recognised as having the power to seize the reality of both desire and death. I have had occasion to say: "I think you would benefit from undertaking analysis (to work on such and such a problem). But I cannot do this work with you. You came to see me because of an experience that was not a pathology, and our meetings concern that experience. In order to respect our agreement, you have to see another analyst. Of course, I can recommend some people I trust completely."

So far, I have never been wrong about the pathological nature of a mourning process. If this should happen tomorrow, my response would be the same. I would say that I was wrong, that the way in which the subject is experiencing the death of his loved one is probably rooted in pathological deprivation in his childhood, and that psychoanalysis is needed. And I would add that I cannot be the analyst with whom he can work because this was not what I believed the nature of his initial request to be, and that this misunderstanding should be respected.

Why be so rigorous? If I do this, am I not repeating the trauma by inflicting another loss? Would it not be more reasonable to believe that the subject gives us access to his pathological stumbling blocks thanks to the trust acquired in the course of the work we did together? Is there not a sadistic dimension to the analyst's refusal to continue, which will be experienced as yet another abandonment?

These objections are foreseeable and have a certain relevance. In effect, they define the line to be drawn between other forms of therapy and psychoanalysis, where the analyst's place in the relation is that of a *subject in his own right*. His commitments and his errors are part of the work accomplished, since both can serve to reveal the mode used by the patient to build his or her relation to the other.

Obviously, we have to recognise that the refusal to continue can be traumatic, and that we must let the subject take the time he needs. We are helped in this by a certain crucial knowledge. We know that every human subject determines, at least in part, what happens to him, in the same way that the dreamer "writes" the script of his dream. We can say, with reasonable assurance, that the traumatic clinical situation was enacted by the subject. We can agree that the text was supplied by his unconscious, but this does not change anything. Or rather, since we, psychoanalysts, are well acquainted with the unconscious, we ask ourselves what is it that the subject is playing out, what *is being repeated* in this *dramatisation* where a satisfactory relation – in this case, the relation with the analyst – turns into a source of suffering and becomes impossible.[1]

In other words, for consciousness, in the dwelling of the Ego, everything seems tragic, but what is the unconscious script which holds the subject hostage? And, if the analyst agrees to continue working with this subject in the new setting – a situation which would be as paradoxical as the refusal to undertake analysis – why not consider the possibility that the new paradox set in place may permanently prevent the subject from establishing a genuine relation to speech? Can we forget the traps that masochism, present in all of us, is able to invent so that nothing changes, so that life remains embedded in the monotony of the unchanged?

Based on the logic of representations, meaning cannot be brought into doubt. If, after having told someone that the pain he is experiencing is part of his emotional health, we agree to engage in analytic work, what credence can be given to the initial statement? Is it strategy of seduction designed to trap the subject in a dependent relationship? Is it a lie? And in addition, how can one believe in the possibility of another who is trustworthy if the words that brought new life are betrayed by the one who spoke them?

There is one more thing left to consider. Because we are not in the business of experimenting, we do not disqualify the moment of the encounter when the subject came to us in good emotional health. Even if later, as was the case in your work with this woman, pathological mourning becomes apparent, there is no reason to discount the period when the pain was related to the actual, present experience. What we have to tell the subject is this: that these two levels are both valid – the one where he was reacting within the limits of emotional health, and the one where the pathological aspect became dominant. Therefore, accepting to work with him in analysis would mean that you no longer consider him capable of emotional health. He may or may not understand. But no matter, the important thing is for him to hear this. In any case, his unconscious knows.

This is not all. More in my next letter.

Your friend,

Note

1   See the clinical case presented in Letter 10, *Winnicott's concept of* continuity of being: *transference and treatment of trauma.*

The divine part of man

Dear friend,

The reason for discussing the relation between psychoanalysis and psychopathology in such detail is that this relation is fundamental. We often forget that the scandal of Freudian thought, which still exists today, lies in the assertion of infantile sexuality, its amorality and its insistence that the normal and the pathological are not to be placed in a hierarchical relation.

Regarding this last point, we are forced to see that the dialogue between psychiatry and psychoanalysis, so productive in the 1970s in Europe, has ultimately resulted in a narrow, phobic medical practice, which has unfortunately attracted some of our colleagues, disheartened by the silence of their analysts.

Let me then come back to our work with this pain whose nature is not pathological, in a psychoanalytic setting. After discussing the situation you encountered, where a serious psychic pathology became apparent, I would like to shed more light on the less complex scenario I described to you in the letter before last. This type of situation requires careful handling as well. Moreover, the difficulties encountered by the subject in *separating* from the interlocutor he has found in the analyst illustrate a number of interesting issues to consider.

What types of ties does the analytic process create when someone comes to see you one or two times a week to share the effects of a borderline situation likely to occur in every life? Upon reflection, one can quickly conclude that these are ties of *friendship*, but it is only through experience that we realise that this very fact, this nature of the relationship, is what will make separation possible, and make it possible to end this very particular kind of analytic process. In other words, if we remain faithful to the Freudian idea of continuity between the normal and the pathological, this work conducted in a context of emotional health illustrates the ethical paradigm for every psychoanalysis.

This raises a question I have often tried to answer: is there a difference between this type of analytic work and a relation of friendship?

Let me remind you what Freud says about the relation between friendship and psychoanalysis in *Analysis Terminable and Interminable*: "Not every good relation between an analyst and his subject during and after analysis was to be regarded as transference. There were also friendly relations which were based on reality and which proved to be viable." Let me point out, as well, that this statement echoes his assertion that we must not reject the idea that transference love can be described as real love. But to come back to our discussion, if the analytic work is carried out in a context of friendship, what reason would there be for it to stop?

This question is essential. We could say that if the analytic process creates friendship, it also creates the conditions it needs to have access to and treat unconscious representations. These conditions require that the analyst be completely available to the analysand, in order to help him or her recognise, think about and work through that which is his or her crucial problem. For the person seen in analysis, this subjective focus has incalculable value; at the same time, the relational asymmetry involved is fruitful for the process and for its target, the unconscious, but is opposed to the usual practice of friendship where reciprocity and mutual reversal of positions are the rule. The apparent paradox is that the more akin to friendship the analytic relation becomes, the more difficult it is to maintain the asymmetry.

This is a natural consequence of the presence of friendship, of the coherence of its existence. There is a moment when the end of analysis and the requirement of truth in friendship coincide. We will come back to this question later.

Although this perspective has a certain relevance, it is my belief, as I said earlier, that the analytic process is not completely devoid of reciprocity. In fact, it would be surprising for this process to result in something very antithetical to its own character. The analyst and the analysand share the joy of discovering unconscious content, the joy of thinking about this discovery and working it through. (Of course, feelings other than joy are present as well. I chose to speak of joy because it evokes pleasure, jubilation, and accomplishment.) Moreover, in the course of the work that eventually allows access to unconscious representations, subjective positions may sometimes be inverted, when the analysand makes his discoveries before the analyst does. Finally, the analyst's reflection while he is engaged in supporting the patient's psychic elaboration, and in theorising what is at stake in the clinical encounter, is another pleasure that can be shared, even if it has to be considerably postponed.

If we pursue this line of thought, we are forced to conclude that asymmetry cannot be the element that distinguishes the analytic process from friendship. A friendship devoid of any asymmetry would be the equivalent of symbiosis. Experience teaches us that without an asymmetric subjective position the friend cannot be treated as another, his singularity cannot be confirmed by coming face-to-face with that which most intimately defines us as dissimilar subjects. This is what is required in order for the friend who is host to another to become a witness, he is a reference point – he gathers and accompanies the experience, he is the place of storage, of proof, of the reality status of a particular moment in someone's history. The witness signifies exteriority, the outside, divergence, and alterity from the Ego.

In other words, the alterity involved in friendship concerns role reversibility: the friend who listens today will be the one listened to tomorrow. There is no doubt that this reversibility, this type of reciprocity, is *most certainly possible* in the psychoanalytic relation. To pretend the contrary would be to deny that psychoanalysis can be transmitted, and consequently, that psychoanalysts can be trained. In fact, Freud considered the analytic process the means *par excellence* of learning the practice precisely because he presumed that there is continuity between the position of analysand and that of analyst. In short, in psychoanalysis, the reciprocity founded on role reversibility is not something rendered impossible by the *structure* of the relation between the two protagonists. The fact that it is not implemented is simply a question of *method*.

All things considered, what differentiates the analyst from a friend is the place of anxiety in the relation. Since the analyst strives to alleviate, before eliminating altogether, the pathological causes of anxiety, since he strives to contain or defuse the destructuring effects of inevitable or necessary anxiety on a deprived or fragile Ego, he creates the illusion that he can constitute a barrier against anxiety, or guarantee its future disappearance. Although, admittedly, this illusion plays a role in the analysis, allowing fundamental structuring of the psychic space, when analysis is ending this illusion must be redefined, and reconsidered, and anxiety must be recognised for what it is: the twin of desire, a tool for identifying limits; and the stimulus for widening the field of possibilities. (I am well aware that the conception of analysis I am presenting is not shared by most of our colleagues.)[1]

The conclusion of the analytic process with this man who came to see me after the death of his wife illustrates a type of resistance present when the relation with the analyst is ending – even if the process was not, strictly speaking, psychoanalysis.

We had been meeting for several months. He had resumed the course of his life, the pain had become more bearable, and he had projects underway. I wanted to know why he continued to see me. To my surprise, he said: "I will stop coming when all the anxiety is gone."

Since he had an excellent knowledge of the Bible, I invented the following story for him – and often used it subsequently:

> When God finished creating the world, he wanted to rest. But that was easier said than done, since God suffered from insomnia – understandably, of course.
>
> Being God, he quickly realised that what prevented him sleeping was anxiety. So, to put an end to his divine insomnia, he had a divine idea: he decided to share it with all future generations of humans on Earth. He lost no time carrying out his plan, and he was able to sleep and dream. Therefore, anxiety is the divine part of man. This is why, instead of fighting it, we must learn to welcome this prestigious guest and put his presence to good use.

Warm regards,

Note

1 Letter 19, *Transference and friendship*, deals with this question as well.

Loup Verlet

Psychoanalysis as a revolution of the conceptual framework

My dear friend,

Your ex-religious fanatic patient first reminded me of an analysis that exhausted me, as well as two supervisors I had at the time, both exceptional. I started to conduct analysis with a twenty-five year-old man who suffered repetitive asthma attacks and sometimes needed urgent hospitalisation two or three times a week. Using Pankow's method of therapy, I had him make drawings and clay sculptures, and in a short time the asthma disappeared. I was very proud of my therapeutic prowess – but I had no idea what was going on.

This situation lasted for years. He spoke essentially of two things: his childhood in a house full of brothers and sisters, and his present life. During the analysis, he met a woman, had three children and built a successful professional life. And yet, for me, none of this made sense. When I started my first supervision concerning this patient, I had already understood, before meeting the "elder", that I held the place of the asthma-control medication Ventolin, that I was not a person but rather a bizarre, heterogenous object that acted as a narcissistic crutch. I had also understood the perverse dimension of transference.

In addition, I have to mention the very particular emotional atmosphere of the sessions. Although at the end of each of our meetings I felt completely desperate – because, in my view, we had made no progress – during the session I felt well, entirely available to him and interested. The pathetic style he sometimes displayed did not diminish his intelligence, he had no sense of humour but was not overly serious, and he managed to be engaging without being outright likeable.

At the end of one year, the first "elder" jokingly suggested that I throw this man out the window. But since both of us knew the tragic consequences of such abandonment, we agreed that I would probably keep seeing this patient all my life. And we worked on another analysis, which actually had time to be concluded before the dead-end situation with this patient was sorted out.

With the second "elder", things went more quickly. He praised me for my patience and questioned what he called my selflessness. Together, we tried to identify possible "benefits" I might be drawing from this impasse, technical errors or misunderstandings that might have occurred earlier in the analysis – subjects which had already been explored in my work with the previous supervisor. Very soon, the second "elder" told me that all of this bored him deeply and that, just like me, he was running out of ideas concerning this patient. He suggested we work on another analysis.

The patient was also running out of anything useful to bring to the process. One day, he lay down and said: "My father died during the night. This doesn't change anything." I stopped the session – it is the only short session I conducted in my life. He was surprised, but my initiative did not lead to a more elaborate discussion about his father. Another time, after a long silence, which was unusual for him, he started listing things that came to his mind: a cloud; the sea; a ship; some fish; the sky; the moon; the sun. I said that I had the impression he was listing the elements that might have composed a child's drawing that he had not been able to draw as a child. To my astonishment, he burst into tears. After years of analysis, this was the first expression of intense emotion he had shown.

For the entire duration of the analysis, up until then, I had seen him on Tuesdays, Thursdays and Fridays. Due to our respective schedules, I had changed our appointments to Monday, Wednesday and Friday – which I liked better, since the sessions were more evenly spaced throughout the week. One Friday, as he was leaving, I said: "See you on Monday." He replied, obviously surprised: "But next Monday is Easter Monday." And, who knows why, I answered: "This is not church, so see you Monday."

The following Monday he came to his appointment and told me how stunned he had been by my remark. And he added something regarding the period he had spent in seminary school. Now, it was my turn to be stunned and I told him how amazed I was that he had never mentioned attending seminary school. He informed me that he had lived at the seminary between the ages of eight and twenty-four – that is, until six months before starting analysis with me. I was overwhelmed with emotion. As calmly as possible, with the diplomacy of someone who can handle something both very fragile and extremely dangerous, even explosive, I asked him why, in the course of all these years, he had never said anything about this lengthy period of his life. He replied that there was nothing to say about the seminary, that it was always the same thing, the same boredom, the same routine. Could he tell me something about this routine? "Well, like in all seminaries, when you are small you get fucked, and when you are older you fuck others." This terse statement marked the start of our analytic work.[1]

Of course, I am not suggesting that you pay no attention to the perverse dimension of your religious patient, but the most important thing about these subjects is the difficulty they have changing their frame of thought. As I had already seen, for my patient I was a substitute for Ventolin; what I had not seen, was that I was – above all – God… a particular kind of God, of course – the fucked fucker – but still a God.

What I want to discuss in this letter is this difficulty of changing one's frame of reference. To do so, I will rely on the reflections of my friend Loup Verlet.

I met Loup Verlet by chance, when I was attending seminars given by the "Fédération des ateliers de psychanalyse". I was curious to listen to a presentation given by someone who was going to talk about music, an unusual subject for this type of meeting. But I was cautious: I sat at the back of the room, near the door, so that I could leave discreetly, just in case... Loup Verlet was talking about, among other things, the relation between a singer acting in a play and the pianist accompanying him – in this case, himself. Without insisting, he was comparing the conditions of this exchange to those of the dialogue between the psychoanalyst and the patient. It was not an analogy, nor was it a metaphor, but rather the indication of a resonance or a coincidence. For me, the essence of what he was saying lay in his relationship with music, which I sensed to be solid and intimate; as I listened, I felt he was sharing with us his personal manner of being an analyst, and this was gently – yes, gently – bringing to my mind certain difficulties I was having at the time with some of my patients.

But the most important thing for me was the quality of his presence, which combined serenity, strength and a ceaseless whirl of ideas.

I was certain that he had come to psychoanalysis after extensive involvement with music, an involvement I presumed to be ongoing. Because I am convinced that the practice of psychoanalysis should follow another type of practice, and because Verlet reinforced my belief, I asked a friend we had in common to tell me more about this touching character. What I learned astonished me even more.

My friend confirmed that music was fundamental in Loup Verlet's life, but she informed me that he was also a physicist. Liquid state physics. He was research director at the National Center for Scientific Research. She was surprised that I had not heard of his book *La Malle de Newton* (Newton's Trunk). It is about a trunk that had belonged to Newton and which, locked and intact, had survived for centuries and was discovered in the 1930s. The book talks about Newton and the things stored in his trunk.

I went over to the table where a bookstore had set out various books. I told myself that a work about Newton, written by an analyst who was also a physicist, must be fascinating. The book was there. "Bibliothèque des sciences humaines", published by Gallimard. The same collection in which I had read Foucault – *Les Mots et les Choses* (The Order of Things) and *L'Archéologie du savoir* (The Archaeology of Knowledge) – as well as Devreux, Galbraith, Lefort, Panofsky, and which also publishes authors like Aron, Dumézil and Louis Dumont, whom I have not read.

On the back cover, I read: "In 1936, a public auction revealed the contents of a trunk in which Newton had stored his manuscripts. To everyone's surprise, next to the learned man's scientific texts, there were also biblical exegesis and texts on alchemy. This revealed not only a hidden side of an exceptional scientific genius, but, beyond the mystery of one man, the shared secret governing our universe, as demonstrated by this original interpretation of the birth of modern physics." And further down: "As witnessed by his secret writings, Newton was constantly inspired by the global vision of a world governed by the invisible, but he sacrificed this vision in order to found his law of universal gravitation on mathematical principles."

At first, one might think that the book is a reflection on the relation between the subject of science and the subject of the unconscious. Of course, Loup Verlet discusses this in his book, but his project is far more ambitious. The last sentence of the back cover text summarises it as follows: "Newton's trunk lies before us gaping and empty. And yet, is it not here that, to answer the call of an absent God, we must invent our answers?" This, then, is how I met Loup Verlet.[2]

I will not presume to give you a summary of this book which must be read slowly and attentively, to prolong the joy of accompanying its powerful pondering as it unfolds, expressed with the simplicity and clarity acquired after extensive reflection on a wide range of subjects. I will try to present this reflection based on some of the questions stemming from the surprising themes the author formulates and develops.

As Loup Verlet points out, Newton dispenses "science of the obligation to respond to any demands from other domains and […] from this point on, makes it accountable only to itself" (p. 219). Newton considers that "the principles on which theory is built are founded exclusively on experience" (p. 244). Loup Verlet adds that:

> Despite Newton's intention to found his physics proceeding by induction based on measurable reality, his theory contained two essential elements that could not be supported by any experience: absolute time and absolute space, which had to be postulated in order to produce an unequivocal formulation of the fundamental equation of [his theory of] dynamics. Thus, the spacio-temporal context of Newtonian theory testified to divine presence in the world: "by being ever-present everywhere", God "constitutes space and duration". Newton's descendants were to forget the religious aspect of a hypothesis that appeared to be the essential foundation of the theoretical edifice. Kant was to see this as the prototype of the *a priori* conditions for knowledge, which precede any experience and can be called "transcendental".
>
> We might ask ourselves how [Newton's] postulated empiricism, which led him, essentially, to replace religion with an atheist science, was compatible with religious faith." The solution to this paradox lies in something we have already discussed. "For Newton, the primacy granted to experience is not a sign of distancing oneself from God but, on the contrary, the best way to come closer to Him, as much as it is possible for Man to do so.
>
> (p. 246)

In other words, by founding science as an autonomous field of knowledge, Newton eliminates the religious order. In fact, he suggests a new *frame for thought*. "Fortunately for him, he does not know it: although he is fully aware of the capital importance of his discovery, he cannot assess all its consequences, which will become apparent over time, in retrospect." Why does Loup Verlet write "fortunately"?

The question of the *frame for thought* identified by Verlet constitutes a paradox: Newton cannot be aware that he is in the process of changing the conceptual framework that has been in place in his culture up until that time without destroying his own frame for reflection, the frame which allows him to establish the mathematical foundations of physics. And his personal frame for reflection is that of his era, in which God and religion are at the centre. One of the divisive functions of the trunk is to keep alive the two aspects of the paradox: the unthinkable called alchemy stored in the trunk, while a creative form of thinking develops a theory that renders the hypothesis of God unnecessary – a hypothesis that would have been unthinkable for Newton.

When Loup Verlet says of the heirs of Newtonian theory that they "forget the religious aspect of a hypothesis that appeared to be the essential foundation of the theoretical edifice", he is not making a criticism, but is pointing out a real difficulty that he attempts to elucidate: the difficulty for us to imagine a world, Newton's world, where religion was a compulsory reference, inescapable – where it constituted the frame for thought, the ideological framework which, for this very reason, cannot be recognised.

Verlet supports his argument by referring to Marcel Gauchet's book *Le Désenchantement du monde* (The Disenchantment of the World); the author, following in the footsteps of Max Weber, shows how "the development of religion led to the end of the religious order" (p. 226). According to Marcel Gauchet, "religion was not an epiphenomenon, but a *determining guiding principle* which throughout human history has shaped man's relation to nature, the forms of his thinking, the modes of his co-existence with other men and his political structures – and it was only starting in the 18th century (the century that followed Newton's lifetime) that religion could become a private affair in an essentially atheist society" (p. 227). Therefore, says Gauchet, "for us to understand the novelty of our present, we must make a detour via religion, the key to our entire past". All "primitive" societies are governed by religion. This universal primacy of the religious is very probably due to the conditions of existence and survival in stateless societies.

> In these societies, cohesion must be established and maintained through mechanisms needing no active intervention by society members. [This cohesion] is based on a radical distancing of fundamental principles and, at the same time, on the complete abolition of this distance, since these principles govern all actions of daily life. The primitive religious order is built on a founding paradox enacted by religious proceedings: rites that revive the originary past, a past that, by definition, has never been present, since the immutable law it created escapes the hold of time
>
> (p. 230)

The first and perhaps most decisive stage of the process through which the religious order was transformed originated with the development of the State. Before the State, the religious division was situated between man and his origin.

Once the State was in place, "it began to be situated in the midst of men, between them, separating them from one another: [...] those who were on the side of God and those who were not" (p. 230).

The second stage of the process, in the middle of the first century BC, was "characterised by the appearance of great spiritual masters [...] who, each in his own way, oriented religion toward transcendence, by divesting the other of anthropomorphic representations [...] proposing that the search for the Other take place not in the outside world, but inside oneself." The next step after a division between men is an internal division within man, "*a fracture of the being*" (p. 230).

The third stage started with the *birth of God*, thanks to an obscure nomadic tribe led by Moses. For the first time in history, man was accountable to God for his deeds.

The last stage consisted of the emergence of Christianity, which Gauchet sees as *the religion to end religion*. Christ is:

> consubstantial with the Father as on the divine plane, and consubstantial with man on the human plane [...] In the case of Christianity, the founding paradox takes a central place. Psychic and institutional forces that normally contribute to repress the sense of absurd on which faith is built were given free reign and they reinforced instability and dissociation. Once proclaimed, Christ's nature immediately placed the Christian in an awkward position in the world. It subjected him to the contradictory *demand of remaining outside a world in which he must accept to live*. As Gauchet correctly points out, this is the inescapable doctrine of explicit incarnation, the constitutive aporia of Christian life: how to escape from a world which is impossible to leave
>
> (p. 230).

But what, might you ask, does all this have to do with psychoanalysis? Loup Verlet replies: "Regarding frame for thought (a concept which remains unclear except in physics, but which I discuss in an upcoming book), changing this frame (in analysis, for example) is very problematic. When the old frame becomes shaky but the new frame is not yet in place, the "founder" finds himself in a very uncomfortable intermediary space. How can he think in these conditions? He must construct as best he can a scaffolding of sorts, made of bits and pieces" (private correspondence).

Thus, Loup Verlet considers that psychoanalysis can cause the subject to change his frame for thought, that is, bring about a revolution. He agrees with Freud (and many others) that the analytic process can produce radical changes in the psychic life of a subject, changes that can be compared to scientific revolutions.

This book which I am presenting very summarily, but which is extremely rich, illustrates Verlet's lively reflection and, I hope, the centrality of the question of frame for thought. Reading Loup Verlet helped me to understand why attempts to relate the sphere of the unconscious to the social sphere have been unsuccessful. Most often, these attempts were based on two lines of reasoning: Marxism and psychoanalysis. Loup Verlet, on the other hand, allowed me to build bridges between the two fields starting from the *inconceived content* that governs the frame for thought of either the individual subject or the social subject. The two conceptual frameworks are different, of course, just as the unthinkable is different in each case. What is important, however, is to have identified, for each field, a constitutive paradoxical relation between the two terms *what remains unthought in every conceptual framework.*

Setting in place a new conceptual framework is a frightening experience for the subject. To help you understand this experience, I suggest that we use the concept of an *interim*. This interim is the time needed between the moment when the subject starts to abandon a frame for thought and the moment when a new set of references is constituted. To describe this interim, Verlet uses the concepts of crossing and paradox. When a subject takes the risk of going beyond the limits imposed by a conceptual paradigm, and ventures towards the unthinkable that doing so involves, as does any "creative thinking, the more or less radical suspension of the epistemological premises on which the frame for thought is built" (p. 283) and requires that he "seek grounding *in that which (does) not yet (exist)*" (p. 354).

This suspension may last no more than an instant, in which case it "is reversible and usually goes unnoticed" (p. 283). But when this suspension lasts much longer, for instance, when "the object of the passion of the [subject] offers the same resistance as that of a child to his parents, [when this object] becomes akin to an autonomous living being with whom true dialogue is established" (p. 71), then the founding subject can maintain himself "for years above the abyss of logic that *separates* two incompatible frames for thought" (p. 286, my emphasis). (Of course, in the psychoanalytic setting, the analysand can count on transference and on the analyst.)

Verlet emphasises that crossing the boundaries of a frame for thought means plunging into the paradox of a *discontinuity* of logic. To conceptualise this paradox, Loup Verlet refers to the notion of a *transitional object*. Winnicott describes this object as paradoxical because it is, at the same time, part of the internal world of the child and part of the external world. In other words, to maintain oneself in the interim above the abyss in order to cross from one set of references to another, the subject must accept the paradox of being, at the same time, inside the frame of reference whose limits he is overstepping, and inside a new frame whose limits he does not yet know.

Let us remember that, for Winnicott, psychic health, which implies creativity, is closer to madness than to normalcy. (Verlet presents a very moving description of the links between passion, madness and creativity on pages 294–295.) Winnicott's description of the relation between the *good-enough mother* – that is, not too persecutory – and her baby is also paradoxical: the mother is able to bear a necessary illness, which allows her to adapt so perfectly to her baby's psychic needs that she becomes indistinguishable from him, and at the same time is able to recognise her child as distinct from herself, as another. This ability to identify with the psychic needs of her child is an ego-support function of the mother, an ego which, in Winnicott's view as opposed to Lacan's, does not have a specular origin.[3]

You will remember that according to Lacan it is when the baby sees his image with his mother in a mirror that he recognises for the first time his own body as a unity. Lacan postulates that the origin of the ego is in the recognition of this form. He points out that recognising the image of his body as a unity precedes considerably the time when the baby will experience himself as a whole being – a subject, as we have come to say in France since Lacan. In Lacan's view, the anticipation triggered by the image of a unity in the mirror is a crucial experience for a human being. But he also believes that the ego function takes on the importance that the image had in this anticipation. This identification with the image, Lacan believes, makes the ego the origin of the structural alienation that leads us to represent ourselves as integrated and contained beings.

Loup Verlet's discussion of Lacan's *The Mirror Stage*[4] is remarkable for several reasons. Returning to Henri Wallon's work, which was Lacan's starting point, Verlet suggests that the child's experience when he encounters his image in the mirror for the first time can be seen as a paradoxical experience that might serve as a paradigm for any experience of overturning a frame for thought (pp. 293–294 and 428). At this point, Verlet makes in passing – we might say very discreetly – two enlightening remarks about Lacanian formulations, formulations that focus on a paradox that tends to remain unnoted while the anticipation of unity provided by the image creates the ego and its alienating functioning, the words spoken by the mother about this unitary bodily form create the self, the subject.

Loup Verlet does not outline the terms of the paradox, since he assumes the reader is familiar with them, he provides comments on it straight away. The first comment: "Lacan admits that a paradox cannot be overcome without a discontinuity in logic [...] But as soon as he alludes to the paradox, he attempts to ward off its devastating effects by providing three-fold protection" (p. 295). Second comment: "In *The Mirror Stage*, Lacan only exposes the founding paradox once splitting has rendered it harmless." And Verlet goes on to ask the question: "What was there prior to the paradoxical crossing that led to this splitting?" Later in the book (p. 300), having admitted the fictional character of the ego, Loup Verlet enquires in his discreet manner: "But is it detestable for this reason? Must we aim to abolish it in the name of truth?"

These remarks remind me of what Loup Verlet says about Hofstadter's law of *undecidable statements*. According to this law,

> when such a statement will be made in the course of theoretical progress, it will not be possible to establish its truth or falsity based on formally established axioms [...] Therefore, the theory is fundamentally incomplete and its development involves choices that must be made by mathematicians. Thus, mathematics *irrevocably loses its monolithic coherence*, already threatened by non-Euclidian geometry, but *it gains the advantage of developing like a living organism, branching out each time "undecidable" propositions appear.*
>
> (p. 304, my emphasis)

This comparison gives me the opportunity, once again,[5] but this time with Verlet, to point out that Lacan:

– rejected the function of the illusory, just as Newton rejected fiction;
– refused to accept the *mixing of types of logic* (p. 304) within the same space: for instance, the transitional space (although he postulated the *intrication* of the real, the symbolic and the imaginary);
– made a theoretical choice favouring a unidirectional formulation over suspension of thought, over the undecidable with its many repercussions (repertoried in Lacanian theory), a theoretical choice that excludes from the real field of encounter – and therefore from its elaboration – all anxiety or tension in the face of the unformed, which, together with risk, constitute the material needed for any creative psychic adventure.

Loup Verlet's view of what is involved in conducting analysis – thanks to his approach to the questions of setting, paradox and crossing over – leads me to reconsider Lacanian theory regarding *unbeing* as the end of analysis.[6] While the analytic process can lead to re-foundation of the subject, the question of *unbeing* is necessarily related to anxiety about crossing over, to the discontinuity between two systems of interpretation of the real. From this point of view, this moment is not that of the end of analysis but, on the contrary, it is the epicentre of the process, the moment of change when, more than ever before, the analyst's presence is needed. What I wrote you about the reorganisation of negativity is altogether pertinent here. For the duration of this intermediary period, *the analyst serves as a protective shield.*[7] The end of analysis takes place beyond this (these) crossing-point(s), of course, when anxiety is no longer a persecutory element in the thought process, and becomes, thanks to the analytic experience of crossing over, a tool for exploring the world, an ally of desire, a support for reflection and for commitment in a love relationship.

In 1935, Fernando Pessoa, the brilliant poet (and mathematician), wrote this tiny poem: "Newton's binomial formula is as beautiful as the Venus de Milo. The problem is that few people realise it." In the last 150 pages of his book, Loup Verlet succeeds in making this assertion clear to non-initiated readers like us; he arouses our passionate interest – like a good mystery novel – in the importance and the limits of Descartes' work, in the hatred that Newton conceived of him, in the reasons that led Leibniz to oppose Newton's views.

Enigma: why was Leibniz not wrong when he pointed out a contradiction between the fact that Newton denounced the idolatry of the Eucharistic rite – the miraculous union of God and nature – while his theory postulated action exerted from a distance by a body on another body across a void? (Answer: Newton avoided the question by rooting physics in mathematical language.)

Enigma: from another perspective, how was it possible for Leibniz to consider Newtonian theory, with good reason, to be a heresy, just as Voltaire would a century later? (Answer: because, although Newton asserted the permanent transcendence of God, the mathematical language created by Newton to define physics separated science from religion once and for all.)

Then there is the description of Newton's master stroke, the fact that instead of looking for the cause of gravity, he formulated its laws. And there is also a discussion of the shock that Einstein's thought provoked throughout the world. Verlet then outlines the complex relations between classical Newtonian theory and the two new theoretical frames of reference: relativity and quantum physics.

In more general terms, speaking of a founding act, Loup Verlet observes that the founder always erases the moment of crossing over. *Erasing the crossing* means erasing the *terror* that was present – that is present – when one leaves a frame for thought to advance across an abyss. This erasure is linked to the founder's concern, his desire for universal relevance: what he discovered is not new, it has always been there, his only contribution is to have recognised it. In other words, instead of acknowledging his founding act for what it is – a widening of the field of possibilities, a new relation to the reality of the world – the founder treats it as if it were a return of the repressed. By doing so, he fosters ignorance among the heirs, who will forget that each symbol, each concept, is a victory over the unthinkable (p. 356). But, whether it be "myth or reality the act of foundation requires the exclusion of an accursed part" (p. 485). The accursed part of Newton, stored in the trunk, is the fictional content – which Freud and Einstein were to reintroduce explicitly into the experience of thought.

But it would be a mistake to think that the trunk was hermetically sealed. A little before his death, Newton remarked: "I seem to have been only like a boy playing on the seashore and diverting myself in now and then finding a smoother pebble or a prettier shell than ordinary; whilst the great ocean of truth lay all undiscovered before me."[8]

And Loup Verlet adds:

> But behind this boy stands [...] a child who has not forgotten that he is a magician: in this secret part of himself, this child marvels at the miracles he brings about, the symbols he animates, the images he awakens and the ideas he creates and manipulates. It is in this enchanted realm that Newton discovers atoms, certain that they exist although he has never seen them; it is in this preserved paradise that he hopes to contemplate the presence of God in the world and grasp the action of His hand, it is in this secret den that he witnesses the spectacle of the alchemical transformations whose mysteries he attempts to comprehend.
>
> (p. 70)

I wish you dreams full of stars and galaxies.

Notes

1   I believe that all the years I spent listening to him without understanding why he continued to come to his sessions were, of course, fundamental. During this time, he brought together and connected the fragmented portions of his ego. There was the

fortuitous incident of Easter Monday, but it was the long period during which he was contained by the analyst that made it possible to speak the naked truth directly related to the horror.

2 Verlet, L. (1993), *La Malle de Newton*. Paris: Gallimard, coll., "Bibliothèque des Sciences humaines". The page numbers indicated in parantheses in this letter refer to this edition.

3 For a discussion of Winnicott's theory of the ego, see my book *De l'Amour à la pensée*, op. cit.

4 Lacan, J. (1977), "The Mirror Stage as formative of the function of the I as revealed in psychoanalytic experience" (trans. A. Sheridan) in *Écrits : A Selection*, New York: W. W. Norton.

5 Ibid.

6 Ibid.

7 For such a subject, during the process of redistributing the energy of this negativity without which the psychic apparatus could not exist, the analyst acts as a protective shield. See Note 8 of Letter 11, *Reading* Beyond the Pleasure Principle: *the insistence of Eros*.

8 Verlet, L. (1993), *La Malle de Newton*. Paris: Gallimard, coll., "Bibliothèque des Sciences humaines".

The inner mother

Dear friend,

I have great admiration for the way you formulated your interpretation regarding the mother of your psychotic patient: "Why do you think that your mother always tells you the truth?" Congratulations! The difficulty in these clinical contexts is that although we have to acknowledge the cruelty of these mothers, we must not forget that the unconscious representation of a mother is built on a number of factors among which the reality of the actual experience is not always the predominant element. The remarkable thing about your formulation is that you preserve the possibility that this mother might have been, at least once in her life, truthful with her daughter. It matters little that this probability is very slim. What interests us concerns less about what actually took place rather than the supposition that something took place that allowed the emergence in the psyche of the idea of a good mother. And one of the conditions required for this "something" to be rediscovered is the analyst's relatively kind treatment of who the mother is in reality.

I am always astounded by these people who, mistreated and terrorised by a mad, cruel mother since childhood, are still able, like your patient, to muster up the courage of attempting to have their own thoughts and feelings. It is disconcerting how long it can take me to identify the psychic space in which this attempt originates. (I can see that you are now struggling with the same questions.)

As I said, this wait for an answer can last months, even years, and accepting it is what makes analytic work possible. Accepting to defer the answer means ensuring that you will eventually discover it.

What does this lengthy patience allow you to learn? That there was a nanny who spent a few hours a day with the child until he was three; or that there was a neighbour the child visited at times; or an uncle in a distant town. I knew a man who remembered that a feral cat would come to keep him company when his mother forced him to spend winter nights outside. (Soon after he rediscovered this cat that he had entrusted with his hope for some humanity, he stopped coming to see me and I made no attempt to bring him back – no doubt this reunion was enough to give him a different foundation for his life.)

I encourage you not to underestimate or consider negligible the existence of these occasional others who helped the subject patch together an existence, a space of refuge from murderous violence – these occasional others who lent him the materials needed to build a space from which to form a *point of view* about what he was experiencing, an evaluation of the mother's psychic functioning. These occasional others harbour *the unthought* that allows the child to survive. Analysis makes it possible to integrate this unthought material, and it is for this reason that analysis is a revolution, as Loup Verlet points out.

Your interpretation – "Why do you think that your mother always tells you the truth?" – is extraordinary because it is reminiscent of questions your patient must have asked herself when she was little. Let us imagine the child who hears his mother screaming all the time, or the one who is forced to swallow his vomit, or clean his wounds with bleach, and so on – try to imagine the tragic dilemma that tears them apart. To begin with, if the child has developed a point of view, he knows that his mother is not telling the truth, that she is insane. (He cannot name insanity, but he recognises it, thanks to those occasional others with whom his relation is not insane.) But, he asks himself, what can one do with this knowledge and this feeling, when one depends entirely – being a child – on this mother? Invariably, the child chooses the same answer to his dilemma: he sets aside his knowledge and his feelings. By doing so, he refuses to consider this environment as specific and "processes" it as universal.

What will develop – and the work you are doing now with your patient has an important role to play here – will depend on the vigour with which the child "set aside" that which his point of view was able to recognize. This "setting aside" of the unthought is not to be confused with repression – a phenomenon that Freud discovered to be the fundamental mechanism in neurosis. A totally different functioning is present in people who have suffered massive trauma. They are constantly tormented by that which they have set aside: the trauma and the tools serving to recognise it. This is not content that attempts "to return" to consciousness, like repressed representations. Here, fragments of reality coexist constantly in the subject, but are stored in a zone not accessible to psychic processing based on the principles of our usual functioning. (Pankow teaches us that these fragments of the Real are also fragments of the body.) Whether analytic work is possible depends on the extent to which these fragments of the Real were *cut away*. (We owe the term to Françoise Davoine.)

Your observations about the father of the patient are altogether relevant. For convenience, the mother is identified as the sole agent of trauma – probably because we speak of distortions of the subject's protective barrier, the ego, which comes into being at the earliest period of life, a time when, in principle, the caregiver is the mother. Winnicott is right to call this period the "primary maternal environment", to emphasize a *function* that cannot be reduced to a person: a function of creation; protection; integration; and differentiation of the infant's psychic space. Like all choices based on convenience, this designation has theoretical and clinical effects that cloud comprehension. As a result, to "compensate", the concept of the mother as the sole agent of trauma is supplemented by a corollary notion positing an absent or weak father. However, clinical experience invalidates this hypothesis and bears witness to the active participation of the father in the massacre – a phenomenon I call the *deadly pact between the parents*.

I am reminded of a dreadful joke: an old couple is appearing before the judge to ask for a divorce. He is ninety-nine years old: she is one year younger. The judge tries to dissuade them: "But your age, your children, your grandchildren…"

They answer: "There are no children or grandchildren. We waited until they were all dead."

I was telling you earlier that the rediscovery of these occasional others in the history of your patients is not to be deemed negligible, because the outcome of their analysis depends on it. Of course, this rediscovery in itself does not guarantee success, but at least it can orient the process towards disengagement from the person's infantile past. In this context, there is a good chance that the psychoanalyst can transmit the inconceived that will allow the recognition and setting in place of an inner mother whom I define as a protective barrier for the subject, a space from which he can formulate a point of view about the other and about the world.

If the opposite occurs, if these occasional others do not reappear and the subject in analysis can only draw near the zone where the unthought was set aside, cut away, transference could take on a persecutory tone. This is a difficult situation to handle, since it takes all the skill and diplomacy one has to avoid a configuration where the analyst is placed in the role of the persecutor – a situation which would require ending the analysis.

I am reflecting on your patient, whose intellectual subtlety clearly shows that she could have gained access to this perspective, and that she set aside the space from which she could have thought about her family environment. What she calls her "nastiness" – aggressing you violently after a session in which you worked particularly well, or disappearing for several days – is part of this strategy of bypassing the zone where there is vibrant life (but which also houses the trauma). This strategy concerns, first of all, the insane mother, who remains protected as such. If those occasional others who constituted good presences are the ancestors of this new quality of relation experienced in analysis, avoiding their reappearance or attacking the relation with the analyst are governed by the same unconscious reason – avoiding the enormous psychic work that would be required by taking the unthought into consideration and integrating it, which would mean recognising the insane mother, detaching oneself from her, bearing the guilt of having a loving relationship with another being, recognising the parents' hate and one's own hate of them, separating internally from the murderous parents, carrying into the world that which is felt, thought and named in analysis. The list is far from complete.

Once again, congratulations!

Your friend,

Writing

Dear friend,

I appreciated the questions you asked about writing. The point I consider essential is this: the true difficulty when starting to write is to accept that all your usual relations to the world – your relation to time, to others, to words – will be circumscribed within the limits imposed by the ferocious demands of writing. Writing demands absolute and exclusive loyalty.

We are familiar with the romantic notion of an opposition between writing and life. But since it is not possible to both write and not write, it stands to reason that when one writes, everything inevitably becomes writing.

Of course, there is some difficulty involved in leaving the infinite world of perceptions. As you have possibly already noticed, the loss associated with writing does not consist in what we abandon in order to write – as impostors often claim. What appears lost is all the time spent without writing, all this time in which our desire to meet the world and other people has maintained itself without this element which renders what is real deeper.

A few years ago, I spent an afternoon in the country in Aix-en-Province trying to find the rhythm of a sentence in an essay I was writing at the time. Later, I realised that it had been a matter of choosing between a period and a comma. For four hours, while I was strolling with friends, I weighed these possibilities. I had never been so aware of my surroundings. Writing does not change the world, but it brings its mystery closer.

Writing is, first of all, writing for oneself. Finding a question, answering another, formulating or understanding a concept, internalising an experience. If it does this, a text can sometimes move the reader, accomplish an act of transmission.

"What does it mean, today, to write about psychoanalysis?" you ask.

I realise that the answer I will try to give you will begin in a highly paradoxical manner. I think that one must always write about psychoanalysis from the point of view of that which constitutes one's singularity as an analyst. The paradox is that much time will be needed for you to recognise your personal, unique manner of practicing this profession.

To arrive at this, think and write about your patients as much as possible. Of course, to write you can rely on your clinical notes, but above all, and as often as possible, write about the emotional tone of a session that surprised you or moved you in a special way. Try to determine exactly what interested you in what was being said to you and in what you thought, formulated or imagined. Clearly, all this will be related to a particular patient, but after a time, because your sensitivity is the most useful instrument in your work, you will come to recognise that which is constant, that which insists, revealing the unconscious elements that allow the Thing to take hold of you.

Read and reread Freud. Prepare presentations about these texts, examine them in detail, copy the passages that have impressed you most, and study them until you gain mastery of them. If you have worked well and written extensively, you can consult your notes from time-to-time during your presentation, while remaining open to being surprised by what you may say without having planned to do so.

Do not worry about originality. On the contrary, do not hesitate to say things in the most conventional way possible. Never forget that your dialogue is primarily with Freud, and your colleagues are guests witnessing this informal conversation between you, on questions that you find essential.

Another time, I will talk to you about the importance of texts that amaze you, fill you with awe and move you. These discoveries are essential in shaping what is called a style.

Before ending this letter, I want to point out once again that psychoanalysis is a practice of the spoken word. All the work that we do, including the work of writing, is only meaningful if it sustains, attends to and refines our *way of speaking* to our patients.

Your friend,

Hallucination as a defence and Claude Lanzmann's triple knowledge

Dear friend,

I am glad that you bring up the question of madness as a means to escape hell, as we have seen in Françoise Davoine and Jean-Max Gaudillière's work.

You probably remember that in 1988 I edited *Le Psychanalyste sous la terreur* (The Psychoanalyst under Terror) (published by Matrice-Rocinante), a book in which Latin-American analysts describe their experiences under terrorist regimes.

They point out that the silence imposed by the terrorist State is intended to bring about the assassination of death. In the book, Gilou Garcia Reinoso phrases this observation very astutely: "You must not notice the murder being carried out on the person of your son, your father, your mother or your neighbour. You must not think of it, talk about it or remember it. What you are experiencing has never taken place. This experience disappears, it must disappear at the very moment when it enters the sphere of reality." Life no longer in the field of vision has never existed: it is gone. Life that goes on will never end: it is eternal. Such is the will of the State. The State occupies all places. The whole space is filled up. There are no openings. Those in power are all-powerful, the reign of terror ensures their absolute power. In Argentina, it was not until the advent of the mothers of the Plaza de Mayo – "the crazy women", as they called themselves – that an opening appeared in this closed space of time, and a movement took shape, and grew and gained momentum.

According to Latin American psychoanalysts, the expression "the crazy women" of the Plaza de Mayo corresponds to a clinical reality: to speak of the inclusion of this silence concerning the assassination of death in the psyche – a silence echoing the silence governing the social body – confronts the subject to the structures he has set in place to survive in an extreme situation of constant horror. To accept the injunction affirming that a life never has an end but simply disappears, and that life which continues is not mortal but eternal, means rejecting all the parameters that normally define human existence. Of course, this also renders impossible the usual psychic investment of representations of the pleasures needed for living, as well as representations of superfluous pleasure. But, since a speaking being cannot forego either one of these representations, in order to continue living he is forced to create them on a hallucinatory plane. To speak in a situation of horror is an act of elaboration that involves going through psychic pain. The work of representation of psychic pain is woven into words that immediately concern the entire social body. In fact, the initial pain is the pain of bearing witness because this is the position where the survivor, the assassin and all the dead converge. Thus, to speak is to give voice to the dead. But to speak is, above all, to reveal the hallucination that made survival possible. This is a knowledge.

Then, the psychoanalyst *knows*, even before he encounters the one who comes to talk to him, that the truth of the reality of the subject cannot be limited to the account given by the subject; the analyst knows that this truth escapes the subject. So much so that the latter needs to meet with someone – a psychoanalyst – so that this person will listen to him and help him repossess a truth (still unknown to him) about a life experience – a story – that is his own.

But I believe that the Latin American psychoanalysts who were able to help some of their patients gain access to such an articulation of pain, relied primarily on the fictional dimension of the analytic setting.

In the same way, Claude Lanzmann *knew*, when he started working on his film *Shoah*, that the survivors were not in possession of the truth about their experience. He knew that they would only be able to take hold of any portion of it if they spoke to someone who had not lived through their experience. This explains how Lanzmann could be both warm and ruthless in his questioning of survivors. This is Lanzmann's first knowledge.

His second knowledge concerns the importance of the space of fiction. The film *Shoah* shows us that all those who were subjected to horror never recovered from this experience.[1]

Miguel Estrella is an Argentinean pianist who spent a long time in the sinister prison "Libertad" (Freedom) in Uruguay. Repeated torture caused him to lose sensitivity in his fingers. He feared he would never regain normal feeling in his fingers, and that he would never be able to play the piano again – his life's passion. In secret, he drew a keyboard on paper, and attempted to play from memory; fragments of music would come back to him: a particular piece, then a blank, then another fragment. The blanks persisted, the feeling in his fingers did not return.

One day, he received a gift from the Queen of England – a silent keyboard, but a real keyboard. The international movement organized to free him, as well as this exceptional royal gift, provided protection from his jailors. As a result, Miguel was able to keep the keyboard in his cell. He practiced, regained sensitivity in his fingers, and reconnected with music and the memory of music.

Miguel Estrella was telling me this during a dinner where we met for the first time, after a concert he had given. I told him that I had "become acquainted" with him when I saw the film *The Eyes of the Birds*, which depicts life in the "Libertad" prison, and which is based primarily on Miguel's account.

He told me that he had waited a long time before seeing the film, despite the directors' insistence. At long last, he went to a private screening with a friend, who had been a prisoner at "Libertad" as well. After seeing the first reel, he found the film moving, although he felt an essential dimension was missing: the constant state of vigilance; the nerves; and the senses in a constant state of alert.

Then came the scene where he received the silent keyboard. He realised the actor was playing Schumann and he, Miguel, had the music in his head. At that moment, the music was audible in the space of the film. "I started to scream, I could not stop screaming. It was only then that I understood the horror of what I lived through."

In other words, it was only when the music entered the fictional space of the film that Miguel could recognise that it had not existed in the space of the real during his immersion in horror. It existed, of course, in his memory, and thanks to this he could create the fiction that it existed in the world as well. The fiction of the film made it possible for him to recognise for the first time the fiction that allowed him to survive, but in so doing it also revealed the hallucinatory character of this fiction. The pain expressed by the scream signals the abolition, the end of the hallucination: from that moment on, and until the end of his life, he would be able to speak of his experience. The possibility of narrating this experience is inextricably linked with a loss; from then on, he would no longer be able to hallucinate the reality of a pleasure; instead, to obtain this pleasure he would have to come into contact with the reality of another being.

I said earlier that the film *Shoah* shows us that those who experienced horror never recovered. A very fine line separates them from this scene that they have never left, while they wait for an unimaginable other to bring them a fiction that will allow them to leave at last the hallucinated world thanks to which they were able to sustain the impossible narrative of the witness. Lanzmann knew that by giving the witnesses a space of fiction – that of the film – he was giving them a setting in which to risk revealing their pain. He knew that to situate his desire to know, in the fictional setting provided by the space of the movie, designated this desire as coming from another who is concerned with the question he is asking, but who remains external to the experience he is exploring. He knew that the gift of his request could provide a counterpart to the hallucinatory pleasure making it possible for survivors to go through the experience of horror and to bear witness. Voicing for the first time, on the unique occasion of the filming of the movie, the emotional expression of the horror they experienced is, at the same time, expressing pain, abandoning hallucination, integrating the entire experience as real, giving voice to the dead. I am convinced – and Miguel Estrella is a clear illustration – that after having spoken with Lanzmann during the filming, none of the witnesses went back to speaking as they did before. And thanks to this participation in fiction, they would not be able to stop speaking. From then on, they would speak of an experience which is their own, but which does not define them, from which they have stepped back. The awareness that their thinking has been mutilated causes them to fear (unknowingly) that abandoning the hallucination will destroy all possibility for them to speak. Once they are able to abandon hallucination because someone gives them the gift of his passionate interest, they become open to the constant possibility of an encounter.

I believe that in the process of re-democratisation undertaken today by certain societies, the new institutional mediators (that civil society must set in place in order to refuse the forgetting of the horror and mutilations inflicted by the terrorist State) must take into account this dimension of fiction, the dimension that offers an alternate setting. In other words, given the immensity and unprecedented nature of the task, the political sphere is forced to include the unconscious dimension in its work. Otherwise, future generations will suffer the same ravages that today's political system is attempting to heal in the social sphere.

Claude Lanzmann's third knowledge concerns the inadequacy of Sadian philosophy for working through the question of pain. According to Sade, two options can be considered: either the erotisation of suffering – and we have masochism – or the awareness of the entanglement of death and pleasure. This awareness would make the sadist an agent of Kant's categorical imperative, stated briefly as follows: "You want pleasure, then die!" Reducing pleasure to its libidinal manifestation means defining the victim as an unconscious accomplice, this oversimplification eliminates any reflection on psychic pain, a question which leads to that of the unrepresented portion of experience in the psychic space. The Sadian scene, which omits this question, is a naturalistic scene whose script presumes to summarise the elements involved in the fluctuation of human desire. By contrast, Lanzmann's scene is the scene of fiction. As a result, the place held by the one who knows changes as well, although he knows that the other is not in possession of the truth of his experience, Lanzmann does not presume to possess this truth. What he solicits is not a naturalistic narrative that would reinforce the victim's desire to remain forever complacent in his position as a victim. Lanzmann is looking for a narrative that transforms the survivor into a witness for whom, after the filming of the scene in the movie, the concrete reality of the experience is forever lost as such. Giving expression to psychic pain means locating it in a place other than the space of the body; locating it first in the space of fiction (the content of the movie), as well as in the exchange of words and in the space of the encounter. But in order to make such expression possible, we must be aware, unlike Sade, that there is pleasure associated with the experience of pain, under terror, a pleasure that cannot be reduced to the erotisation of suffering, a pleasure produced by constant hallucinatory activity that allows both the permanent perception of pain and its negation. Re-examining the naturalistic Sadian scene based on these observations reveals this scene for what it is: pure fantasy. Those who saw Lanzmann as a remorseless interviewer identifying with Sade are not merely making a mistake, they are ignoring the connection between hallucination and trauma – only one of a number of questions raised by the movie *Shoah*.

Your friend,

Note

1 In Letter 23, *Françoise Davoine and Jean-Max Gaudillière: history beyond trauma*, I wrote "no forgetting of an experience of horror is possible". It is thanks to Claude Lanzmann's 1985 film *Shoah* that I was able to formulate this fact I had always *known*.

Totalitarian regimes and psychosis

Dear friend,

The treatment of the corpse is what changes a group of bipedal primates into a human community. Celebrating the dead grants his existence a place among the living; mourning his disappearance pays homage to relations of all kinds: imaginary, symbolic and real – that have been established with the former inhabitant of the body being buried.

Rituals involving the body of the dead serve to establish or call attention to the separation between two worlds, the world of the living and that of the dead. Although phenomenologically this is an undisputable fact, at the symbolic level things are much less obvious.

The fact is that in order for such a separation to exist – let us suppose for the first time – the deceased has to *cross over* from one world to another. Recourse to rituals related to the treatment of the body are indispensable to ensure this *crossing*; at the same time, their organisation emphasises the need for efficiency: they must allow the subject to cross the border between the two worlds definitively. It stands to reason that this presumes the existence of a very clear conception of the world of the dead, with its system of rules, and that the conditions for admittance to this world and the requirements for dwelling there have irrevocably been clearly defined.

Every human community has its own methods of treating the dead, and these methods quickly become customs that *safeguard* the distinction between the world of the living and the world of the dead. Respecting these customs allows the living to acknowledge their debt to past generations. The acknowledgement of this debt, together with the prohibition of murder and incest, is part of the triple foundation of the laws of a civilisation.

From this perspective, a totalitarian country is not, or is no longer, a civilised nation. When the representatives of political power carry out their murders with impunity – individual and collective murders – the effectiveness of any human action (social, political, economic or cultural) is measured by its contribution to re-establishing respect for the dead. In Latin America, while totalitarian regimes were in power, cultural agents – political activists and psychoanalysts, for instance – understood that they must *first* speak about the dead, or about the risk of dying, if they wanted to help those in their care to recover their dignity as human beings. When death and murder become commonplace, not only does this involve the social and legal spheres, but consequences at the individual level amount to nothing less than the destruction of any symbolic frame of reference.

Any outward sign serving as a reminder of the distinction between life and death, or simply of the fact that the death of a particular subject is a major event for the community as a whole, is threatening for a totalitarian regime.

Totalitarian systems are perfectly aware of the need to separate death from life in order to recognise their intrication – "the life of the Spirit... endures [death] and maintains itself in it" (Hegel). In Argentina, under the most recent dictatorship, the military junta devised a diabolical scheme: they caused a large number of bodies of assassinated opponents of the regime to disappear. As a result, an unimaginable number of subjects – humanitarian agencies speak of 30,000 – were neither living nor dead; they were the "disappeared", belonging to a third dimension, a strange dimension between two worlds: ghosts, the living dead; and the dead who live. Eventually, this strangeness involved the entire population. Although someone who had disappeared could reappear dead, alive or in ghostly form at any moment, those who were located in a particular space remained, nevertheless, uncertain of their ontological status; present today, they could disappear tomorrow and come to belong to this zone of "strangeness".

The impossibility of knowing whether others are alive or not deprives people of the possibility of defining themselves in relation to life and death. They become zombies, they embody the supreme accomplishment of a terrorist regime.

A zombie has no desire to be counted among the living again, for good reason. As a zombie, he feels no hunger or thirst, he does not fear death, he regrets no losses (friends, family, his home, his work, etc.). Dying, surviving or killing, all have the same value for a psyche in a permanent state of shock. Returning to life means becoming mortal again, recognising violence and fearing it, remembering and burying one's dead, desiring and suffering. What, then, is the use of so much psychic pain?

In these circumstances, the priority is to create the conditions allowing the subject to deal with the consequences of having been a zombie, or having been tempted to become one, or of having considered the possibility of no longer being one. In other words, an intervention in the realm of reality provides an opportunity at the individual level to deal with the imaginary, symbolic and present status of the dead body (or dead bodies) dwelling in the psyche.

This is the perspective from which we have come to view the practice of Brazilian healers, a practice wrongly considered irrational, or even fraudulent, due to its extreme character.

It is clear to us – and our reasons will become obvious – that the work of a healer shares essential characteristics with psychoanalytic psychotherapy as it is practiced with psychotic patients. Moreover, in certain clinical situations – the most serious – the aim of the analyst and that of the healer are identical for a long while. This unusual comparison between the psychoanalyst's work and that of the healer becomes possible once we resolve a persistent and widespread misunderstanding: the healer, in the exercise of his functions, does not possess the entire range of references defining his culture, even when his knowledge of them is excellent. In some cases, his knowledge is very limited or altogether absent. A healer is one who can separate, in the zombie, the dead from the living, one who knows (or can invent) the passages allowing the dead to go – or return – to the world of the dead, one who knows (or can invent) the laws allowing the dead to organise themselves and remain among themselves, as well as the laws allowing the living not to envy the peace of the dead, and not to submit to their devastating rule. This is why, strictly speaking, there is no difference between the therapeutic work a psychoanalyst carries out with a psychotic and the work of a healer with the sick. Both practitioners could be called *metaphorisers*; they create metaphors allowing the passage from the particular to the universal, from trauma to taboo, from the confusion of languages and times to the separation of psychic spaces. It is just as unfounded to suppose that the healer heals because he provides a belief – in fact, what he offers each time is a myth about the origins – as to presume that the myth to which the psychoanalyst has recourse is always the same.

When dealing with psychosis, healers and analysts are faced with intergenerational short circuits that in themselves constitute an autonomous "culture", with its own values, codes and taboos taken as universal certainties by an entire group of people. The work of separating the deadly from the life-giving in order to give, or give back, to death its rightful place – immense but circumscribed – makes every psychoanalyst and every healer an ethnographer of the ancestors, an archaeologist exploring the realm of these particular dead whose traces, not to say mummies, clutter the psyche of the despairing subject who asks him for help. Refusing to consider these aspects of the practice denotes ignorance about psychoanalysts (let us reread Freud!) as well as about healers.

Let us say it again: treating a psychotic subject means making it possible for him to rid himself of the hatred of the dead who burden him, to bury the bodies that prevent him from having his own skin, his own body – without which there is no distinction between the space of life and the space of death; it is the absence of this distinction that defines madness.

What, then, is the difference between the practice of the psychoanalyst and that of the healer? If we leave aside the question of payment – in fact, healers are often paid in kind (food, clothing, lodgings, etc.) – what remains is transference, the analysis of transference, to be exact, which is not part of the healer's practice. But the comparable nature of the two practices has produced undeniable results: in Salvador de Bahia, we have seen psychotic patients considered incurable by traditional psychiatry and by psychoanalysis be cured by *Mae Senhora*. But since the healing process did not include any analysis of transference, for these subjects, the only way to repay their *symbolic debt* was to become healers themselves ("Mae" or "Pai de Santo", "Mother" or "Father of the Saint").

However, in the psychoanalytic domain strictly speaking, the problem remains to be solved. At present, we do not yet have a clearly defined theory about this type of analysis and about the end of psychotic transference. However, every analyst who works with psychotics certainly strives to establish a theoretical formulation – and this, in fact, constitutes an essential difference between the two practices. As for the symbolic debt originating in the end of transference, the stakes seem clearer in the sphere of neurosis. Still, a considerable number of neurotic patients end their analysis by becoming… psychoanalysts.

Finally, having looked at these two modes of therapy and having compared their methods, what temporary conclusion can we offer for further reflection?

As things stand, we can only say… Saravá![1]

So I wish you Saravá as well,

Note

1 Afro-Brazilian term meaning "good luck!".

True love

Dear friend,

Please forgive this long silence. I was very touched by your letter and wanted to take the time to answer it in the fullest way possible. Taking time gave me the opportunity to formulate my thinking regarding this very important subject.

I think you will agree that in modern times love tends to be considered outdated. You will understand as you read what follows that I do not share this pessimistic view. But I know that the analytic community has observed that it has become very rare to see people whose desire for analysis is motivated by concerns with love. In fact, not only do we encounter the resistance offered by society – the old, familiar resistance we all know, but we also have to contend with the limited interest, not to say indifference, shown by silent psychoanalysts to affects, feelings and emotions. Thus, if welcoming the divine is no longer what interests psychoanalysts, it is not surprising that we are turning to therapies dealing only with symptoms, or to religions, which amounts to the same thing. This will become clear later.

Freud defined emotional health as the ability to love *and* to work. This concept applies, of course, to a subject after successful analysis. In this context, what exactly is meant by love?

Love and friendship

As poets well know, love is the enthusiastic welcoming of the advent of presence. Presence of the reality of the world, real presence to the reality of the world. Real presence of the other, real presence to the reality of the other.

Most of the time, people speak of friendship to designate the symbolic aspect of love. I do not disagree, as long as we think of friendship as providing a companion with whom we can share enthusiasm, throw caution to the wind and transgress all conventions.

Remembering these essential characteristics reveals the usual opposition between love and passion: a strategy designed to temper love by imprisoning it in a cowardly rationality. This confinement, this reduction of love to pity, devoid of excess, is the triumph of the type of sensitivity created by the mediocrity long promoted as the norm by the alliance of the Church and the ruling classes.

Equally as suspect is the attempt, in the name of the importance of the symbolic, to do away with love because of its imaginary aspects. This conception is no doubt one of the scars left by the injuries inflicted when structuralism entered the fields dedicated to psychoanalytic reflection. In fact, from a purely structuralist perspective, it is possible to avoid reference to the imaginary when reflecting on the elements that structure the symbolic dimension of a given culture. But transposing this conception to the domains of transference and encounter is devastating. In this context, rejecting the imaginary amounts to amputating the encounter and the transference of the particular subtleties that confer their uniqueness. However, certain theoreticians have considered for some time that disqualifying the imaginary elements of an encounter is proof of intellectual integrity. From this point of view, the affective elements in transference should be disregarded, since they are of no interest. Thus, according to these theoreticians, transference love, which Freud does not distinguish from real love, has no importance and is reduced to the status of a purely imaginary phenomenon. As you know, this concern with "integrity" has become rooted in today's culture thanks to the favourable reception it was given by the cultural agents of the postmodern era. But we forget that throughout history this conception has served the interests of religion, since complete openness to the Real, which is the founding principle of love, undermines the closed world religion requires for its ready-made transcendence, and without which the role and privileges of the clergy would be compromised.

Friendship accompanies love. Sometimes it is already present when love suddenly appears, while at other times it develops later. Friendship and love are two distinct forms of encounter and it is important to be aware of the different types of relations that can exist between them. To begin with, we should define the emotional nature of each form of encounter. Afterwards, we will try to describe the ways in which these two forms of encounter combine, modify and nourish each other and mutually reinforce each other's autonomy.

It is generally agreed that tenderness is the main emotional characteristic of friendship. As for love, it's defining characteristic is anxiety. The one who loves is one who is able to contain anxiety. The anxiety that must be contained is one of the consequences of the hiatus that has come to characterise his relation to all things. This hiatus is created by his limitless desire for the loved one.

But anxiety is not absent from friendship either. Here, Winnicott can be of great help. Winnicott sees both friendship and play as belonging to the transitional space. In fact, play can contain a certain degree of anxiety – even intense anxiety. When the intensity rooted in instinctual activity is added to this anxiety, a threshold is crossed and the ego takes over. Although love must deal with the anxiety created by the desire for endlessness, the lover's feelings of friendship for the beloved constitute a space of respite. This space serves to receive and integrate the results of the lover's psychic elaboration, an infinite labour of representation of his relationship to the real–reality of the other.

Thus, the hiatus created by desire produces anxiety and, at the same time, triggers an intense psychic activity of representation. This activity enlarges the field of possibilities and increases the strength with which thought takes hold of the reality of the world. To love is to desire, and to love is to think.

It is conceivable that the psychic space which allows the lover to love the openness of this hiatus is not the same space as that in which his thoughts reconstitute the experience of this love. Although love is the front-runner that leads the being to the limits of his own unknown spheres, the celebration of the scope of the voyage and the distance travelled is not a matter that concerns the being. The one who is summoned to this reconstitution of an unprecedented experience, who is invited to formulate it as an idea, is the subject. Of course, we are speaking of a subject held in the power of captative love by his love object, a subject who must find another space in which to structure into thought the excessive experience that his being has forced him to live through. I am borrowing the concept of "captation" from Françoise Dolto to describe the situation in which friendship intercedes to allow the subject to take hold, at least in part, of his unprecedented experience. Living the experience in a captative mode applies to the lover's relationship to himself, his narcissism, as well as to the way in which the two lovers together construct the story of the experience. This elaboration, which tempers the unprecedented nature of the encounter with the real, facilitates its redirection and mitigates the traumatic aspects of the experience. In effect, the advent of love, which always disturbs the previous organisation of the psychic space, is always traumatic. True love is a catastrophe. A salutary catastrophe. The desire for endlessness that accompanies love produces a tension linked to the handling of anxiety, a tension that would be unbearable were it not relieved by friendship. As long as friendship maintains its independent function, the reprieve it offers to the lovers serves to renew passion.

But the relation between friendship and love goes beyond their complementarity in psychic functioning. This relation is conflictual as well. While friendship strives to reduce tension, to restore peace, passion works to maintain the opening through which the Real of the other can burst in at any moment, sometimes painfully. Clinical experience, just like life, clearly shows that when friendship crosses over onto the terrain of love, love fades and all aspects of the Real become peaceful once again. Thus, the excess associated with any experience of true love involves complementarity and conflict between friendship and love. Without friendship, there is no joy in passionate love. Without a space of respite, we are plunged into raw passion with its neurotic or psychotic manifestations. But when respite from excess is too lengthy, desire fades.

The need for the experience of love to be carried over into friendship is also apparent in its relation to language. The language used by the lover to pay homage to the extraordinary passion he is experiencing is, from his own point of view, an impoverished language. This impression of inadequacy is inevitable. Made of the desire which gives it wings and bewilders it at the same time, this language is constantly filled with fragments of the real it designates: "I love you"; "I love the scent of your body"; "I love your arms"; "I love your belly"; "I love your thighs"; "I love your penis"; "I love your hands"; "I love your hands on my body"; "I love your face"; "I love your gaze"; "I love your hair"; "I love the shade of your skin"; "I love to love you". Thus, it is from the place of captation that the lover will be able to formulate, in a language sprinkled with bits of his encounter, that which is impossible to say, without straying too far from the reality this language celebrates. For instance, "I love as love loves. I know no other reason to love you than to love you. What more do you want me to say than I love you, when what I want to say is that I love you? When I speak to you, it makes me suffer that you answer my words, not my love" (Fernando Pessoa, "Primeiro Fausto").

While anticipating the presence of the other fills the lover with joy, imagining the possibility of losing his beloved is always a source of pain. The advent of the beloved is more than a profound transformation of life, it is life itself. The thought of his disappearance is a glimpse into the absurdity of death, a prelude to paralysis of the senses, to stupefaction. There is no difference between the need for the actual presence of the other and the desire for this presence. The being who is in love has become so profoundly other that if the other disappears, there does not really remain a being.

The beloved merges with external reality. "Love is a joy with the accompanying idea of an external cause" (Spinoza).[1] The place of the beloved is the same as that of the unconscious for a subject at the end of his analysis. The external is a source of supreme joy tied to a love of oneself never before experienced: an expansion of the self accompanies an extraordinary impression of expansion of the peaceful presence of the world and of the other. An expansion and self-affirmation created by the strength of desire rooted in the joy of knowing the unconscious, and by the intense joy rooted in the desire to know the unconscious. The powerful joy of desire.[2]

The psychic functioning rooted in this new joy afforded by the simple experience of existing and loving life does not exclude any affect, yet it encompasses all other feelings and emotions. The joy of loving is always accompanied by the pain of loss. This is so because the insurmountable otherness on which love is founded is also a permanent source of suffering – the only certainty is one's own love.

The impossibility of being certain of the love of the other is not a function of doubt, nor of some mysterious masochistic tendency of the ego. This uncertainty is inherent to the love's dilemma. In fact, if the other is the reason for my life, being certain that he loves me is equivalent to seeing myself as the reason of the reason for my life. Freud recognised the imaginary figures involved in the real stakes present here; in *On Narcissism: An Introduction*, he speaks of the inevitable idealisation of the beloved. I will come back to this Freudian concept, but for the moment let us continue to examine the real dimension of the experience of love.

In my opinion, it is the combination of desire and love that constitutes true love. This opinion is not widely shared. Perhaps the reservations it elicits in France are related to the character of the French: "never sincere, always intimidated, unable to say honestly what they think, who love money above all things and never sin out of love or hate. For someone with this character, it is not intelligible to be driven to despair by love, for he cherishes that absurd courage known as resignation." This is the harsh portrait of the French painted in *The Charterhouse of Parma* by Stendhal,[3] a man well-versed in matters of love – love, the sublime madness, as he called it.

But our esteemed Henri Beyle did not succeed in avoiding contradictions altogether. The loves of his remarkable characters: Gina del Dongo, known as the Duchess Sanseverina, or Count Mosca, or Fabrizio, or Clélia, are depicted as living very intensely and in an amoral fashion, but their loves are always unhappy or star-crossed.

For instance, what happens after Clélia summons Fabrizio and speaks the famous words you may remember: "It is I," said a beloved voice, "who have come here to tell you I love you, and to ask if you are willing to obey me […] I have made a vow to the Madonna, as you know, never to see you; that is why I am receiving you in this darkness. I want you to know that if you ever forced me to look at you in daylight, everything would be over between us."

What happens, then, when the characters are bold enough to risk living the devastating psychological experience of desire associated with love? Stendhal's answer is as follows: "Here we shall ask permission to pass, without saying a single word about them, over an interval of three years."

In other words, when love with its accompanying desire is possible, Stendhal has nothing more to say and asks our indulgence for his silence. In fact, the book ends shortly thereafter, rather abruptly. It is not far-fetched to suppose that Lacan might have been inspired by it when he made a separation between love and desire.

Mystical love

True love, the combination of love and desire, includes ecstasy. Ecstasy brings to mind mystical love, whose study makes it clear that for the lover, the beloved is God. If I love, there is a God. The encounter with the beloved is the origin of a new being and of a new world. Thus, the place of the beloved in love rooted in desire is no different than his place in mystical love. But, in this type of love, since the beloved is in the world and sexuality makes it possible for him to be literally devoured by love, ecstasy has an expression, orgasm, for its realisation and its renewal.

As far as the lovers are concerned, their positions are very different. The mystical lover places his relation to the other in the sphere of the Real of delusion. In passionate love, on the other hand, the Real occupies an intermediary space, between the lover and the beloved. This Real includes the possibility that the beloved may stop loving me, or may disappoint me – which would set in motion a dis-idealizing process. Both possibilities would cause psychological pain, a pain with no possible representation, most often leading to despair or melancholia.

Love rooted in desire is, in a certain sense, less psychologically demanding than mystical love: it does not require the hallucinatory generation of the beloved.

But the psychic work required in passionate love is just as arduous. Of course, there is the feeling that the beloved is everywhere in the world, causing the lover to recognise his beloved a thousand times when he sees a gesture, a gait, a particular feature of a stranger – but this impression does not erase the awareness of the beloved's actual absence. Paradoxically, this awareness contributes to the feeling of joy associated with this kind of recognition: if I think I see my beloved in places where he is not, it means that he is with me everywhere.

The presence of the beloved rekindles primary traces to such an extent that there is no point in trying to distinguish the state of being in love from a dream state. Thus, there is a certain parallel between this state and the hallucinatory satisfaction of desire. The actual existence of the beloved is at once so necessary and so magical that the subject is never certain that he is not hallucinating, while at the same time there is no doubt as to the beloved's existence in the reality of world.

In terms of the subject's psychic economy, the beloved occupies a very problematic place. A place on the border, on the edge, at the frontier between inside and outside – explaining why the beloved is invested as a transitional object would be. But this place is also at the intersection of the real, the symbolic and the imaginary – and this is why disinvesting the beloved makes reality meaningless, dead, propelling the lover into melancholic madness.

This place of the beloved reflects the intolerable aspect of all passionate love, the absolute and permanent need for the physical presence of the other. The physical presence of the other embodies the radical difference between the lover and the beloved. The radical difference of the beloved, the complexity of his otherness, is what makes sensual love possible. This difference is what excludes any illusion of completeness. To love and desire someone means loving this difference, loving this complexity, loving the distance that separates you and distinguishes you from the beloved, while you wish with all your heart to abolish this distance. The fact that this distance is a source of anxiety, suffering and pain is only one aspect of the experience of love – a fundamental aspect. But, at the same time, orgasm and friendship make this distance malleable, liveable, "containable", and therefore enriching for the subject.

Often, when this suffering, this pain, is not relieved by any pleasure or orgasm, it is recognised as sublime mystical love with its particular ecstasy. The figure that best personifies this concept is Saint Teresa of Avila,[4] who was no doubt an exceptional woman. As a little girl, she dreamed of being a martyr; at the age of seven, she made a plan to run away "to the country of the Moors, begging her way for the love of God, in hopes that she might be beheaded there" – which gives us an idea of her times and brings to mind dreams of martyrdom in our own times. As an adult woman full of vitality, Saint Teresa of Avila rejected her unbounded sensuality which persisted, despite all manner of penance and mortification, in the form of hallucinatory voices and visions of God, her lover. This illusory completeness, this saturation of the being by the constant tension between love for an impossible presence and the impossible accomplishment of desire for this presence, has been used to construct the paradigm of *jouissance*.

This paradigmatic concept of *jouissance* has served – and still serves – as a pretext for some analysts to remain unconcerned with the unhappiness, sadness and despair of their patients. The paradigm of *jouissance* rooted in the pain of incompleteness follows logically from the reduction of love to the imaginary. To reduce love to the imaginary is to act as if love were simply a hysterical symptom among others. From this point of view, mystical love is nothing more than hysteria rendered more noble by a touch of psychosis. Reducing the sublime to the *jouissance* connected with the tragic – which brings to mind the passion of Christ – authorises indifference to the joys of this world, blindness to feelings and emotions, sets up an absurd opposition between the symbolic and real life, and paves the way to the rejection of the Freudian theory of drives.

But, since Freud considered that only representations of sexual drives can be repressed in the unconscious, rejecting the theory of drives amounts to imagining an unconscious from which sexuality is excluded.

What is the place of the sublime in love rooted in desire? And what exactly is the sublime? It is undeniable that the joys associated with being in love, tempered or not by anxiety, are numerous; they are exquisite, delectable, sublime. But restricting the experience of the sublime to ecstasy, or to the state preceding or following ecstasy, would be disregarding the essential. However, it is important to specify that what makes ecstasy possible in the state of being in love – and is also an aspect of the sublime – is the impossibility of distinguishing between need and desire. Separating my need of the beloved from my desire for the beloved is simply not possible. Much the same way as it is not possible, beyond a certain threshold, to distinguish between hunger and appetite, to say which of the two enhances the taste and makes the smell more subtle. The desire's appetite of the lover for the beloved expands the time that leads to orgasmic satisfaction. Desire for the body of the other reawakens the sexual need for appeasement of the senses, creating a rhythm that in no way resembles that imposed by instinctual discharge.

In passionate love, the sublime is not a consequence of a certain mode of relating to the other. What is sublime is the very existence of the beloved. Everything concerning his existence produces an erotic effect: his gaze; the tone of his voice; or his silence. Or anything. The dizzying effect of abandoning all restraint. The beloved's existence makes life simple, light, carefree. How could life be otherwise, since there is a God. The relation between the lover and the beloved is a relation between God and a poet. Like two children, they take the world and the things of the world by the hand, and the four of them play together. And just as is the case for children who love and feel loved, there is no difference between play, laughter, desire and thought. As you will see a little later, the metapsychology of this circularity is fascinating.

Love and truth

There is a relation between urgency and truth that concerns love.

The amorous encounter is a moment of truth *par excellence*. The beloved's entrance into someone's life is a break-in – a violent gust of wind pushing open a door to reveal a sun-drenched landscape. The beloved is pure exteriority.[5] Going to meet him means venturing into an outside where another me, whom I do not know, who is a stranger, is waiting for me. It is urgent to respond to this call of a truth about myself located beyond the opening created by the beloved in the monolith of the real. Dwelling in urgency takes all my strength, all my energy, all my concentration, because in order for me to meet this other whom I shall be, who waits for me outside and calls to me, I must modify the usual frame of thought that allowed me to accompany myself so far.[6] This same state of dwelling in urgency characterizes writing, when writing changes the writer, transforming him as he follows the thread of a reflection that he comes to know as he writes, and which reflects his most profound truth, a truth waiting to meet him outside, in the act of writing.[7] This is why when a writer writes, he wants to do nothing else, can do nothing else than respond to this emergency, live this demanding and exalting experience, catch hold of the inscription of a transformation, his own, whose shape and limits are as yet unknown to him.

Reflecting on love with Freud

The first Freudian concept of true love consisted of integrating the tender dimension and the sexual dimension, to achieve harmony between tenderness and sexuality.

Freud described the two manifestations of Oedipal love: impotence caused by idealisation; and debasement of the object of sexual desire; in short, for a neurotic man, the woman occupies either the place of the mother or that of the whore. Speaking of women, Freud described frigidity and hatred of men – two consequences of penis envy.[8]

But right from the start of *On Narcissism: An Introduction*, Freud presents a hypothesis similar to my own perspective on the subject: "The highest phase of development of which object-libido is capable is seen in the state of being in love, when the subject seems to give up his own personality in favour of an object-cathexis."[9] A little further, Freud makes two other observations that confirm my thinking and grant the Real a privileged position in the state of being in love: "The sexual instincts are at the outset attached to the satisfaction of the ego-instincts; only later do they become independent of these, and even then we have an indication of that original attachment in the fact that the persons who are concerned with a child's feeding, care, and protection become his earliest sexual objects: that is to say, in the first instance his mother or a substitute for her."[10] In other words, if there is a continuity between the earliest sexual objects and the fact that they coincide with the persons who tend to the body and the needs of the subject, it is reasonable to say that an intense sexual life is the foundation of equally intense feelings of love, and that in this situation there is no distinction between desire and need. In this context, the beloved is external to the subject, and his idealisation is founded on the paradigm of the love of an entirely real mother for her entirely real child. In fact, in the same text, Freud takes into account this dimension of the real in the creation of the ideal: "This ideal ego is now the target of the self-love which was enjoyed in childhood by the [*real*] *ego*" (my emphasis).[11]

But Freud's constant focus on a theory of intrapsychic functioning (his monad) would soon cause him to introduce nuances that modified these strong statements. He wrote: "Complete object-love of the attachment type is, properly speaking, characteristic of the male. It displays the marked sexual over-evaluation which is doubtless derived from the child's original narcissism and thus corresponds to a *transference of that narcissism* to the sexual object. This sexual over-evaluation is the origin of the peculiar state of being in love, a state suggestive of a neurotic compulsion, which is thus traceable to an impoverishment of the ego as regards libido in favour of the love-object" (my emphasis).[12] In short, *no more* other, *no more* exteriority. I believed that I loved someone but in fact I was only loving myself at the stage of my early childhood. This is what explains the over-evaluation of the beloved, and his idealisation. Neither depends on his particular qualities, nor on the unprecedented, extraordinary nature of this new encounter. Everything is reduced to the imaginary – keep moving, there is nothing new to see – love is merely a fantasy, and the love object merely the support for the transference of my infantile megalomania.

It might be said that Freud moved back and forth between these two conceptions, one that recognises the otherness of the beloved, while the other relegates the beloved to the realm of the imaginary, associating him with a mere intrapsychic operation. Of course, no choice needs to be made, since both conceptions are fundamental. And yet, for the sake of clinical focus on a theory of fantasy, Freud often favoured the imaginary. But by making this choice, he overlooked the significant psychic transformations that can be brought about by a real, present, intense and never before experienced sexual life in the history of a subject. These transformations involve the restructuring of identity configuration and narcissistic organisation, and what follows as a result: the inscription of new psychic representations.

This impasse to which Freud arrives is consistent with a theory that reduces transference to the repetition of past relationships. Given that it leaves out all elements not repeated in the sphere of transference, this theory does not integrate the possibility of inscribing new representations, a possibility created precisely because the real and present relation with the analyst has unprecedented, novel and non-repetitive characteristics. We are all aware that reducing the analysis of transference to that which repeats itself in analysis has always been the choice of those who refuse to pay the psychic price demanded by the work of an analyst. To describe this imposture as an intellectualisation of the process is misplaced courtesy; in fact, what we are seeing is an attempt to make mediocrity the measure of truth. Moreover, we have seen the same analysts insist that transference never ends as a way of justifying their hold on patients – and interpret any enthusiasm or passion as a sign of perverse residues – as a way of protecting the reassuring comfort of their lacklustre lives in which sexuality and desire are but shameful memories. In addition, because working with psychotics requires the analyst to have a gift for recognising the never-before-seen and for divesting this unknown of its frightening character, reducing the conception of transference to the repetition of past experiences means excluding psychotics from the domain of analysis.

Love and sublimation

Reflecting on the state of being in love from a psychoanalytic perspective and with a focus on the dimension of the real means adopting a theoretical position vis-à-vis the sublimation process. But first, given that idealisation of the beloved is a fundamental characteristic of love, it might be useful to examine the relation between idealisation, sexuality and sublimation.

According to Freud, sublimation concerns the sexual drive and idealisation concerns the object. In *On Narcissism: An Introduction*, he writes: "Sublimation is a process that concerns object-libido and consists in the instinct's directing itself towards an aim other than, and remote from, that of sexual satisfaction; *in this process the accent falls upon deflection from sexuality*. Idealization is a process that concerns the *object*; by it that object, without any alteration in its nature, is aggrandised and exalted in the subject's mind. Idealization is possible in the sphere of ego-libido as well as in that of object-libido. For example, the sexual over-evaluation of an object is an idealization of it. *In so far as sublimation describes something that has to do with the instinct and idealization something to do with the object, the two concepts are to be distinguished from each other*" (my emphasis).[13]

Freud points out that: "The formation of an ego ideal is often confused with the sublimation of instinct, to the detriment of our understanding of the facts." He notes: "A man who has exchanged his narcissism for homage to a high ego ideal has not necessarily on that account succeeded in sublimating his libidinal instincts." But he concedes that: "It is true that the ego ideal demands such sublimation, but it cannot enforce it; sublimation remains a special process *which may be prompted by the ideal but the execution of which is entirely independent of any such prompting*."[14]

Based on these premises, we can say that idealisation of the beloved acts as an incitement to sublimation of the sexual experience. The suggestion that friendship be considered a space of respite for the lovers is consistent with this economy. But as I said earlier, if friendship trespasses on the territory of sexual desire, this desire fades and all aspects of the real are appeased. In that case, what type of relation can we imagine between sublimation and sexual desire in the state of being in love, so as to preserve the sharpness of desire that places the subject in a totally new relation to the world? What metapsychological explanation corresponds to the experience that the more the lover desires the beloved, the greater is his desire for a new mode of existing in the world?

We know that the encounter with the beloved is the start of a sexual life that would have been unimaginable up to that moment. In other words, the sexuality that accompanies the state of being in love exceeds the frame of reference that was available to the subject until then. As a result, this new experience will impose psychic work of re-elaboration of previous sexual ideals. This allows us to conclude, as Freud did, that the bringing into question of sexual ideals will unavoidably affect all ideal representations that govern the subject's self-regard and his relation to the world.

Having said all this, we are much closer to understanding why idealisation of the beloved is inextricably linked with the sublimation process. Given that the experience of desire exceeds the limits of the previous framework of sexual ideals, the over-evaluation of the beloved – his idealisation – depends in greater measure on the real nature of this experience than on its imaginary characteristics. Thus, while the extraordinary nature of the experience of desire explains idealisation, the fact that this experience had been unimaginable up until then requires the immediate construction of a new representational framework that can contain and process the experience – calling forth sublimation processes. This is necessary in order to prevent anxiety from overwhelming the ego, and to allow the experience to continue and retain all the characteristics we have described. Processing the experience is therefore a matter of rearranging ideals, which involves introjection of the qualities of the beloved.

This summarises, in metapsychological terms, the stages that lead from the unimaginable encounter with the other – which calls into question all existing representations – to the idealisation of the beloved, which involves the creation of a new representational framework of ideals. This new framework, which relies on sublimation processes, is what prevents real and inevitable anxiety from exceeding tolerable intensity.

The effects of the amorous encounter are no less surprising at the level of narcissistic economy. This encounter also invalidates all self-representations that had previously determined the subject's experiences of pleasure and enjoyment. What happens to the portion of this pleasure and enjoyment that exceeds the former narcissistic economy? No doubt a portion of the energy "in excess" – "in excess" relative to the capacity of the previous representational framework – will be used for the inscription of new ideal representations. The latter enable the transformation necessary in the narcissistic economy to prevent the experience of being in love from causing depersonalisation, and to allow this experience to be integrated into the ego ideal.

At this point, another passage of Freud's *On Narcissism* helps to deepen our understanding: "Here we may even venture to touch on the question of what *makes it necessary* at all for our mental life to pass beyond the limits of narcissism and to attach the libido to objects. The answer which would follow from our line of thought would once more be that this necessity arises when the cathexis of the ego with libido *exceeds a certain amount.* A strong egoism is a protection against falling ill, *but in the last resort we must begin to love in order not to fall ill,* and we are bound to fall ill if, in consequence of frustration, we are unable to love. This follows somewhat on the lines of Heine's picture of psychogenesis of the Creation" (my emphasis).[15]

Based on this remark, we can fill out the metapsychology of the circularity set in motion by an amorous encounter: exhilarating narcissistic revelry prompts the investment of the beloved, which creates a new representational framework of the world and of the self, a framework that makes possible a new economy in which anxiety is tolerable, and the narcissistic revelry can begin again, renewing libidinal investment in the beloved and in the world, and so on...

As you no doubt noticed, in this passage of Freud's text sublimation is not presented as occurring at the expense of sexuality, but is, in fact, a continuation of it, a direct consequence of sexuality, described as *necessary*. Therefore, sublimation cannot be seen as a mere process of desexualisation; in fact, the *creation* of a new world of internal and external representations relies on the same components of sexuality. It is also noteworthy that in this context sublimation, before it applies to the object, is the result of a "surplus" of energy in the narcissistic economy, a "surplus" that must find release. From this point of view, sublimation is a release of tension, without any change in the quality of the affect underlying this tension. Winnicott employed the term *ego-orgasm* to describe this psychic experience.

In fact, in a text entitled *Contributions to the Psychology of Erotic Life*, written in 1912 before *On Narcissism*, Freud had already introduced this idea of necessity. But here the necessity was not tied to an excess in the narcissistic economy, but rather to the very nature of the sexual drive. In Freud's words: "Surprising as it may sound, I think that one would have to deal with the possibility that there is *something in the nature of the sexual drive itself that is unfavourable to the achievement of complete satisfaction*." And he goes on to say: "The same incapacity of the sexual drive to yield complete satisfaction once it is subjected to the first demands of civilization becomes the source of the greatest cultural achievements, which are brought about as the result of a sublimation, pushed even further onwards, of its drive components. For, what reason would people have for putting the sexual drive-forces to other uses if, by some distribution of those forces, they could have provided complete satisfaction of desire?" (my emphasis).[16]

What stands out, above all, is the accent placed on the untameable, insatiable nature of the drive, its insistence. This insistence was discussed again eight years later, when Freud presented the notions of death drive and repetition compulsion. But what interests us at the moment is that here this insistence, this compulsion, refers to sexual drives, which in Freud's second drive theory were classified among the life instincts. Speaking of the sexual drive, Freud refers to "something", "a drive-force", insatiable and untameable, that will serve to achieve sublimation. Once again, sublimation is not presented as a process of desexualisation. It is not seen as having a faith separate from the sexual drive, but rather the faith of a permanent and inevitable *residue* of this drive, after it has achieved its aim. To be perfectly clear, the character of this residue, in which bisexuality holds a predominant place, in no way differs from the affective character attributed to instinct energy; in fact, it is precisely this character that makes sublimation possible. In other words, if what sublimation must process is loss, it is Eros that will process it, not Thanatos.

From this perspective, sublimation is not seen as a successful retake of failed object cathexes or of inadequate repression of pregenital drives, nor as a way out of inhibition, depression or introversion of the libido. Here, sublimation processes are the logical outcome of successful object cathexis. What is highlighted here is the flow between narcissistic libido, object libido and sublimation. In other words, what we have here is an illustration of the thinking process when the psychic health functions at its best.[17]

I believe I have already given many indications to show that the conception of love I am putting forward does not contradict the concept developed by Freud. Still, it is true that most of the time Freud stresses that "libidinal object-cathexis does not raise self-regard. The effect of dependence upon the loved object is to lower that feeling: a person in love is humble." From this point of view, being loved in return is seen simply as the recovery of the portion of ego-libido forfeited in libidinal cathexis. Moreover, Freud went so far as to associate love with perversion: "Being in love consists in a flowing-over of ego-libido on the object. It has the power to remove repression and re-instate perversion."[18]

But Freud also provides a different perspective on love's economy: speaking specifically of the relation between self-regard and libido, he refers to "*a real happy love* [...] *in which object-libido and ego-libido cannot be distinguished*" (my emphasis).[19]

Given this indistinction, it becomes possible to show that the essential characteristic of the relation between the lover and the beloved is the rejoicing in the existence of the other. The other in whom one rejoices is the one called forth by the amorous encounter: the most important other, the primary environment, a place and time in which my existence coincides with the framework of the world, which it symbolises. This statement can be demonstrated – and we acknowledge our indebtedness (mine and Freud's) to Spinoza, but we will leave the demonstration for another occasion.[20]

How do we explain such variations in Freudian theorisations? I believe that they point to neurotic solutions to the difficulty of loving, on the one hand, and true love, on the other hand. The excess of desire in true love requires excellent psychic health if the subject is to satisfy all the demands of the psychic work involved, at the level of ego economics, of libidinal investment of the beloved, of thinking about oneself, the other and the world. The psychic work is enormous, infinite and as vast as life itself.

The apparent contradictions between Freudian concepts of love are due to the fact that Freud alternates between two worlds when he reflects on the state of being in love: his starting point is sometimes the ego-libido, and sometimes the object-libido. In my view, all contradictions disappear when he defines "a real happy love [as that] in which object-libido and ego-libido cannot be distinguished". This indistinction between ego-libido and object-libido defines his conception of the *real*.[21]

When Freud speaks of happy love, he does not forget to underline the enormity of the psychic effort required by loving *really*. He writes: "So it seems that it is the *irreducible differences between the demands of the two drives* – the sexual and the egoistic – that make people capable of ever higher accomplishments, *although there is always the constant danger to which weaker individuals are at present subject in the form of neurosis*" (my emphasis).[22] These considerations bring to mind those of Winnicott and of Freud himself in *The Loss of Reality in Neurosis and Psychosis* – which describe psychic health as being closer to madness than to normality.

One more comment. We have already seen that all these manifestations of libidinal economy in the ego's relationship with another often require reorganisation of representational ideals. In fact, these readjustments always concern the ego ideal. But what kind of superego can go hand-in-hand with this flexibility of the ego-ideal? Is a superego capable of tolerating so much upheaval compatible with the intolerant, critical nature of this agency as it is usually described in Freudian theory? The answer, of course, is no and I will discuss this at length another time.[23] For now, I would simply like to point out that Freud gives us an implicit theory of a loving and supportive superego, which concerns the mother and which he left in suspense... because "in order to simplify [the] presentation [he only discusses] identification with the father".[24] Freud was to make his most incisive criticism of an exclusively cruel superego in his 1927 text *Humour*.[25]

One last observation. You may have noticed that nowhere in this discussion did I mention hate. The fact is that I find it absurd to consider hate the opposite of love. The opposite of love is madness. But what is the relation between love and hate?

If God, the beloved, stops existing, the subject is propelled into the void. To counteract the pain of the void, hate steps in. I think that when separation from the beloved takes place, the aggression that was bound to love and desire now becomes unbound and attaches itself to anger and hate. This new coupling of aggression is useful in the work of separation from the loved object. (Let us remember that Freud was referring to the real loss of a loved one, to his death. He never formulated a theory about separation from a person one loves, who continues to live in the real world.) This coupling is possible when everything goes well, that is, when the subject has the resources or the good fortune to be able to set in motion a process of separation. Otherwise, as I said, madness takes over: hate is turned against oneself and, therefore, against the world.

Your friend,

Notes

1   Spinoza, B. (1996), *Ethics*. Translated by Edwin Curley, London: Penguin Classics, Part III, *Definitions of the Affects*, Definition VI, p. 105.
2   Psychic functioning in true love is akin to what Spinoza called the third kind of knowledge. See Letter 36, *Freud and Spinoza.*
3   Stendhal, *The Charterhouse of Parma*. New York: The Modern Library, 2000, p. xiv, pp. 488–489.
4   Renault, E. (1970), *Sainte Thérèse d'Avila et l'Expérience mystique,* Seuil, Paris, coll. "Maîtres spirituels", p. 9.
5   At the same time, he is part of the lover's internal world. This paradox is intrinsic to the state of being in love.
6   See Letter 28, *Loup Verlet: Psychoanalysis as a revolution of the conceptual framework.*

7   The same relation exists between the painter and his painting, the composer and his music, any artist or researcher and his work.

8   Freud, S. *Contributions to the Psychology of Love: A Special Type of Choice of Object made by Men* (1910); *On the Universal Tendency to Debasement in the Sphere of Love* (1912); and *The Taboo of Virginity* (1918). S.E., 11, London: Hogarth.

9   Freud, S. (1914), *On Narcissism: An Introduction*. S.E., 14: p. 76, London: Hogarth. Ibid., p. 87.

10 Ibid., p. 94.

11 Ibid., p. 88.

12 Ibid., p. 94.

13 Ibid., p. 95.

14 Ibid., p. 85.

15 Freud, *On the Universal Tendency to Debasement in the Sphere of Love*, op. cit., pp. 259–260.

16 Freud, S., *On Narcissism: An Introduction*, op. cit., p. 98.

17 See Letter 11, *Reading Beyond the Pleasure Principle: the insistence of Eros*.

18 Freud, S., *On Narcissism: An Introduction*, op. cit., p. 100.

19 Freud uses the term "real love" in his text "Observations on Transference Love" in *Further Recommendations on the Technique of Psychoanalysis*. S.E., 12: pp. 157–171, 1915. I prefer "true love" to "real love", because the former alludes to the truth of what is spoken.

20 See Letter 36, *Freud and Spinoza*.

21 Freud, *On the Universal Tendency to Debasement on the Sphere of Love*, op. cit., p. 260.

22 Freud, S. (1912), *Contributions to the Psychology of Erotic Life*, S.E., 11: 183. London: Hogarth.

23 See Letter 35, *The Celestina superego and the Dulcinea superego*.

24 Freud, S. (1923), *The Ego and the Id*. S.E., 19, note 9, p. 26, London: Hogarth. Let us note that this "simplification" leaves aside the caregiving mother as an object of identification, giving priority to the phallic mother.

25 Freud, S. (1927), *Humour*, S.E., 21: 160–166. London: Hogarth.

Hate

My dear friend,

I would be glad to take up the discussion of hate from the point where I left it off in my last letter. You say that you agree with my idea that the opposite of love is not hate, but rather madness. But you have trouble understanding the way I see hate as an agent facilitating the work of separation from the beloved. As you so aptly observe, since this work tends to depend on coupling with aggression, which is now unbound from desire for love, hate becomes secondary.

I do not consider you "a pain in the neck guardian of the temple" because you draw attention to the fact that Freud considered hate a primary emotion. On the contrary, as I often say, reference to the Freudian texts is always essential. What analyst could deny the constant need for this dialogue?

Since Freud, many authors have discussed the economy of hate in the space of transference. All of them raise the same questions: is there a place for hate in transference? If there is, what is this place and what purpose does it serve? The patient's hate is conceivable, but is the analyst authorised to feel hate, is such hate desirable? And what of the effects of the real hate of the parents towards the subject: do these effects have a place in psychoanalysis? Can they be treated? If so, what conditions are needed? This incomplete list comprises the questions asked by psychoanalysts who exclude psychotic subjects from the analytic relation. As for those who dare to work with madmen, treating hate in transference is not optional, it is an obvious necessity, a requirement.

First, there is the hate of the parents, which the patient will bring into analysis by mistreating his analyst as he was mistreated. But contrary to the child the patient once was, the psychoanalyst can speak of the effects of this hatred on his psychic life. And there is a good chance that, thanks to this, the patient will begin thinking about the psychic life of his parents, and about his own pain.

Self-hatred, a consequence of the internalisation of the parents' hatred, is associated with immense guilt. This guilt has been assumed by the child *instead of the parents*, in whom it is absent. The emergence of this guilt in the domain of transference is a fascinating process. It is a completely unconscious means used by the patient to cause the analyst to feel guilty towards him. This is accomplished through strange unconscious acts committed by the analyst, like the example I recounted at the start of our correspondence about the incident when I failed to wake up in time for my session with a patient.[1]

The aim of these unconscious manoeuvres – described by Melanie Klein who designated their functioning as "projective identification", is to transform the analyst into a persecutor. The elements of reality in the relation with the analyst – his irritation, his nodding off, his acting-out and other failings – will serve to prevent the recognition of the projective aspects involved (projecting onto the analyst the characteristics of parental violence).

These manoeuvres attempt to validate the unconscious theory that the psychoanalyst, like anyone else, is just like the parents – which can cause the analysis to end in disappointment. Such an outcome offers several benefits: not having to recognise the analyst as someone who can provide protection, who feels no hate, makes it possible to keep the internal parents blameless. This refusal to know makes it possible to prevent them from taking vengeance for having lost their control over the child the patient once was. (Control is a form of hate.) But the greatest benefit is that this refusal to know exempts the patient from confronting the guilt that would necessarily accompany his recognition of his parents' sadism, a recognition that would *initially* awaken the feeling of having abandoned them. (We must not forget that the child was aware of being his parents' therapist, as well as their medication, the psychic body that acted as a container in which the parents' impulses landed with a crash.)

If the analyst is able to avoid the clinical traps set by the patient's unconscious in transference, the patient will finally be able to feel, without guilt, anger and even hate towards his parents.

Sometimes the analyst feels outright hatred towards the patient. This hatred without guilt is provoked by the sadistic attacks to which the patient subjects his relationship with the therapist by adopting perverse or psychopathic behaviours. In his famous paper *Hate in the Countertransference*, Winnicott describes the handling of this situation in analysis. He demonstrates that in order to work through what transpires in transference, it is imperative to admit this feeling of hate to the patient.[2]

From the psychoanalyst's perspective, the worst situation is that in which his guilt finds no rational explanation in any actual failing, and is the direct result of the hate he feels towards the patient, without being able to identify its causes. In these cases, the patient has transferred massively to the internal world of the analyst the vague feelings of hate he experienced in response to his parents' cruelty. (In his book *Countertransference and Related Subjects*, Harold Searles points out that if as early as the first meeting with the patient the analyst feels besieged with guilt, he is dealing with the massive guilt transfer of a patient who is probably psychotic.)[3]

Another possibility – and the list can go on and on – is the case where the analyst is faced with the insensitivity of a patient. Rejection of any form of emotion corresponds to two subjective positions: the coldness of the parents; and the child's hyperactive thinking, since he is constantly in a state of heightened alertness that allows him to foresee a possible outbreak of deadly violence. (The extremely precocious maturity seen in children of psychotic parents is the result of this combination of coldness and violence.) In this clinical situation, the analyst is transformed into an *analytic machine* by a patient attempting to reduce the therapeutic encounter to an intellectual exercise devoid of any emotion. This attempt is a continuation of the need he had as a child to split his mental functioning from any contact with the sensoriality of the body.

The drowsiness that suddenly envelops the analyst during a session is often a clinical sign of the hate that crushes him and that he has to contain. Let us look at a clinical example: a woman, a patient of mine, is just beginning to bury her dead. (The work of burying the dead is fundamental, as I described recently.)[4] As the session begins, she says that her body is full of words and I am happy to hear it. In a little while, I find myself fighting an irresistible desire to sleep. In order to stay awake, I speak: "The experience you are describing must have been very difficult." Towards the end of the session, and again in order to keep myself from falling asleep, I ask: "Do you realise what a heavy burden of expectations you place on other people?", "Sometimes," she says. "But I can see that you are falling asleep!"

I tell her she is right and I add: "I think that you wanted to keep for yourself the things we were talking about at the start of the session, and so much the better. You are afraid I will steal them from you, so you are assailing my thoughts."

She exclaims: "That's right. But it's nothing compared to what my mother used to do to me!"

Thus, we are dealing with the relation to a child. Not the child that the patient once was, but the relation that he might have with his own child based on his identifications with the modes of violence exercised by his father and/or mother towards him. *The analyst occupies the place of the generation to come.* As such, he guarantees the possibility of a future and constitutes the proof that the patient can, in turn, cause someone else to suffer. (Obviously, the analytic work becomes considerably more complex when the subject actually has children. In that case, the faster the analyst understands that he occupies the place of the patient's offspring, the sooner the violent or sadistic acts against the real children can diminish.[5])

This brings us to the question of truth. There is a very strong relation between hate and truth. Like love, hate encounters truth in the outside world, but truth does not bring it into question; on the contrary, the one who hates reconfirms himself as unchanged. Love is a tie; hate is a glue – impossible to live with it, impossible to live without it. Hatred's relation with truth involves no urgency; it takes place without any need for movement. Hatred arrives at truth within immobilised thought. Hatred does not seize truth, it encloses it in still thought where nothing more can be transformed, where everything is immutable: the one who hates sails on a sea of certainties.

Let us go back to Freud. Hatred is part of the paradoxical segments of Freudian theory. I will go over two directions taken by Freud's research: the genesis of hate; and its place in paranoia.

In its genesis, hate is associated with displeasure. What is disliked is rejected and this operation brings into being the external, the outside. Therefore, initially the outside is constituted of the unpleasant, of the bad, of the hateful. Thanks to your usual astuteness, you no doubt noticed the shift from displeasure to hate. The idea is not mine, but comes from the Freudian body of thought.

Let us think about this original operation of rejection. Initially, there is an experience marked by displeasure, which must be eliminated to guarantee the pleasurable functioning of the psychic system of the organism. Three things must be noted:

a   pleasure requires functioning in a closed circuit;
b   closure is achieved by expulsion of displeasure;
c   the inside (the psychic system closed in on itself) is constituted at the same time as the outside.

In this monadic view, there is no need for the other. But even from a monadic perspective, there remains one problem. Unpleasure, the bad or the hateful have to be expulsed. But what energy is summoned to do this?

Melanie Klein must have recognised this problem, since she answered the question without formulating it outright. In her view, it is the death instinct which expulses unpleasure, the hateful, which in effect expulses itself to the outside. Very well.

However, when Freud developed his theory on hate, he had not yet formulated the concept of the death instinct. But we can suppose this energy to originate in self-preservative impulses, which coincided with libidinal impulses at that stage of elaboration of Freudian theory. Once again, granted.

But how are we to imagine an energy that exists (whether we call it death instinct or self-preservative impulse) and needs to constitute an outside of the psychic being, since given that it already exists, it does not need to perform such an operation in order to exist? Must we then postulate the closing in on itself of the psychic system before this energy can be made available for expulsion? But, in these conditions, it would no longer be the rejection of the unpleasant, the bad and the hateful that would constitute the outside. Have we encountered a dilemma? Yes, because energy as such can exist without differentiating between an internal and an external space. Energy serves needs or reacts to stimuli; this is its function at the level of animality. The dilemma is inherent to the theory supporting the hypothesis of the creation of the internal and the external world by self-generation.

Contrary to animal life, a topical difference between inside and outside is a logical requirement for reflecting on the psyche, and therefore on the human. But since the human is not created by energy, since the human is created by the human, we must admit that my theoretical conception, which views the mother, from the start, as an ego-support filter, filtering excitations from the external world, *makes her the guarantor of an interiority which differentiates, from the start, the psychic space from corporeal maturation processes.*

Concerning what I have just discussed and particularly what will follow, I would like to quote Montaigne: "This is not my doctrine, it is my study; nor is it the lesson of another, but my own."[6] The only difference is that my study is my doctrine and that I am much indebted to my patients for my lesson.

Let us look at *Instincts and their Vicissitudes*[7] in which, as you remember, Freud characterises hate as primary. My first thought is that Freud has replaced displeasure with hate in his conception of the creation of an exterior, and that consequently it is hate that must be expulsed in order to create an outside. This idea is well-founded, but two other observations made by Freud raise some difficulties: the first is that hate must always concern a total object; the second is that hate is not an instinct.

If hate always concerns total objects, it can no longer be primary. In truth, how is it possible to recognise the outside when there is not yet an internal space belonging to the subject? As a result, from now on we shall not speak of hate before the baby can recognise objects as total, that is, separate from him, external to him – and this takes some time. But from this perspective, it is no longer the expulsion of hate that creates the outside, but rather the outside is the condition required for hate to exist.

The existence of the environment – mother as an ego-support filter of the world – does not solve the problem. Based on this theory, it is the mother who guarantees the constitution of the baby's own psychic space and therefore, once again, it is impossible to define hate as primary in the *infant*, since hate can only exist starting at the stage where it can be tolerated by the ego. Dilemma or paradox?

If it is a paradox, it can be resolved by supposing that hate is primary in the relation between a mother and her baby, who is a total object. It can be postulated that *hate exists at the origin in the mother's psychic reality*. Hate is the *operator* of the necessary separation, of the essential otherness whose recognition is so painful for the mother. In this context, this primary hate in the mother will constitute the *infant* as exterior to her – by opening the possibility for him to create in his turn objects, the world and others as realities separate from him. But, since an infant does not exist independently from maternal care, and since at the start of life the psychic space of the baby and that of the mother are fused, primary hate in the mother renders hate in the baby primary. And there you are!

We must keep in mind that in this context we are speaking of the unconscious maternal representations at work in the theoretical formation of a subject. These representations become manifest in reality in the guise of subtle events whose low intensity requires numerous repetitions before they can accomplish their separating function. I hope that the reminder of these repetitive manifestations will prevent this complex hypothesis from being reduced to a traumatogenic theory of the formation of the subject. Now that we have specified these aspects of the hypothesis, we can go on to say that we can easily conceive of a mother who unconsciously hates her baby at the very moment when she holds him for the first time. In truth, she would really love to eat the perfect little feet, the pretty little hands of the baby, the skin that is so soft. But if she were to give in to her cannibalistic instinct, there would be no more baby. This makes the mother very sad. She hates this impossibility of eating her baby without causing him to disappear. From a strictly unconscious point of view, according to Freud, this hate is necessary to make it possible for the mother to love her baby as someone truly different from herself. In this perspective, we can say that without hate there could be no psychic health for the child – because there would be no child. Here, hate is not a destructive factor; it is part of the symbol-generating function of the death instinct, it creates difference, allows otherness, establishes the possibility of considering the child as another, and opens onto the possibilities of being. But, in that case, why continue to call *hate* or *death instinct* the agency that makes all this possible? The question deserves to be examined.

Freud concluded that hate is not an impulse. What is it then? Is it the quintessential affect? An affect with no representation? You can see that it would be impossible to postulate that an affect without representation could be the opposite of passionate love with its investment in a multitude of intersecting psychic representations. But leaving this aside, let us consider this quality without a memory trace (I am using the capital letter to emphasise the opacity of the difficult question we are examining.) Unpleasure is also a quality and, as such, it has to be expulsed in order for the metapsychological monad to be theorised exclusively in quantitative terms. (You will note that we come upon the same problem that Michel Neyraut identified relative to transference.)[8]

To conceive of hate as primary in the infant means to stipulate an affect prior to any representation. But, in that case, how can Freudian theory postulating an unconscious constituted solely by representations of memory traces, in which affect plays no role, describe this affect? It cannot. Here, the importance of Piera Aulagnier's work becomes more evident. By defining the pictogram as a representation of affect and as the affect of representation, she grants affect – and transference – a new place in the metapsychology. By making the pictogram the consequence of the pleasant or unpleasant encounter between an object and its complementary zone-object (the breast, the mouth), she also renders the pictogram dependent on the degree to which the baby is or is not an object of maternal libidinal investment, and a source of pleasure during the encounter. Once it is integrated into the theory in this fashion, hate becomes conceivable at the level of originary processes.[9]

The Freudian stumbling blocks and paradoxes regarding hate that I have just outlined are presented in his theory of paranoia. According to Freud, the paranoid subject encounters hate coming from the outside. This hate is, in fact, his own hate that he projects. The cause of the projection is repressed homosexual love for the father. We should remember that his book about Schreber, which constitutes his theory of paranoia, was written during a period of conflict with Jung, which rekindled his conflicts with Fliess, whose paranoia cannot be doubted, and that both relations were charged with homosexual libido.

Among the texts making a critique of Freudian theory on paranoia – I am including a selected bibliography – Herbert Rosenfeld's article on the relation between homosexuality and paranoia is fundamental.[10] His paranoid homosexual patient can function as long as his relationship with his older partner is maintained. When these ties of love weaken, the patient's internal world becomes dominated by persecutory components and his relation to the feminine take the grotesque form of dressing in drag. Rosenfeld shows that homosexual investment constitutes libidinal protection against the fear of being swallowed up in a femininity rendered insane by hate of the father.

Without this libidinal recourse, Schreber is condemned to the delusion of being a woman, a delusion which keeps together – for a long time – the fragments remaining after the massacre. Philippe Réfabert pointed out that in these conditions Schreber cannot recognise hate.[11] But where has hate gone?

If my hypothesis is correct – that it is symbolisation of hate by the mother that allows the child to exist – we can say that in paranoid subjects hate is not symbolised, and that its symbolisation is impossible. In Freud's theory of paranoia, hate holds the same place as the place it is assigned in the theory relative to the genesis of the psychic apparatus: it is expulsed to the outside; rejected; and projected. And the outside is bad, unpleasant, dangerous and persecutory. The paranoid subject's relation to his hatred is of the same nature as the relation between the theory of impulses and hatred as a primary affect: something utterly unthinkable. But is the exteriority of hate a requirement for understanding hate, or is the Freudian conceptual framework preventing us from understanding it differently?

While we await an answer, we can observe that it seems unbearable for narcissistic balance to recognise hate not integrated into libidinal drives as simply available affect. When hate is made part of the libidinal stakes, it causes conflict but it has its place, a recognised and uncontested place in the fantasies of the envious, the resentful, the revenge seeker, the sadist and the masochist.

In consonance with narcissism, hate assassinates. The assassin merely repeats the murder perpetrated against him, the murder that produced the psychic cadaver he is.

Cruelty is the attempt to transform the other into the tomb of the fragments of this cadaver, or to scatter them to the four winds. Thus, the effects of the real hate of the parents on the psychic life of the child vary depending on the degree of interiorisation of this cadaver. The range extends from indifference to the advent of cruelty. Here we are no longer speaking of pleasure or libido, but of the extent of the massacre.

The paranoid subject's inability to recognise hate is related to his insensitivity to violence. This insensitivity is the result of introjections of parental cruelty. It is a solution to which the child arrives late, after painful, repeated experiences of his powerlessness to instrumentalise his anger in response to his murderous parents. This powerlessness is associated with the prohibition against questioning the legitimacy of his suffering.[12]

Freud's theory of an essentially cruel superego is shaped by his conception of hate. I shall develop this at greater length after you read Fernando de Rojas' play *La Celestina*.

With my warmest regards,

Notes

1 See Letter 10, *Winnicott's concept of* continuity *of being: Transference and the treatment of trauma.*

2 Winnicott, D. W. (1958), *Collected Papers. Through Paediatrics to Psycho-Analysis*, London: Tavistock Publications.

3 Searles, H. (1979), "Feelings of Guilt in the Psychoanalyst", in *Countertransference and Related Subjects.* New York: International Universities Press.

4 See Letter 32, *Totalitarian regimes and psychosis.*

5 I have given an illustration of this observation in Chapter III of my book *De l'Amour à la pensée*, op. cit.

6 Montaigne, M. de (1958), "The Complete Essays of Montaigne", (trans. D. M. Frame). Stanford, CA: Stanford University Press.

7 Freud, S. (1915), *Instincts and their Vicissitudes* S.E., 14: 219, London: Hogarth.

8 See Letter 16, *Freud, Michel Neyraut, Piera Aulagnier: Anxiety Between Theory and Practice.*

9 Ibid.

10 Rosenfeld, H. A. (1949) "Remarks on the relation of male homosexuality to paranoia", *International Journal of Psychoanalysis*, 30: 36–47. Reprinted in *Psychotic States*, London: Hogarth Press, 1965; Eduardo Prado De Oliveira, "L'invention de Schreber" in *Le Cas Schreber.* Paris: PUF, coll. "Bibliothèque de psychanalyse", 1979; Chauvé Azouri, *J'ai réussi là où le paranoïaque échoue...*, Paris: Denoel, 1991; Micheline Enriquez, *Aux carrefours de la haine.* Paris: EPI/Desclée de Browwer, 1984.

11 See Letter 14, *Paranoia as seen by Philippe Réfabert.*

12 For Winnicott, the primary factor in children is not hate but aggression in the service of motor skill development. This aggression must be distinguished from that tied to libidinal drives, to which Winnicott also attributes great importance. Aggression connected to motor skills is present before the earliest integrations and should not be confused with aggression resulting from frustration, which can even become anger, indicating that a certain level of integration has already been achieved. This *aggression tied to motor skills is an integrative factor: it is what makes possible early recognition of the external world* – that is, a world not belonging to the ego.

Thus, there is a *potential of primary motor capacity*, synonymous with activity in the infant, whose aggression is what *embodies* the sense of reality of libidinal experiences. And we can add a corollary: libidinal experiences with a limited aggressive component associated with motor skills do not reinforce the sense of reality or of existing. In other words, aggression associated to motor skills precedes the erotic component; in a subject whose environment was respectful of the logic of his requirements as an infant, *motor capacities became attached to the libido, and not the reverse.* In this case, there is certainly *a firmly established early grounding of the ego* (the unconscious ego) – that is, of an initial capacity to interpret the failings of the environment in a way that facilitates better integration. This aggression tied to motor function does not lose all its autonomy when it is integrated into libidinal instincts. For instance, we can attribute to it the pleasant and reassuring impression made upon us by people we describe as spontaneous, at ease and seemingly able to accomplish their goals effortlessly. (Such spontaneity can give rise to murderous intentions.) When a subject is disconnected from the primal aggression associated with motor function, he will likely have an impoverished experience of the real: motor activities are the source of the discovery and rediscovery of the environment, of the world.

Winnicott's conception of an aggressive component tied to motor skills and distinct from the aggression intrinsic to the libido invalidates the attempt to reduce primal narcissism to a space closed in on itself. In addition, this distinction between aggression linked with motor capacity and aggression connected with sexuality makes it possible to solve the problem of the ego's own energy. The Winnicottian perspective does not make a qualitative difference between aggression in the service of motor activities, in other words, of the unconscious ego, and aggression associated with sexuality. The difference between them is related both to the origin and to the relation connecting aggression to the two distinct functions, each with its own requirements. The specific requirements of each function – motor skills and sexuality – determine the exact manner of their coupling with aggression. In other words, it is possible for aggression in the service of motor skills to be invested in the libido, and vice versa. Thus, passing from one to the other is not a problem: Winnicott insists on a logical hierarchy and on the autonomy of each function. (As well as on the risk of lack of integration between psyche and soma if this passage from one to the other takes place in the absence of certain conditions of development, or before a certain capacity to transpose sensations is acquired.)

The Celestina superego and the Dulcinea superego

Dear friend,

I am very happy that you are reading *La Celestina*. This text gives us the opportunity to start working on the theory of the superego, which according to Freud himself is still a partial theory. This work will inevitably bring us to ask ourselves what we mean when we speak of the ethics of psychoanalysis. But let us start with the play and its main character.

The first surprising thing is the date when the play was written, 1499, as well as the fact that the play was performed in Spain during the Inquisition. That at the time the performance consisted of a reading of the text by a single actor, before a selected audience, does not change the fact that the very existence of the play is extraordinary. On the contrary, it is particularly surprising given that this selected audience represented the intelligence and power of Spanish society, that is, those who accepted and made use of inquisitorial methods. The fact that the author, Rojas, used every possible trick to see the play performed does not explain anything either, since these subterfuges were probably known by everyone, and especially by those entrusted with supervising, prohibiting and punishing all forms of expression opposing official dogma.

Rojas' subterfuges were far from subtle. The fact that Fernando de Rojas, a Marrano (converted Jew), should have claimed that he found this text in some forgotten corner of the world is the least precautionary measure to be expected of a Marrano, but it does not explain why the play was not blacklisted. And it was certainly not the pacifying epilogue of the play, which praised the "educational" values of a story that teaches young people the dangers of love – that would have misled the torturers' henchmen.

The play deals with love, but not just any kind of love. It is about love tied to sexuality, about the way love and sex always go together, and about the fact that no matter what we say, men and women think of nothing else. The play demonstrates this hypothesis. Freud could have written it himself.

The main feminine character is amazingly modern: an active, sensual woman who takes pleasure in her sexuality, who takes charge of her love life and her social life, who, in every situation is more courageous than most men – because her attitude towards the reality of the world is less defensive; because she is more aware of this reality. She is a woman who searches for the truth, like all those who have endured oppression – because it is a matter of survival, of knowing where the next violence could come from – and she therefore recognises lies. And since lies and political power often go together, and power is in the hands of men, she has perfected her knowledge of men – of their lies and their ignorance about the sexuality of women.

Given that only a "demon" can reveal all this reality that should not be seen, Rojas confers this dramatic function to a woman. By doing so, he creates a character in conformity with the manner in which the religious society of his time portrayed women: lecherous and demonic – witches.

Celestina is an old whore, a procurer. She is also a witch, a witch who intimidates demons, who threatens them and makes them obey. Of course, such a portrayal of a witch is a very subtle, intelligent way of mocking inquisitorial procedures: by judging a woman for witchcraft, it is not a servant or an accomplice of the Devil who is condemned, but her Master. Thus, Rojas goes further than the Church in describing the witch, he makes an absurd suggestion: that a human being could be more powerful in the practice of evil than Satan. From this perspective, what is absurd is not so much the definition of a "witch", but rather the very existence of this concept – in other words, what is absurd is the Inquisition. Well done!

If we set aside the dramatic function of the Celestina character – "revealer" of what is repressed in a religious society, interpreter of this society – to consider the life and personality of this woman, we have to admit that we would love to meet her, horrible as she might be – for there is no doubt that this woman is horrible and dangerous; but we are analysts and are therefore particularly interested in the strange lives human beings can live.

Celestina is familiar with desire in all its forms – she knows the joys, the pains and the anxiety that it can produce – and she engages with it literally and figuratively, that is, she makes it part of her life. She is paid to tell women what they already know – that for them love is sexual desire – and to tell men what they do not want to hear – that they are afraid to associate love with sexuality. She is paid for her intransigence in the use of this knowledge, for her tenacity in uncovering under infinitely varied disguises the reluctance to recognise these truths. Her sense of reality and her strength are rooted in the periods of misery she lived through – in short, in her experience of traumatic suffering. She has much in common with psychoanalysts, in fact. As for those who say that a real analyst "does not know anything", such statements are the invention of ideologues who consider any use of power to be abuse of power. In truth, and fortunately, analysts do have knowledge. Our reasons for not considering Celestina an analyst – despite the traits mentioned above, are of a different nature. I shall come back to this.[1]

I became acquainted with *La Celestina* through Françoise Davoine, when I attended her seminar on *Don Quixote*. She considers love to be the key to reading *Don Quixote*. From her point of view, *Don Quixote* tells the story of the analysis of a psychotic, with Sancho playing the role of therapist. Part I describes Don

Quixote's delirious escape into psychosis; Part II describes his recovery, after he encounters and recognises perversion. Believe me, this reading is not at all simplistic; on the contrary, it opens the interpretation of the work to a multitude of perspectives. And like all judicious interpretations, this one becomes indispensable, it determines our relation to the text.

But what is Don Quixote escaping from? From perversion. Fortunately, since Françoise Davoine forgets to be a psychopathologist, she considers that *insanity is a response to perversion*, a way to keep life alive. In fact, the multitude of beings encountered by the hero created by Cervantes – who draws a portrait of the Spain of his era, the portrait of humanity – can be divided into two types: those who see Don Quixote, despite his madness, as a subject with his integrity intact; and those who laugh at his madness, who make a mockery of it. The latter are perverse beings who reinstate the traumatic situation, and the Celestina character, obviously known to Cervantes – is the paradigm representing them, as Françoise Davoine rigorously demonstrates.

At this level of interpretation, Françoise Davoine analyses the dynamics of the relation between Celestina and her interlocutors. Whether stated briefly or at length, her aim is that no one shall resist her. Celestina uses her knowledge about sexuality, and about all the strategies employed by human beings to avoid knowing the truth regarding their desire, to acquire a hold on others. She does not precede her interlocutor in order to wait for him at the place where he must necessarily arrive; she harasses him despite all the energy he employs to refuse recognising his desire, to avoid being aware of it.

Celestina, who can make demons obey her, who is therefore absolute Evil, is the ideal of all perverts. Celestina is frightening and fascinating due to her ability to precipitate the other into the deepest anxiety by confronting him without warning to the truth that constitutes him. Her hypnotic power is based on this violence, as well as on the enjoyment of her cruelty, which is evident to her victims. But the most frightening characteristic of a pervert, like that of any totalitarian regime, is not so much what he does to us, but what we imagine that he is still capable of doing.

Celestina always addresses the infantile component of anyone she meets. She *knows* that this is the supreme means of gaining hold on another person. By revealing his secret wish to avert the anxiety accompanying any true desire, Celestina presents herself as one who can fulfil a promise of endless *jouissance* – and by so doing she becomes the sole authority in matters of prohibition, limits and reality. This is the position held by the parents of a psychotic subject in relation to their child, who is their toy, their little thing, the partial object dispensing the perverse pleasure they need in order not to drown in the deadly emptiness handed down to them through countless generations.

But how is it that Don Quixote is not crushed, torn to pieces, by the Celestinas of the world? Because he has Sancho, his therapist, and above all Dulcinea. According to Françoise Davoine, Don Quixote's love for Dulcinea is the symbolic value that sustains him. I completely agree with this hypothesis, which seems obvious. In Françoise Davoine's seminar, I often underlined these distinctions by speaking of a *Celestina superego* and a *Dulcinea superego*. The Celestina superego comprises everything destructive, hateful and cruel in the subject's experience. The Dulcinea superego includes everything that connects, everything that allows life and Eros to triumph over the deadly Thanatos. Contrary to Celestina, who targets the infantile in people in order to establish her hold over them, the Dulcinea superego cares for the wounded child and is interested in the childhood years of life. In the work allowing the subject to separate from trauma, the analyst is a Dulcinea superego, careful not to have the therapeutic situation repeat the trauma, so that it can constitute a novel experience of encounter in the patient's life.

The Celestina superego is related to attachments to parental cruelty, while the Dulcinea superego refers to a space of dreaming and detachment from unbearable suffering and permanent, insidious persecution. Each of these superegos contains an Ideal which, very briefly, could be resumed as follows: life as a work of destruction, life as a work of creation. And although psychoanalysts are in a position to know that freeing oneself from parental cruelty is far from easy, they work "for" Dulcinea. I believe this to be a clinical reality, the unquestionable truth of our daily practice. Some of us even consider this our ethical code. However, in view of the psychoanalytic theory available today, our perspective requires constant reaffirmation.

According to Freud, the symbolic is transmitted from one generation to another through the superego. The superego is "*actually the legitimate heir*" of the parental agency. "[T]*he super-ego takes the place of the parental agency and observes, directs and threatens the ego in exactly the same way as earlier parents did with the child.*" But, "*The super-ego seems to have made a one-sided choice and to have picked out only the parents' strictness and severity, their prohibiting and punitive function, whereas their loving care seems not to have been taken over and maintained*" (New Introductory Lectures XXXI, my emphasis.)[2]

At this point, the foundations of subsequent theoretical developments are established; their expansion will only reinforce their characteristics: the superego will be cruel and its dynamic relation to the ego will be based on the delusional model of feeling observed, and the model of identification to the parents will be that of pathological mourning – melancholia. On the instinctual level, the superego will group together the effects of the death instinct theory, the violence of the father of the primitive horde, as well as all of the child's aggression towards his parents, no less. In short, Freud's formulated theory of the superego makes it possible to understand Celestina, but not Dulcinea.

When Lacan reformulated Freud's theory of the superego, he did not overstep any boundaries by promoting Celestinian cruelty. Nor did he contest the established doctrine when he inscribed the superego in the paternal line exclusively. But Lacan was an astute reader who was aware that his loyalty concerned the established body of Freud's work – and not the status of the question we have inherited from Freud. Each time Freud decided upon a doctrine regarding a certain question, he had the honesty to review the aspects of the question not yet formulated or theorised. Lacan's definitive approach often leads him to make categorical, absolute choices which weaken the strength of Freudian stakes, diminish the flexibility of Freud's thought and "ideologise" its ramifications.

As far as the superego is concerned, what Lacan leaves out is precisely the *hesitation* indicated by Freud who states that the superego "seems" to have made a "one-sided choice". In fact, just as the dreamer is the author of his dream, here Freud invents the concept of superego, defining its content and its consequences. Thus, *it is Freud who is aware of making a one-sided choice when, in defining the superego, he focuses on the strictness and severity of the parents*, without integrating "their loving care" to provide theoretical "continuation".

If we wish to find in the Freudian texts the material that can constitute the theory allowing a clinical practice of the Dulcinea superego type, as well as its extension to a symbolic system based on love, we need to search for the thread of recurrences of this hesitation in Freud's work. Given the ease with which certain analysts embody the *Celestina superego* today – the "vow" of silence and the refusal to interpret the transference being two of the most grotesque examples of the cruelty shown to patients – this search would be very useful. And I would be happy if you could accompany me on this journey.

In this regard, I can tell you that this Freudian hesitation is an effect of something that you will hear described as Freud's change of direction in the 1920s. At that time, in his clinical practice due to traumatic war dreams, and in his personal life due to the death of his daughter Sophie, Freud had to admit that the functioning of the psychic "apparatus" is not always dedicated to obtaining pleasure. Certain psychic elaborations require durable engagement with unpleasure, suffering and pain; these elaborations cause the psychic "apparatus" to function on another level, *beyond the pleasure principle*. Based on this observation, Freud brought into question his first instinctual duality theory (*ego instincts, sexual instincts* – the ego being the agency responsible for repression) and suggested a second duality: *death instincts and life instincts,* Thanatos and Eros. Wanting to draw attention to the specificity of his discovery of the death instinct – since he feared that it could be confused with mere resistance, or with a barrier to obtaining pleasure – Freud abandoned altogether his theorising on Eros, insisting instead on the destructive, irresistible and primordial character of Thanatos. As a result of this choice in the elaboration of the doctrine, a theory of Eros, and a theory regarding the interaction between *life instincts* and *death instincts* in the psyche, remain to be formulated. In other words, Dulcinea has been abandoned along the way.

This abandonment occurred very early, immediately following the appearance of the concept, although it was presented as temporary, as merely a consequence of the pedagogical structure of the text. The following explanation is to be found in *The Ego and The Id*:

> Perhaps it would be safer to say "with the parents"[3]; for before a child has arrived at definite knowledge of the difference between the sexes, the lack of a penis, it does not distinguish in value between its father and its mother. I recently came across the instance of a young married woman whose story

showed that, after noticing the lack of penis in herself, she had supposed it to be absent not in all women, but only in those women she regarded as inferior, and had still supposed that her mother possessed one. *In order to simplify my presentation I shall discuss only identification with the father* (my emphasis).[4]

If a double identification of the child with the parents is recognised, why does Freud prefer to discuss – at first – "to simplify [the] presentation", identification with the father?

The reasons are of two kinds. The first has to do with the relatively late introduction of the concept of superego in the theoretical corpus, when the place of the father of the horde, after his prohibitive function in Oedipian theory, is well-defined; when the theory of cruelty in melancholia due to the splitting of the subject has been formulated; and when the deadly aspects of repetition compulsion are becoming obvious. In other words, when the concept of superego has to be defined, Freud refers at first to the clearly formulated theoretical texts already available. It is simpler and more efficient to do this, keeping in mind the unpredictability of death; if Freud were to die before completing his theory of the superego, at least he would have left a portion of the theory well integrated in the corpus of his work. But there are other reasons.

Reasons of another kind have to do with the Freudian conception of the mother. Let us go back to the passage of *The Ego and the Id* quoted above. We note that the manner in which the ideas are presented emphasises primary identification with a phallic mother (who has or does not have a penis), rather than identification with the mother as a caregiver, a holding and tender mother – whom Freud had, nevertheless, described very early, for instance in this passage from *Formulations Regarding the Two Principles in Mental Functioning,* that I often quote:

> … an organisation which was a slave to the pleasure principle and neglected the reality of the external world could not survive [...] The employment of a fiction like this is, however, justified when one considers that the infant – provided one includes with it the care it receives from its mother – does almost realise a psychical system of this kind.[5]

Later, in *The Basic Writings*, Freud admitted that, by her care of the baby, the mother's importance is: "unique, without parallel, established unalterably for a whole lifetime, as the prototype of all later love-relations."[6]

(After having chosen these quotes, I realised that these passages concerning the mother are usually associated with the formation of the ego. And in fact, the problem with a partial formulation of the superego – that I am now reviewing with you – is marked by Freud's refusal to imagine its origins in continuity with the organisation of the ego as a protective shield, as protective of the subject, as a protector of the innermost being.)

But it is often the case that in Freudian texts this recognition of the positive nature of the loving relation with the mother suggests an idea of mother-infant mastering (*instinct for mastery*). How does this shift happen? It happens because in maternal love and care there is also seduction. Whether tenderness precedes seduction or occurs simultaneously with it is a question that Freud answered in two different ways. In his descriptions of the relation between the mother and her baby, he opted for giving tenderness priority – and Winnicott used these descriptions as the foundation of his primary environment concept. But Freud the theoretician gave precedence to the aspects of seduction in maternal care. Was this a way of guarding against Jungian distortions on the part of his disciples? Was it loyalty to Goethe who considered that the subject must free himself from the reign of mothers? The important thing for our discussion is to note that in theorising about the manner in which the child frees himself from maternal attachment so that he may emerge as a subject, it is justifiable to suppose that there are powerful counter-investments preventing the child from being swallowed up in the quagmire of the maternal. From this point of view, the theory giving primacy to the paternal reference in personality structuring based on identification with the superego is justified; the father becomes the bastion which protects the subject by preventing him from succumbing to the fusional, deadly forgetfulness of devouring mothers. (It is noteworthy that Freud himself felt uncomfortable being the object of maternal transference.)

It is not surprising that the word *bastion* came to mind: of course, a bastion against the mother, but in a context emphasising the protective nature of the superego. And now, let us look at Freud's 1927 article *Humour*. Strachey, Freud's English translator, remarked that here Freud presents the superego as "likeable" for the first time.[7]

In fact, at the end of the article Freud presents the superego as trying to console the ego through humour, and to protect it from suffering. He adds that this does not contradict the superego's origin in the parental agency. Of course, parental agency is to be understood as the mother and the father, but above all as a loveable and loving father. Finally, Freud comments that recognition of this function of the superego teaches us that we still have a great deal to learn about this entity.

Although we agree that it is better late than never, we cannot fail to notice (and regret) the ravaging effects of such delayed understanding on clinical practice. If we add to this the time that it takes to publish translations – the French version of this text came out in 1994! – one can imagine the consequences, the number of misinterpretations and misunderstandings, and the extent of the disaster. For instance, you can see how this has facilitated the collusion between the loyal members and the "boy scouts" of the analytic establishment, those who defend the temple of the severe superego, those who would see to it that Ferenczi, Balint, Winnicott and Bion – who have given thought to the loving roots of the superego – be viewed as tolerated eccentrics. Moreover, this gives you an idea of the debt we owe to the salutary resistance these pioneers of psychoanalysis offered to inanity, to conformity, to intellectual laziness and to the denial of indisputable clinical facts.

I shall not dwell on the implications of Lacan's first theory of the superego. In his book *Fin du dogme paternel*, Michel Tort examined the question exhaustively and revealed, among other things, the religious and authoritarian roots of Lacan's conception of the father. Another very interesting analysis of Lacan's theory of the superego, complementary to Tort's work, is the one made by Bernard Penot.

According to Penot,[8] who compares Freudian and Lacanian texts, Lacan's "obscene and ferocious" superego does not refer to the Freudian father, but rather to a terrifying archaic mother. The superego is a totalitarian power the subject will have to escape in order to become his own person. Penot shows that for Lacan "the ego ideal represents the 'paternal' symbolic agency in the psyche. But in that case, this agency must be distinguished from the narcissistic conformity figures of the ego ideal, while the superego invariably maintains its primary *parental* [totalitarian] nature". "The Name of the father must emerge in the place occupied by the primordial mother." The obscene and ferocious figures of the Lacanian superego, which Penot brings into relation with the supremacy of Freud's dictatorial figure of the superego in *Group Psychology and the Analysis of the Ego*, "essentially reveal the limitations, not to say failure, of the symbolisation process".

What is noteworthy here is the fact that Penot maintains the idea of the parental couple. It is as if he was returning to the initial text on the superego, in *The Ego and the Id*, where identifications to the likeable Freudian father later portrayed in *Humour* were intended to bring about the formation of the ego ideal. (Penot does not mention the text on humour; I am the one who is trying to find the theoretical sideroads that could have led to the formulation of a loving primary identification to the parents before the text written in 1927.) We must point out that this division of labour between ferocious superego and structuring ego, discovered by Penot in the Lacanian texts, is present in Freud's work as well. In fact, Freud often presents the ego ideal, portrayed as a protective agency, as being synonymous with the superego; at times, the ego ideal is even presented as existing before the superego. This confusion highlights the effects of the "simplification" that left out of the original conception of the superego the likeable mother and father – a notion reintroduced in the text on humour.

One misinterpretation consists in identification to a prehistoric father, a hypothesis considered fundamental by many analysts from various schools, which is consistent with the genesis of the superego based on the prohibition of incest and on the concept of a prohibitive father. I have no difficulty accepting the Freudian hypothesis of the *real murder* of the prehistoric father – although I do not imagine him solely as a tyrant. The trace of this murder is apparent in its results: the circulation of women and the prohibition of incest. But the Freudian notion of transmission of the memory trace of this *murder even to the infant* seems to me to belong to the metaphysical domain or to the sphere of magic.

I am not denying the possibility that a subject may have a direct grip on the trace of a real event, and even on the event itself, without recourse to language. This is, in fact, a component of psychic suffering. I also know that this component can constitute a quality in the encounter with the other. I am thinking of the state of being in love, and of certain borderline clinical situations. In short, we are speaking of a deeply moving experience of encounter. And so the question is, how could an infant, who does not yet have a psychic space of his own, contain the horror of the reality of murder?

What follows are the last two paragraphs of Freud's text entitled *Humour*:

In other connections we know the super-ego as a severe master. It will be said that it accords ill with such a character that the super-ego should condescend to enabling the ego to obtain a small yield of pleasure. It is true that humorous pleasure never reaches the intensity of the pleasure in the comic or in jokes, that it never finds vent in hearty laughter. It is also true that, in bringing about the humorous attitude, the super-ego is actually repudiating reality and serving an illusion. But (without rightly knowing why) we regard this less intense pleasure as having a character of very high value; we feel it to be especially liberating and elevating. Moreover, the jest made by humour is not the essential thing. It has only the value of a preliminary. The main thing is the intention which humour carries out, whether it is acting in relation to the self or other people. It means: "Look! here is the world, which seems so dangerous! It is nothing but a game for children – just worth making a jest about!"

If it is really the super-ego which, in humour, speaks such kindly words of comfort to the intimidated ego, this will teach us that we have still a great deal to learn about the nature of the super-ego. Furthermore, not everyone is capable of the humorous attitude. It is a rare and precious gift, and many people are even without the capacity to enjoy humorous pleasure that is presented to them. And finally, if the super-ego tries, by means of humour, to console the ego and protect it from suffering, this does not contradict its origin in the parental agency.[9]

(p. 166)

We have come full circle. Initially, to "simplify" his presentation, Freud discussed only identification to the father to explain the genesis of the superego; now he warns us that we have much more to learn about this concept. And, once again, we must thank all those who conducted this research before us, all those who have always questioned and reformulated Freudian metapsychology based on the lessons learned from transferential encounters.

I shall present a partial inventory of the effects of these belated Freudian observations about the superego on the conduct of psychoanalysis. First, the position of the analyst changes from being in line with the incest prohibitive function only, to integrating *a loving, comforting and protective function* as well. (These are Freudian terms.) The analyst is assumed to be capable of using humour, and there is no justification for him to feel obliged to be solemn as a judge, stiff as a frozen shadow, phobic and obsessional about any manifestation of emotion on his own part or in his responses to the affect of his patients. The analyst is not simply a mirror; he must also allow the patient to joke with the world; to do so, he must have the skill – or tact, as Ferenczi called it – to joke with his patient. In this context, we can refer to the famous remarks made by Winnicott:

This sense of humour is evidence of a freedom, the opposite of a rigidity of the defences that characterises illness. A sense of humour is the ally of the therapist, who gets from it a feeling of confidence and a sense of having elbow room for manoeuvring. It is evidence of the child's creative imagination and of happiness.[10]

As well as this:

I am not involved by deliberate intention in the comparison of psychotherapy with psychoanalysis or indeed in any attempt to define these two processes in such a way that would show up a clear line of demarcation between the two. The general principle seems to me to be valid *that psychotherapy is done in the overlap of the two play areas, that of the patient and that of the therapist. If the patient cannot play, then something needs to be done to enable the patient to become able to play, after which psychotherapy may begin.* The reason why play is essential is that it is in playing that the patient is being creative (my emphasis).[11]

I am presenting Winnicott's remarks here as a reminder of the suspicions they aroused, and which after his death reached a shameful level of betrayal. His critics found it suspect for a psychoanalyst to experience such pleasure and joy in his work with patients, to like his occupation so much to say that the analyst's silence does not exclude the possibility of showering the patient with words; is there not a hint of perversion in all this? These critics are the analysts who ceaselessly complain of the "heaviness" of their work, work that constantly bores them, since they never have anything to learn from their patients.

In short, Freud's text on humour redefines the analyst's presence in the analytic process. Lacan recognised the importance Winnicott gives to this presence, but he neither acknowledged his debt to Winnicott nor attempted to understand all the implications of this standpoint. However, Lacan introduced a very fruitful concept when he invited analysts to identify the domain to which the interpretation of transference refers. To draw attention to the fact that the interpretation of transference can refer either to the domain of the Real, the symbolic or the imaginary highlights the plurality of the analyst's qualities of presence in the conduct of the analysis. It is regrettable that Lacanian analysts have shown so little interest in pursuing this field of clinical research, which in my opinion is the most important one that Lacan introduced.

The one remaining thing to say about this new Freudian conception of the superego is that it is impossible to make it fit into a tragic ethical perspective of psychoanalysis. However, our views on the presence and receptivity of the analyst, founded on this new conception, are coherent with the line of thought I have been advocating for some time, and which makes friendship the ethical foundation of our practice.

Moreover, we may want to examine the logical ties existing between humour and transference. In my view, humour is either part of the analysis when the latter constitutes a transitional space between the analyst and the patient, or is part of the psychic environment offered by the analyst to a patient who is engaged in transference, but not yet in analysis. In this case, humour is a psychic and intellectual agent facilitating the construction of a transitional space, or the creation of the analysis as transitional space – which is the same thing. In other words, while a good transferential relation can encourage humour on the part of both protagonists, sometimes it is humour which will make it possible for transference to be recognised as such.[12]

In conclusion, and to illustrate, I will give you a clinical example described to me by our friend Annie Topalov. It concerns a patient perceived by the analyst as being very confused, having trouble recognising her place in her life and in the world. A seemingly unimportant event caused her to describe for the first time a very strange relationship with her father. The latter would walk around naked in the house, sit on the toilet without closing the bathroom door, and tease his daughter who locked herself in when she showered, instead of letting her Dad see her pretty breasts. When she visits her parents, her father always comes to fetch her at the airport and, in response to his daughter's discreet distance, he argues that they are a close-knit family, that he is her father and that she should talk freely about her life. This prompts the analyst to remark that she understands now why the analysand is sometimes so confused, and why she moved to another city.

This was followed by elaboration concerning the incestuous father. At the end of the session the analyst said: "The next time you visit your parents, be sure to ask your father to meet you at the airport naked." The patient burst out laughing.

What I find remarkable about this interpretation based on the Dulcinea superego is that it operates on several levels: it prohibits incest; it involves incestuous madness; and it serves to create enormous opening. In my view, this is precisely the aim of psychoanalysis.

As you can see, I am merely giving you a glimpse of the vast territory that remains to be explored.

Till next time then!

Notes

1 What constitutes the paradoxical nature of the dramatic character Celestina is this: while her modernity serves to reveal the hypocrisy of her society, unconsciously her position is that of the perverse subject – since she participates in, and benefits from, the world she exposes.
2 Freud, S. (1932–1936), *New Introductory Lectures*, Lecture XXXI, S.E., 22: 57–80. London: Hogarth.
3 Perhaps it would be safer to say "with the parents". In order to simplify my presentation I shall discuss only identification with the father." (My emphasis.)
4 Freud, S. *The Ego and the Id*, op. cit., p. 26.

5 Freud, S. (1911), *Formulations Regarding the Two Principles in Mental Functioning* S.E., 12: 218–226. London: Hogarth.

6 Freud, S. (1938), *The Basic Writings of Sigmund Freud*, First English Edition, (trans. Dr A. A. Brill) The Modern Library.

7 Freud, S. *Humour*, op. cit. 4. Freud, *Humour*, op. cit. pp. 160–166.

8 Penot, B. (1995), "L'instance du Surmoi dans les Écrits de Jacques Lacan", in *Surmoi II, Monographies de la Revue Française de Psychanalyse*. Paris: PUF.

9 Freud, S. *Humour*, op. cit. pp. 166.

10 Winnicott, D. W. (1971), *Therapeutic Consultations in Child Psychiatry*. London: Hogarth Press, p. 32.

11 Winnicott, D. W. (1971), *Playing and Reality*. London: Routledge, p. 72.

12 See Letter 13, *Humour*.

Freud and Spinoza

Dear friend,

Thank you for your generous appraisal of my last two letters. Now, you are the one who acts as my interlocutor. I appreciate the good fortune of having an attentive reader like you – so I am now writing for you.

You are so right to recognise in my conception of the superego, which expands on the conception formulated in Freud's later work, and in my reflections on the insistence of Eros, my appreciation of Spinoza, and of a Spinozian perspective on the conduct of psychoanalysis and on the ethics on which our practice is founded.

I shall try to respond to your request and describe how both men contribute to my thinking. As I said earlier, I am happy that you asked me to explain the relation between the two perspectives, and I do so gladly, but this is no easy task. I would like to be as exhaustive as possible, without overwhelming you with a multitude of quotations. I would like to speak simply, without being simplistic, and be concise without losing clarity. In short, what follows is the result of trying to reconcile all these demands.

I shall start with your last question. Yes, of course Freud was familiar with the work of Spinoza. He knew it intimately. However, in his own work he only made explicit mention of it on three occasions, which have been cited by Yovel, an author of whom we have already spoken.[1] Freud alludes to Spinoza often indirectly, by referring to Heine, who was a Spinozist; moreover, he no doubt had occasion to speak of him with Lou Andreas-Salomé, who had great admiration for Spinoza's thought, to which she had certainly been exposed by Nietzsche.

But the three instances where Freud speaks of Spinoza, identified by Yovel, show the fundamental importance of Spinoza's work for the elaboration of Freudian thought. The first of these appears in *Leonardo da Vinci: A Memory of His Childhood* (1910): "Because of his insatiable and indefatigable thirst for knowledge Leonardo has been called the Italian Faust. But... the view may be hazarded that Leonardo's development approaches Spinoza's mode of thinking."[2]

The second reference is to be found in a letter in which Freud declines an invitation to contribute an article to a book commemorating the tricentennial of Spinoza's birth (1932): "Throughout my long life, I (timidly) sustained an extraordinarily high respect for the person as well as for the results of the thought of the great philosopher Spinoza."[3]

The third reference occurs in a letter to Lothar Bickel, a Spinozist psychoanalyst, who had asked Freud to specify his debt to Spinoza and to explain why he so rarely cited him. This is Freud's answer, in a letter dated 28 June 1931: "I readily admit my dependence on Spinoza's doctrine. There was no reason why I should expressly mention his name, since I conceived my hypotheses from an atmosphere created by him, rather than from the study of his work. Moreover, I did not seek a philosophical legitimation."[4]

This "atmosphere" is related to the fact that Freud was a man belonging to the Jewish diaspora. At the time, and especially for a Jewish intellectual, this meant being familiar with the Bible and the writings of Maimonides, as well as with Spinoza's interpretations of biblical texts and the texts of Maimonides. Freud and Spinoza were also men whose "situation" in life was very similar: both were atheist Jews; both were ahead of their time, each of them opening a vast new field of enquiry into the human condition; both completely alone, and at times totally isolated. In Freud's words: "Nor is it perhaps entirely a matter of chance that the first advocate of psycho-analysis was a Jew. To profess belief in this new theory called for a certain degree of readiness to accept a situation of solitary opposition – a situation with which no one is more familiar than a Jew."[5]

When Spinoza equated divine identity with nature, he carried out the assassination of God, which Nietzsche proclaimed three centuries later. Subsequently, Freud was to demonstrate the relation between the greatest human accomplishments and infantile sexuality, a concept which, as he himself admitted, constituted a considerable injury to culture.

As for Freud's isolation as a non-religious Jew, it must be said that he inherited the benefits of Spinoza's hard-won struggle. Being a Jew and a non-believer caused Spinoza to be ex-communicated, to be rejected and ostracised by his contemporaries of the same faith, and to be regarded with deep mistrust by the rest of his contemporaries, the non-Jews.

In terms of doctrine, it is easy to imagine why Freud would be interested in Spinoza. Like the latter, Freud rejected all transcendence connected to the human condition. Human existence is not a divine creation. In the beginning, there was man and there was the world. Each particular man must formulate the singular reasons for his life, must know himself and determine the relations he wishes to have with the world that preceded him and the world around him.

In addition Freud, like Spinoza, had certain expectations in regard to science. For instance, he hoped that biology would confirm some of his hypotheses. (On the other hand, his conception of phylogenesis as an agent in the transmission of fundamental psychic events was an easy way out, or an intermediary solution, until the theory could be developed more fully – which occurred following Lacan's discussion of the symbolic.)

Having said this, the type of knowledge to which psychoanalysis gives access is not associated with the near religious exaltation found at times in Spinoza's work. For Freud, the joy of knowledge is first and foremost the joy one takes in oneself, a joy that combines love and work. Joy results from the integration of sexuality and of thought, it is embodied joy, the joy of a thought process in which, after psychoanalysis, honest reflection can recognise the central place of sexual life as the origin of all desire.

In other words, at first sight Freud's objective seems more limited and more modest than Spinoza's objective had been. Freud offers a method of attending to the person, while Spinoza is interested in saving him. This salvation relies on a new conception of the world, a conception Spinoza believed to be grounded in science. For Freud, on the other hand, psychoanalysis was not a view of the world, and he warned against the danger of letting science take the alienating place of religion.

This apparent Freudian modesty concerns the therapeutic process, as distinct from the psychoanalysis itself. The therapeutic process involves both the request that a subject brings into analysis based on his symptomatic suffering, and the limits of the therapeutic power of psychoanalysis that Freud recognised in connection with certain patients. He advised young psychoanalysts not to have (great) expectations for their patients; in his opinion, trying to make the resolution of the patient's problems coincide with the analyst's desired outcome for the patient is an expression of the therapist's sadism. In short, Freud believed that it was necessary to admit that certain subjects cannot go beyond a precarious, shaky psychic solution to their conflicts – and the therapist has accomplished his task if the work carried out in the psychoanalytic process enabled the subject to arrive at a symptomatic compromise more comfortable than the one previously in place.

This lack of a value judgement regarding the end of a psychoanalytic therapy does not exclude a very clear and rigorous idea of the optimal results that can be achieved in psychoanalysis. Freud first formulated this idea concisely in a well-known phrase that speaks of transforming neurotic misery to ordinary human unhappiness. At the very least, we can say that the idea of normality as inseparable from the ordinary unhappiness of living is unusual. A few years later, in *The Loss of Reality in Neurosis and Psychosis*, Freud gave a more precise – and more ambitious – definition of normality. In short, normality consists of being at the same time sufficiently neurotic to recognise reality, and sufficiently psychotic to undertake to remodel it. This conception, which excludes any form of resignation, draws Freud closer to Spinoza, paradoxically. (I say "paradoxically" because the definition of emotional health is based on the combination of two "negatives".) In other words, to accept that thinking always supposes a certain degree of anxiety and that the creation of a new representation of the world emerges at the frontier of madness, is the price to pay, in Freudian terms, for making the advent of (Spinozian) joy possible.

This conception of "normality" involves constant and very demanding psychic work. We might add that, without pleasure – or rather if the subject does not associate his pleasure and joy with this demand – the constraint imposed by the superego would be equivalent to that characterising the most highly obsessional organisations.

Thus, numerous factors enter into play in the analytic process to determine whether the subject will arrive at optimal psychic functioning, or achieve only symptom relief that is precarious but more comfortable than the coping system previously in place. In Spinozian terms, we might say that the psychoanalytic experience could produce only knowledge of the second kind, acquired in the course of the analytic process, or could produce a radical change in the subject's relation to himself and to the world. The Freudian equivalent of knowledge of the third kind concerns the analysis itself, that is, the working through which applies not only to symptoms but also to the relation between the productions of the unconscious and the sensitivity of the subject to himself and to the world, and between unconscious desires and the conditions needed to widen the field of the possible.

In the course of psychoanalysis, these two levels of functioning of the psychic apparatus, the analytic process and the analytic elaboration, are simply two stages in the organisation of the transference. As such, they are interchangeable and there is no need to place them in a hierarchical relation. But, at the end of the process, if, as Loup Verlet would say, a change of paradigm has occurred, the psychic work is strictly a work of elaboration. In this sphere, it is not the analyst who carries out the analysis; the latter sustains itself through the desire of the subject in analysis to move forward – through anguish and joy – towards the unknown in himself, making the analyst his witness, giving him this place that only a friend can fill.[6]

In regards to doctrine, an important point on which the two men agree is the unity of mind and body, of psyche and soma. Spinoza, a proponent of immanence, is convinced that there is a relation between bodily states and the mind, between thought processes and all things connected to the body;[7] Freud agrees: desire – a psychic phenomenon *par excellence* – is rooted in the body, the love for another being is an extension of the satisfaction of hunger. Another important point, in Spinoza's doctrine this time, is the major place held by psychology in the *Ethics*.

By contrast, as I said earlier, for Freud joy is of a different nature than joy as described by Spinoza: "The Jew is made for joy and joy for the Jew", he wrote in a letter to his fiancée, Martha in 1882. Freud, whose name in German actually means "joy", unlike his ancestor, does not propose an ascetic attitude towards the affects and passions born of the experience of joy. Freudian joy includes anxiety – the fundamental affect – as well as the acceptance of death (I shall come back to this).[8]

This difference makes it difficult to equate Spinozian *conatus* with Freudian desire. But the term proposed by eminent Spinoza scholars, who translate *conatus* as *desire*, is acceptable since it conveys the power Spinoza attributed to this agent of thought processes, of psychic elaboration.

Both thinkers considered that this force capable of interpreting the world, of distancing itself from existential circumstances, of establishing a rigorous position in regard to truth is in no way connected to any transcendence; it is rooted in the finitude of human life which does not open onto any beyond outside of culture. But for Spinoza *conatus* is connected with an idea of effort and implies a tendency to asceticism, while Freudian desire is sexual, it cannot be imagined independently of the pleasure of its satisfaction – be it delayed satisfaction, and rigorously maintains its relation to the dark side, the impure, the sordid.

What I find surprising and hard to understand is that there has been no recognition of the equivalence which can be made between what Spinoza calls knowledge of the third kind and the relation of a subject with the unconscious after psychoanalysis.

I would say that in Spinoza's view the third kind of knowledge for a subject consists in his awareness of what constitutes his singularity in the world and in his relation to God.

This awareness is not merely rational, even though it must be preceded by an acquisition of knowledge. Because for Spinoza God is not the origin of man, and His essence can only be seized in particular things, such as this particular man for instance, knowing oneself means knowing God. Therefore, this awareness is an intuition which includes and internalises the entire journey travelled to arrive at it. This intuition is associated with an affect of a particular nature: joy.

This psychic experience described by Spinoza is absolutely identical with the Freudian notion of insight (*Einfall*). Insight is the appropriation of the work of transference interpretation, an appropriation allowing the subject to transpose to his relation with himself the emotion involved in his relation to his analyst; the seizing of his unconscious takes the form of an encounter with a self who is another – it is an opening onto the infinity of the world.

From the perspective of a theory of knowledge the two processes cannot be considered equivalent. The Spinozian subject does not have recourse to another to recognise this new mode of relation to oneself and to the world. The equivalence exists at the level of the psychic *quality* of the two experiences. In both cases, the subject *arrives at* a mode of encounter that would not have been possible without the demands of the second kind of knowledge in Spinoza's terms, and without the elaboration of transference in Freudian terms.[9]

The Freudian unconscious as the cause of one's actions is only a phase in conscious processing, the phase in which consciousness intervenes in a relation to something other than itself. When a psychoanalyst tells a patient: "You are impotent with your wife because you take her for your mother", this does not cure the impotence, but opens a field of enquiry for the patient. When the work he carries out in analysis allows this same patient to rediscover the strong sexually-charged emotion he had felt towards his mother, it is very likely that the intense emotion accompanying this return of repressed material will put an end to his impotence in his sexual relations with the woman he loves; but, more importantly, this experience will serve to change his relation to the unconscious: the "exteriority" of the unconscious will disappear and, from then on, knowing himself will mean knowing his unconscious. This explains Freud's statement, which Spinoza would have validated as knowledge of the third kind, and which describes this expansion of the self and of the world: "Where the [unconscious] is, there shall ego be."

Let me present the question from another angle, that of the irreducible opposition between the two doctrines: Spinozian monism and Freudian dualism.

Freud's latter theory of a duality of instincts, the concept of a life instinct and a death instinct, Eros and Thanatos, assumes that the death drive is present from the beginning of life: each person has a death drive particular to him. This idea is expressed in radical terms in *Beyond the Pleasure Principle*: "everything living dies for internal reasons... the aim of all life is death."[10] This is in complete opposition to Spinoza's view, which states that "Each thing, as far as it can by its own power, strives to persevere in its being", and that "No thing can be destroyed except through an external cause" (*Ethics*, III, propositions 6 and 4).[11]

And again, how can we reconcile the Freudian position with Spinoza's fundamental statement "A free man thinks of nothing less than of death, and his wisdom is a meditation on life, not on death"?[12]

And yet, in the context of a psychoanalytic relation, these two positions do not appear irreconcilable. Nor are they incompatible from an end of analysis perspective.

Let us start with clinical practice. Freud understood that the parents' love for their children is an extension of their love for themselves. The wonder felt at the sight of a baby is an extended version of parental narcissism. The French psychoanalyst Serge Leclaire postulated, based on the death instinct, that the murder of this marvellous child is the necessary condition making it possible to assume one's position as a subject.

This proves to be the case in certain psychoanalyses where the work primarily concerns a difficulty to adapt the all-powerful character of desire to the reality of the world and the difference of the other. Nevertheless, it stands to reason that this observation in no way contradicts the obvious fact that it is better for a child to be loved by his parents than the contrary. What counts is the intensity, the quality of the connection between desire and reality. We should note as well that according to Serge Leclaire excessive self-love is morbid, has a deadening quality, and that being freed of this excess renders life more real and more vibrant.

Inversely, in the case of children who were not loved by their parents, or those who survived sustained traumatic violence, clinical work consists of making a place for life, of imagining the possibility of life. Almost always, this means inventing for the patient the marvellous child he would have deserved to be; to do this, the analyst must remain attentive to the insistence of Eros. Our practice, and life experience in general, have demonstrated that those who have been through a murderous experience, either real or psychic, and have been able to relegate it to the past, never think of death, but only of life. And in fact, this subjective position, the one stated by Spinoza when he says "A free man thinks of nothing less than of death, and his wisdom is a meditation on life, not on death", is exactly the same as that which might be seen in a subject after psychoanalysis.

Psychoanalysis forces the subject to undertake very arduous emotional tasks: to recognise the demands of his desire; acknowledge hate; confront the essential reality of the differences between the sexes; and face the thought of death – the most difficult task, according to Hegel. But if this work is carried out, if the subject acknowledges that "the life of the Spirit is ... the life that endures [death] and maintains itself in it",[13] why should it be inconceivable that the subject turn all his interest and energy entirely towards life and towards life's fulfilments, that all his thoughts be turned towards the joy of celebrating the aliveness of life? Why should we suppose such a position to be naïve and pathological – based on defence mechanisms such as denial, splitting or disavowal? Are we to believe that the work done in psychoanalysis, and the end of the analysis, do not bring about any changes in the relations the subject entertained with anxiety, suffering, loss and joy before treatment? Since when does loving life, being glad to be alive, mean being less aware of the vicissitudes of life? Experience proves otherwise: those who live a real life are the best equipped to face and to think through the most weighty demands of real–reality. (I am sure it comes as no surprise to you that this perspective excludes any attempt to conceive of the ethics of psychoanalysis as an ethic of the tragic.)

From a Spinozian point of view, this development ties psychoanalysis to the second kind of knowledge, which is dependent on time. Knowledge of the third kind would combine the propositions in the *Ethics* with Freudian objectives. This type of functioning is a *mode* of relation to oneself and to the world, not a *state* acquired once and for all. Therefore, new life experiences may still be "processed" by the subject through analytic elaboration, that is, in accordance with the second type of Spinozian knowledge, which, contrary to intuition and to insight, involves a thought process that requires time.

In other words, psychic functioning rooted in this new joy of simply living and loving life excludes no affect, even though it encompasses all other affects and emotions. The quality of this new joy is closely tied to a love of oneself that was previously absent: an expansion of the ego accompanying the extraordinary feeling of the expansion of the serene presence of the world and of the other. Expansion is self-affirmation produced by the force of desire. This desire is rooted in the powerful joy produced by knowledge of the unconscious. And the strength of this joy is built on the desire of knowing the unconscious. The strength of the joy of desire.

Living with Spinoza's joyful knowledge of the third kind, or with desire that includes the existence of the unconscious, creates a different relation to time. This is easy to understand if we remember that at this level of psychic functioning achievements and accomplishments occur outside the limits of constraints. The pleasure of thinking and the lived experience associated with it are accomplishments in themselves. Thus, we can say that the subject lives in another time, outside chronological time.

It would be easy to have an ironic reaction to this Spinozian perspective, since it presupposes a relation to the Real, as well as a quality of psychic functioning achieved by a very few, like Spinoza and Freud. But you will agree that I am not proposing a worldview, nor an idealisation of psychoanalysis. Of course we are speaking of an ideal, but an entirely embodied ideal, practical, like that of true love. Moreover, how could a conceptual practice, or any practice, exist without a representation of its ultimate aim, without reference to what it produces as the surpassing of its own limits, without postulating its highest functioning, its ethics?

Best regards,

Notes

1 Yovel, Y. (1992), *Spinoza and Other Heretics*. Princeton, NJ: Princeton University Press.
I owe a debt of gratitude to Robert Misrahi, French translator and commentator of Spinoza, for it was thanks to his work that I was able to read and study the *Ethics*. But my debt to Jovel is just as great. His intelligent, subtle perspective makes it possible to understand the relation between the caution and ambiguity of the Portuguese convert Benedict Espinoza, and the style of his philosophical formulations. This comprehension sheds a powerful light on the meaning of these texts, giving them a different colouring and highlighting the courage needed for such an enterprise. In addition, Jovel allows us to benefit from his immense erudition in perceiving the influence of Spinoza's thought from the Age of Enlightenment to the present day. (Another seminal work, from the bibliographical point of view, is the biography written by Steven Nadler, *Spinoza, A Life*, Cambridge University Press, 2001.)

2 Freud, S. (1910) *Leonardo da Vinci: A Memory of His Childhood*, S.E., 11: 59–137. London: Hogarth

3 Yovel, Y., (1992), *Spinoza and Other Heretics*, Princeton, NJ: Princeton University Press, p. 139.

4 Ibid.

5 Freud, S. *The Resistances to Psycho-Analysis*. S.E., 19: p. 222. London: Hogarth, 1925 (quoted by Jirmiyahu Jovel, *Spinoza and Other Heretics*, op. cit.).

6 Friendship is an eminently Spinozian subject, closely linked to joy, and related to knowledge of the third kind. Let us remember what Freud writes in *Analysis Terminable and Interminable*, op. cit., "Not every good relation between an analyst and his subject during and after analysis was to be regarded as transference; there were also friendly relations which were based on reality and which proved to be viable" (p. 222).
As for Winnicott, he places friendship in the transitional domain. Here then, in brief, is my way of integrating these three approaches, during the course of an analysis, the establishment of the work of analysis as transitional space, an in-between space which separates and unites the patient and the therapist, is also the establishment of friendship as an agent of thought in the elaboration of the transference. More generally, friendship will function as an agent of thought when the encounter between the two protagonists will be taken up with inventing life based on the recognition of the products of the unconscious – a configuration that describes the analysis as such.

7 The following examples illustrate Spinoza's conception of the relation between psyche and soma:

    a "All these things, indeed show clearly that both the decision of the mind and the appetite and the determination of the body by nature exist together – or rather are one and the same thing..." Benedict De Spinoza, *Ethics*. Part III, "Of the Affects", Scholium of Postulate 2, p. 73.

    b "An idea that excludes the existence of our body cannot be in our mind, but is contrary to it." Ibid, Proposition 10, p. 76.

    c "The idea of any thing that increases or diminishes, aids or restrains, our body's power of acting, increases or diminishes, aids or restrains, our mind's power of thinking." Ibid, Proposition 11, p. 76.

    d "Finally, we have shown that the power of the mind by which it imagines things and recollects them also depends on this, that it involves the actual existence of the body. From these things it follows that the present existence of the mind and its power of imagining are taken away as soon as the mind ceases to affirm the present existence of the body." Ibid, Scholium of Proposition 2, pp. 76–77.

8   The term asceticism may be misleading or lead to misinterpretation. I am not saying, of course, that Spinoza aimed at a transcendental state. I am using the term in the context of a biological hierarchy which defines what Robert Misrahi calls the path leading from a primary mode of knowledge to knowledge of the third kind, where the desire to persevere in being is synonymous with the desire for joy and love of life.
Although it is clear that Spinoza's desire for joy has no sexual overtones, it is indisputable that this desire has the greatest force. At the risk of getting caught in a tautology, let us reiterate that from the Spinozian perspective the desire accompanying knowledge based on joy and on love of live presupposes the most highly realised functioning of the mind (the psyche), a functioning in plenitude, where love of oneself is inconceivable without the permanent creation of ties to the other.
If we add a sexual dimension to this functioning, we have all the elements that constitute Freud's theory of sublimation – which finds some of its roots in the Spinozian conception of joyful desire for thought. Lou Andreas-Salomé's 1921 essay "The Dual Orientation of Narcissism" (in *The Psychoanalytic Quarterly*, No. 31, 1–30, 1962) gives a fascinating glimpse onto the combination of Freudian and Spinozian perspectives on sublimation. (See also Letter 33, *True love*.)

9   It is not exactly accurate to say that Spinoza does not refer to the other. In fact, the presence of the other, taking him into consideration, with the creation of ties that this involves – ties of friendship and social ties – is one of the key characteristics of the functioning of the mind (the psyche) based on the third kind of knowledge, that which is created in the joy of desire. But on the path leading from primary knowledge to fully developed psychic functioning, Spinoza's other is not an agent of change (a concept which brings to mind the Freudian monad); on the contrary, the other is a complicating element, a pure externality whose essence cannot be captured, so that the mind (the psyche) can only suffer its effects (passively).
Monique Schneider writes at length about this absence of the other in Spinoza (in *Le Fini, l'Autre et le Savoir chez Spinoza et Freud*, Cahiers Spinoza, 1, Paris: Editions République, 1977). Starting with the Spinozian concept that destructiveness is always external, Monique Schneider arrives at a definition of the encounter as a mutilating, persecutory event. She states: "For Spinoza, the negative only exists in the space between two particular beings." From this perspective, she adds, passion is defined "as a region of exteriority within my own power to exist". But affect is not always negative in Spinoza's view: for a free man, the important thing is not to be subjected to it, to have the determination to persevere in being and to transform passion into desire. Spinoza does not propose the suppression of affect, but rather the transformation of a passive affect (passion) into an active affect (desire). Thus, Monique Schneider's interpretation concerns the first kind of knowledge. S. Freud, *Beyond the Pleasure Principle*, op. cit., p. 38.

10   Spinoza, B. de (1996), *Ethics*. Translated by Edwin Curley, London: Penguin Classics, p. 75.

11   Spinoza, B. de (1996), *Ethics*. Translated by Edwin Curley, London: Penguin Classics, p. 151.

12   The agent allowing the mind (the psyche) to go from passivity to activity – and therefore to the knowledge of joy – is the desire to persevere in being (the *conatus*). This is why the entire third part of the *Ethics* is a remarkable reflection on what Freud would come to recognise as the conceptual sphere of narcissism, in which he was to introduce the concept of ego-libido, to complete Spinoza's notion of self-preservation. Contrary to Freud, who always recognised the real dimension of the affective force, Lacan confined himself to the philosophical context in which Spinoza inscribed the affects, thus remaining in an eminently religious context. He borrowed the Spinozian conception of affects as framed solely by the imagination, which constitutes the

first kind of knowledge, to elaborate his concept of the imaginary order. The widespread result of this choice, persisting among his third-generation disciples, is the non-interpretation of transference, and consequently the overlooking of what takes place in the relation with the other, in this case the analyst.

Another consequence of this choice was to the theorisation of the symbolic level, compared to which the imaginary level has little significance. It would be a serious mistake to consider the relation between these two levels comparable to the relation between Spinoza's second and third kind of knowledge. In Spinoza's conception, there is continuity between the two modalities, while the Lacanian theory relative to these levels reintroduces a Platonic type of transcendence.

In general, Lacan's reading of the *Ethics* is more philosophical than analytical. This distortion is again apparent in Lacan's reflections on Spinoza's *conatus*. Spinoza designated as *conatus* the way in which desire perseveres in a being who follows the path leading the mind (the psyche) from a primary type of knowledge to the knowledge of joy: it is a linear conception which, for this reason, does not disqualify any stage of the function of the mind (the psyche). On the contrary, knowledge of the second kind is a precondition to the stage where the mind (the psyche) functions in plenitude. The notion of *conatus* refers to the constant state of being of the mind, and implies a power whose effects Spinoza describes. Lacan's formulation of the foundation of his ethics is entirely different: it is a matter of not giving up on one's desires. This eminently philosophical formulation – since it concerns the being rather than the conflict – presents from the outset a series of oppositions to which there must be resistance. The marks of this injunction are recognisable in Lacanian disciples with an authoritative attitude and with an exaggerated sensitivity to any objection regarding the entire body of their defensive certainties.

13 Hegel, G. W. F. (1977), "Preface" in *The Phenomenology of Spirit* (trans. A. V. Miller). Oxford: Oxford University Press, p. 19.

Index